Translation's Forgotten History

HARVARD EAST ASIAN MONOGRAPHS 394

Translation's Forgotten History

Russian Literature, Japanese Mediation,
and the Formation of Modern Korean Literature

Heekyoung Cho

Published by the Harvard University Asia Center
Distributed by Harvard University Press
Cambridge (Massachusetts) and London 2016

The Harvard University Asia Center publishes a monograph series and, in coordination with the Fairbank Center for Chinese Studies, the Korea Institute, the Reischauer Institute of Japanese Studies, and other facilities and institutes, administers research projects designed to further scholarly understanding of China, Japan, Vietnam, Korea, and other Asian countries. The Center also sponsors projects addressing multidisciplinary and regional issues in Asia.

Publication of this book was supported by the Sunshik Min Endowment for the Advancement of Korean Literature at the Korea Institute, Harvard University.

Library of Congress Cataloging-in-Publication Data

Cho, Heekyoung.
    Translation's forgotten history : Russian literature, Japanese mediation, and the formation of modern Korean literature / Heekyoung Cho.
        pages cm.— (Harvard East Asian Monographs ; 394)
    Includes bibliographical references and index.
    ISBN 978-0-674-66004-5 (hardcover : acid-free paper)   1. Translating and interpreting—East Asia.   2. Literature and society—East Asia.   3. Korean literature—Translations—History and criticism.   4. Russian literature—Translations—History and criticism.   5. Japanese literature—Translations—History and criticism.   I. Title.
    PN241.5.E18C47 2016
    418'.04095—dc23

                                                                                        2015025981

Index by Anne Holmes

♾ Printed on acid-free paper

Last figure below indicates year of this printing
25 24 23 22 21 20 19 18 17 16

For my parents, Mun Hyeja and Cho Myungje

Contents

Preface

Translation has become a keyword triggering reconsideration of assumptions and interpretations of various cultural phenomena in the field of literary and cultural studies. Yet, despite the increasing awareness of translation's formative role, translated literature is still habitually considered derivative of source texts, that is, not as original as the original. The set of legal regimes surrounding contemporary copyright is one instantiation of this belief and testament to its dominance. In our reading of foreign literature, the work of the translator is often overlooked, and it would hardly seem apropos to include translations of foreign works in the canon of a given nation's literary history. But the formative period of modern literature in East Asia, around the turn of the twentieth century, offers us a different view of translation. During this time, translation was considered a creative and authentic activity that stood alongside other forms of prose writing, both fiction and nonfiction. For most leading East Asian intellectuals of the day, translation was a critical mode of influence on both literary and social discourses. *Translation's Forgotten History* investigates the meanings and functions that translation generated for modern national literatures during this formative period, thereby reconsidering literature as part of a dynamic process of negotiating foreign and local values. Translation was not a supplement to national literature but the kernel of it. Through examination of Korean intellectuals' translation and appropriation of Russian prose in the early twentieth century, I aim to highlight translation as a radical and ineradicable part—not merely a catalyst or complement—of the formation of modern national literature, and thus to begin rethinking the way modern literature developed in Korea and East Asia. Although national canons are often founded on amnesia regarding their process of formation, framing literature from the beginning as a process rather than an entity allows a more complex and accurate understanding of national literature formation in East Asia, and may also provide a model relevant to the situation of world literature today.

This book re-addresses the role of translation in the formation of a modern literature by examining how colonial Koreans appropriated Russian literature, through the medium of Japanese relay translations, while in the process of building their own modern literature in the early twentieth century. Translation has been integral to the formation of most modern literatures, and Korean literature is no exception. Writers appropriated foreign literatures to build a new vernacular language and used foreign literatures and literary figures as a vehicle for creating a new public role for the writer. Within this project, Russian literature had particular importance as an example of a socially engaged literature under an authoritarian regime; it was the most translated of any foreign literature in early twentieth-century Korea, and was one of the most influential literatures in other East Asian countries also.

Korean translations, however, took place through the mediation of Japanese language and culture. Most Korean writers first read Russian literature in an encounter structured by the colonial relationship between Korea and Japan (1910–45). Since only a few Korean intellectuals could translate Russian literature directly from Russian and Japanese translations of Russian literature were in a number of cases already available, Koreans mostly translated and adapted Japanese versions. Thus, Japanese selection of what and how to translate from Russian literature prefigured Korean reception to a significant extent. Through close historical and textual analysis of works that traveled from Russian through Japanese to Korean, I argue that translation was an active and creative form of intellectual work by which colonized intellectuals engaged with their sociopolitical situation, and that Koreans' use of Russian literature formed part of an intellectual community around East Asia, a community that is most prominently visible in a shared use of Russian realist literature in the process of developing a socially committed literature of their own.

Despite the fact that translation was an indispensable element of and process in the formation of both the concept (or consciousness) and the substance of national literature, the process itself has been diminished and forgotten—or intentionally erased by history writing that portrays national literature as an autonomously developed outcome. In post-liberation Korea, Korean scholars engaged, from the 1970s to the early 1990s, in overt and covert debates as to whether modern Korean literature was transplanted or developed autonomously, and whether premodern and modern Korean literatures are continuous or discontinuous. The theory of autonomous development, which emphasizes an internal logic in the development of modern Korean literature was revitalized in the early 1990s during the debate on the true starting point of modern Korean literature—a debate whose central aim was to find the germ of modern literature within traditional literature that had not been affected by colonization.

This nationalist approach can be understood as a meaningful, if not inevitable, part of the process by which national literatures that have experienced (semi-)colonization can recover some sense of cultural sovereignty. But the problem is that in pursuing these arguments, Korean scholars have tended to minimize the impact of foreign literatures, Japan's mediation, and, as a corollary, translation itself, because they assume that literary influence is symptomatic of an immature literature and, by extension, of a weak nation. Concomitantly, this approach has prevented scholars from confronting their colonial legacies and those legacies' impacts on their own ways of conducting research. In the 2000s, however, Korean studies scholars in both Korea and the United States began to pay serious attention to the issue of translation in modern Korean society. The topic has become a valuable line of inquiry among a number of groups of scholars trying to understand the fundamental characteristics of modern Korea. As a pioneering study of the significant relationship between Russian and Korean literature, *Translation's Forgotten History* seeks to account for the meaning and function of translation in modern Korean literature during the process of its formation.

This volume also provides a broader East Asian perspective from which to understand the formation of modern literatures. Both China's May Fourth writers and modern Korean writers relied on Japanese translations of Russian literature. They were deeply affected by an image of Russian literature as a socially engaged body of work—an image that was initially formed in the Japanese literary world—and one that differed markedly from the initial reception of Russian literature in Europe, which emphasized the familiarity of its Victorian style. Thus framed, Russian literature had a unique impact on East Asian intellectuals, who were searching for new models for literature and new ideas about the social role of the writer at a time of immense change. Whether they were writing in a colony (Korea), a semi-colony (China), or an imperialist state (Japan), these writers struggled to present a new vision to their societies; not only in Korea and China but also in Japan, Russian literature was embraced most strongly by anti-imperialist intellectuals. Japanese anti-war writers around the time of the Russo-Japanese War (1904–05) and proletarian writers in the 1920s and 1930s habitually referred to Russia's nineteenth-century realists. This suggests that Russian literature became one element in a form of anti-imperial cosmopolitanism in East Asia in the early twentieth century. In light of the relationships that cohered through Russian literature, *Translation's Forgotten History* thus increases our understanding of a shared literary experience and sensibility in East Asia, which referred to Russia as a significant other in the formation of its own modern literatures.

Beyond Asian literature, this book contributes to the field of translation studies and to studies of (colonial) mediation as well. Translation studies seeks to place significant emphasis on target cultures by rethinking translation as rewriting and refraction rather than reflection or imitation. My research adds a fuller understanding of the relations between translation and the formation of national literature by arguing that the creative force of translation was gradually effaced from literary history as a necessary part of national literature becoming the dominant mode of understanding. It is also relevant to studies of mediation, which in my own study takes the form of relay translations and mediated cultural transmission between Russia and Korea.

While accommodating understandings made possible by previous scholarship, this book thus aims to go beyond the paradigm of national literature yet still find a place for agency and the importance of local meaning through a focus on the constructive process that translation entails. I hope that *Translation's Forgotten History* will also contribute broadly to humanities scholarship by serving as a valuable point of departure for comprehensive studies of the global formation of modern literature, the travel of cultural capital, and colonial studies, and that, in wider terms, it will contribute to such fields as the history of writing and authorship.

Acknowledgments

Writing this book was possible only with the support of many people. The book evolved from my dissertation, and my first thanks go to the professors at the University of Chicago who inspired and encouraged me over the course of many years: Kyeong-Hee Choi, Norma Field, Bruce Cumings, Michael Bourdaghs, and the late Anna Lisa Crone. I also appreciate the generous help and accommodations offered me by scholars in Japan and Korea during the initial research stages of the project: Kojima Naoko, Hotei Toshihiro, Watanabe Naoki, Chŏng Kŭnsik, Kim Yunsik, Kim Oegon, Kim Myŏnghwan, Kim Hŭnggyu, Kim Chaeyong, and Yi Sanggyŏng.

Colleagues and friends at the University of Washington, in the Department of Asian Languages and Literature, the Simpson Center for the Humanities, the Korean Studies Program, the Textual Studies Program, the Translation Studies Research Cluster, and the East Asian Library have given me generous support. I benefited greatly from conversations with Ted Mack, Clark Sorensen, Kathleen Woodward, Davinder Bhowmik, Chris Hamm, Hwasook Nam, Paul Atkins, Jennifer Dubrow, Vicente Rafael, Cynthia Steele, Hyokyoung Yi, and many others. I must also thank all those who, over the years, have offered comments and suggestions in the context of conferences, workshops, and lectures, including Chris Hill, John Treat, and Katerina Clark.

This book has been generously supported by an NEH fellowship for university teachers from the National Endowment for the Humanities, although any views, findings, conclusions, or recommendations expressed in this book do not necessarily reflect those of the National Endowment for the Humanities; an ACLS fellowship from the American Council of Learned Societies; a Royalty Research Fund Award; a Society of Scholars Fellowship from the Simpson Center for the Humanities at the University of Washington; and a postdoctoral fellowship from the Council on East Asian Studies at Yale University.

I am grateful to *U.S.-Japan Women's Journal* for permission to republish portions of Chapter 3.

Without the encouragement of Minhyea, Suyoung, Ji-Eun, and many other friends, the journey of writing this book would have been much more difficult.

My family—my parents, siblings, and nieces and nephews—sustained me with their unfathomable love throughout this long journey. Special thanks go to my husband Justin, who has been the most caring reader and friend, and my daughter Terin, who makes me laugh every single day.

Notes on Transliterations, Names,
and Translations

Korean words are transliterated in the McCune-Reischauer system, Japanese in the Hepburn system, Russian in the Library of Congress system, and Chinese in the Pinyin system, except for the names and words widely known in English by other spellings. For instance, I use Seoul and Tokyo rather than Sŏul and Tōkyō, and Tolstoy and Dostoevsky rather than Tolstoi and Dostoevskii.

Korean, Japanese, and Chinese names are written in the order of surname followed by the given name. I use the surname on the second reference for East Asian names. However, in the case of well-known Japanese authors who are often referred to by their given names, I follow that custom and refer to them by their given names rather than surnames on the second reference. Thus, for instance, I use Shōyō to refer to Tsubouchi Shōyō.

Unless otherwise indicated, translations from Korean, Japanese, and Russian are my own.

INTRODUCTION

Translation and the Formation of Modern Literature

Translation is a mode of generating new meaning and a medium for change in society. It is a genuinely creative activity, whose role becomes particularly evident when a society is undergoing critical historical and cultural change, and early twentieth-century Korea witnessed such a moment. For Korean intellectuals, who felt an urgent responsibility in the era of imperialism, literature was understood as an embodiment of their people's independent spirit as well as an emblem of a newly developed civilization. Literary translation became a way for Korean intellectuals to actively engage with the social and intellectual transformations of early colonial Korea. They translated and adapted, with all the ingenuity of authors, to build a form of modern literature that would respond to their society's historical situation. It has often been assumed that a translated work necessarily lacks the creativity and authenticity of the so-called original, and that the activity of translating does not have a history attesting to its different meanings, functions, and expectations in different societies and periods. But these assumptions, as I will show, are artifacts of the modern concept of national literature, which itself is a historical construct.

What did translation mean in the formation of national literatures in East Asia? When did "literary translation" become a term that designates the rendition of a foreign literary work into a national language? What has made translators and their labor invisible, and established the foreign text as the source, and the translation as derivative? When did the boundary between a nation's *own* literature and another nation's literature become so self-evident—and, relatedly, when did translation become such a specific kind of literary activity?

Translation and nationalism are in an ironic relationship. It was through translation as a medium that both the concept and the substance of national language and literature were constructed and reinforced around the world. Yet translation as a constitutive medium has been forgotten in the collective amnesia of origins that nationalism demands. Nationalism makes it necessary to forget divergent ethnic and linguistic origins in order to imagine a purer nation more worthy of devotion than the social and political reality that preceded it. National literature, which is part of this process, has also forgotten its diverse origins, and this inevitably includes its connections to foreign literatures. The amnesia is confirmed and naturalized by literary histories that assume that national literature has impermeable borders, and these histories have been common in Korea, particularly during the postliberation period from the 1970s to the early 1990s. To understand the work of translation in a place and time in which national literature had not yet been able to forget its origins, we must therefore rethink the field of translation itself.

A Forgotten History: Translation, Nationalism, and National Language and Literature

Benedict Anderson's *Imagined Community* is an epoch-making study of the origin of nationalism. Astonishingly, given the depth of its insights, it also serves as an example of the general blindness to translation that affects studies of nationalism and national language. Anderson takes up vernacularization and "the fatality of human linguistic diversity" as one of the central foci in his explanatory system. This issue cannot properly be discussed without mentioning translation, yet this is something he never brings up. He explains the underlying forces that ended "the imagined community of Christendom" and made it possible to imagine new national communities. For him, "the esotericization of Latin, the Reformation, and the haphazard development of administrative vernaculars" served as the three coordinates in dethroning old communities.[1]

If these three forces were significant for the emergence of the new imagined communities in terms of their contributions to the decline of Latin, Anderson holds, then "what, in a positive sense, made the new communities imaginable was a half-fortuitous, but explosive, interaction between a system of production and productive relations (capitalism), a technology of communications (print), and the fatality of human linguistic diversity."[2] He goes on to explain that it was not the diversity of human languages itself but the "interplay" of these three factors that made it possible to imagine the new national communities. Anderson's "print-languages"—the result of the interplay among fatality, technology, and capitalism—are positioned between Latin and spoken language. Print-languages are not the lingua franca that Latin was. But they have fewer variations than spoken languages. They also form fields of communication among themselves. They allow people to become capable of understanding one another "via print," and they imagine a group of people who understand the same print-language to be a community.[3]

What is missing in Anderson's discussion of nationalism in relation to language is a consideration of the role of translation. First, vernacularization itself, which contributed to "the rise of national consciousness," to use Anderson's words, arose both as a process and as a result of translation. Vernacular language was not a written version of a spoken language but a "translation" of a written language, in this case, Latin. As Karatani Kojin explains:

> When Dante wrote in the vernacular, he did not directly transpose contemporary spoken language into writing. From the various idioms (Saussure) existing all over Italy, he selected one. It is not because he selected the standard idiom, but rather because he wrote in the vernacular as a form of translating Latin, that his écriture later became the standard écriture. That act relegated the other idioms to the status of dialect. The same can be said in the cases of French and German.[4]

This oversight in Anderson's theorization is also present in much recent scholarship into the vernacularization of the Korean and Japanese languages, in its overwhelming focus on the process of bridging the gap between spoken and written language.[5]

Second, it was not only print-languages but also translations that were indispensable in laying the basis for national consciousness. While print-languages allow fellow readers to imagine a linguistic community whose members understand each other via print, these readers become aware of the boundaries of their community through the translation process between languages. As Naoki Sakai argues, "it is not because two different language unities are given that we have to translate (or interpret) one text into another; it is because translation *articulates* languages so that we may postulate the two unities of the translating and the translated languages as if they were autonomous and closed entities through *a certain representation of translation*" (emphasis in original).[6] Translation is the venue where the differences between languages must unavoidably be recognized and negotiated, and those languages are ostensibly represented as closed entities. The locus where translation takes place is therefore the edge of the imagined linguistic community.

Before he discusses print-languages, Anderson emphasizes the crucial role of the novel in the formation of national consciousness, in that it changed the concept of "simultaneity" from a vertical to a horizontal notion and made it possible for people to imagine communities by recognizing the simultaneous existence of other people and events through the readings of novels and newspapers (which are novels without correlation between subplots, according to Anderson).[7] The kind of print-language that is indispensable for novel-writing also came into being through the process of translating foreign languages. The linguistic elements and their interplay with other elements, which Anderson introduces to explain the origins of nation and national consciousness, are thus profoundly intertwined with the issue of translation.

Not only the concept of national language and literature but the substantial form of national literature was forged through the confrontation and negotiation inherent in the process of translation. In his article "Conjectures on World Literature," Franco Moretti tries to formulate a world literary system to explain the connectedness of national literatures. He starts from Goethe and Marx's anticipation of the birth of world literature:

> "Nowadays, national literature doesn't mean much: the age of world literature is beginning, and everybody should contribute to hasten its advent." This was Goethe, of course, talking to Eckermann in 1827; and these are Marx and Engels, twenty years later, in 1848: "National one-sidedness and narrow-mindedness become more and more impossible, and from the many

national and local literatures, a world literature arises." *Weltliteratur*: this is what Goethe and Marx have in mind.[8]

Although he is inspired by Goethe and Marx, Moretti's concept of world literature is not a singular entity. There is "one world literary system (of inter-related literatures)," but this system is "profoundly unequal." His concept of world literature as a system is based on the hypothesis of "the world-system school of economic history, for which international capitalism is a system that is simultaneously *one*, and *unequal*: with a core, and a periphery (and a semiperiphery) that are bound together in a relationship of growing inequality."[9] The inequality means that peripheral literatures are subject to interference from core-culture literatures, but the reverse does not hold true.

Taking his cue from Fredric Jameson's observation that there is a "gap between the raw material of Japanese social experience and these abstract formal patterns of Western novel construction that cannot always be welded together seamlessly," Moretti develops some rules about the birth of the modern novel in a local culture.[10] He argues that "in cultures that belong to the periphery of the literary system (which means almost all cultures, inside and outside Europe), the modern novel first arises not as an autonomous development but as a compromise between a western formal influence (usually French or English) and local materials."[11] He claims that the compromise between the foreign and the local is so common that the Spanish, the French, and the British cases, where the novel form arose independently, are not the rule but the exception.[12] The term "compromise" in Moretti's explanation covers the complicated negotiations that must take place among foreign form (foreign plot), local material (local characters), and local form (local narrative voice). He considers the local narrative voice as the most unstable among the three elements because the narrator plays the role of commentator and evaluator in the site of negotiation of the differences. Cracks develop between "story and discourse, world and worldview: the world goes in the strange direction dictated by an outside power; the worldview tries to make sense of it, and is thrown off balance all the time."[13]

My own interest resides not so much in the distinctions between these three elements as in Moretti's concept of compromise itself. From my perspective, what he means by "compromise" is none other than translation, both as the process and as its result (i.e., translated texts).

The negotiation/compromise that is so integral to any act of translation, most especially in a modern literature's formative period, is well demonstrated in Lydia Liu's book on translingual practice in modern China. By examining the historical linkages and conditions of translation, she discloses the complex process "by which new worlds, meanings, discourses, and modes of representation arise, circulate, and acquire legitimacy within the host language due to, or in spite of, the latter's contact/collision with the guest language."[14] The compromise in the contact between cultures, which was possible only through the process of translation, was an indispensable agent of the birth of "national" language and literature. Further, *Translation's Forgotten History* argues, translation's designation as a derivative and secondary literary act comes out of the need for national languages to hide the negotiated contexts of their birth.

Moretti's secondary/distant reading survey of the birth of modern novels hints that most modern national literatures came into being simultaneously with the category of translation. It was translation that functioned as the constructive force of modern national literature in East Asia. As Naoki Sakai puts it, the birth of national language and literature can be explained by "the regime of translation": "Japanese language was born, or stillborn, in the eighteenth century among a very small portion of literary people, when the schema of configuration came into being. This is to say that the schema of configuration is a means by which a national community represents itself to itself, thereby constituting itself as a subject."[15] Sakai expands his concern to include national literature, arguing that the construction of national literature in modern times has been inseparable from the process of co-figuring. Therefore, from the outset, "the construction of national 'literature' has always already been haunted by that of 'comparative literature': national literature has inherently been comparative literature."[16] In addition to the regime of translation as an explanatory tool for the birth of national literature, the real process of making national literature was conducted through the relentless effort of translation. The concepts of, and distinctions between, foreign literature and national literature were not clearly formed and divided in its formative period. The ongoing process of formation took place through the work of translation, which configured them as separate, equivalent entities, and the resultant translated literature played a significant role in the formation of national literature in East Asia.

Even though translation was an essential element in the formative process of both the concept and the substance of national literature, the process itself has been devalued and forgotten, or deliberately erased by literary histories that represent national literature as an independently developed cultural product. From the 1970s to the early 1990s, Korean scholars were involved, in many different ways, in debates over the independently developed versus transplanted outcome of modern Korean literature and over the (dis-)continuity between premodern and modern Korean literatures. The theory of autonomous development accentuated an internal logic in the development of modern Korean literature and immediately drew enormous scholarly attention and support.[17] In the early 1990s, this theory was invigorated in the form of a debate on the true starting point of modern Korean literature, one of whose principal purposes was to locate the root of modern Korean literature within the Korean literary tradition.[18] Yet the problem is that, while pursuing these arguments, scholars have been inclined to denigrate the interactions between Korean literature and foreign literatures, the impact of Japan's mediation, and, as a corollary, the role of translation in the formative period of modern Korean literature.

This neglect and disparagement of translation go well beyond the debates in Korea over modern Korean literature. As André Lefevere points out, "literary histories, as they have been written until recently, have had little or no time for translations, since for the literary historian translation has had to do with 'language' only, not with literature—another outgrowth of the 'monolingualization' of literary history by Romantic historiographers intent on creating 'national' literatures preferably as uncontaminated as possible by foreign influences."[19]

Apparently, this has been significantly problematic in modern China as well. Liu mentions that, in her study, she has "resisted the temptation of explaining *change* in terms of either foreign impact or indigenous evolution, the choice of which would bring the issue to a premature closure when one ought to be opening up to further inquiry."[20] To avoid the dichotomy of "foreign impact" and "indigenous evolution," which forecloses the scholar from further productive questioning, she pays attention to the process of change: "The notion of *translated modernity* is useful because it allows me to identify and interpret those contingent moments and processes that are reducible neither to foreign impact nor to the self-explanatory logic of the indigenous tradition" (emphasis in original).[21]

In the formative period of modern Korean literature in the 1900s, 1910s, and 1920s, translated texts sometimes exerted a more profound impact than the writings in the still-forming national literature. And part of the writers' creative writing occurred on the very edge of what today would be plagiarism—that is, translation including abridged versions, summaries, adaptations, and appropriations, without referring to the foreign author's name. But it would be improper to devalue these works and exclude them from the history of the local literature. Translation and creation were not separate at this time. Translation *was* creation in the formative period of national literature, and translated texts and creative writings (written in a very new form of modern language) were complementary and mutually influential. This might be visually explicable through Walter Benjamin's vessel analogy.

Benjamin's theory of translation offers an inspiring and unique perspective on translation, one that begins from the complementarity of original and translation. For him, translation is not something subservient to the original but, rather, the original's afterlife.[22] The organic and mutual relationship between the original and translation is better explained in his analogy of a vessel:

> Fragments of a vessel which are to be glued together must match one another in the smallest details, although they need not be like one another. In the same way a translation, instead of resembling the meaning of the original, must lovingly and in detail incorporate the original's mode of significance, thus making both the original and the translation recognizable as fragments of a greater language, just as fragments are part of a vessel.[23]

What Benjamin fundamentally argues is that translation reveals the kinship of languages that are complementary, in harmony under "God's remembrance." Without taking on his mysticism entirely, I would like to emphasize his idea of complementarity between the source text and the translated text. If the original and the translations are not in a unidirectional relationship of authority and subservience but in fact are complementary, then translation also legitimately demands an autonomous space of creation in relation to the source text. Especially at a time when the works of the writer and of the translator were not separated clearly, translation and creative writing were of the same cloth, or vessel. The unavoidable role of translation in a receiving culture becomes clearer when the number of translations exceeds the number of literary works produced by local writers. The Chinese literary historian A Ying (Qian Xingcun) estimates that "of the at least 1,500 published works of fiction in the last decade of the Qing, two-thirds are translations of foreign literature."[24]

Translated texts need to be considered in the history of a given national literature because translation was both the element that served to amplify the repertoire of the literature and a constructive force for modern national literatures—a construction that would be erased after its stabilization. One cannot fully understand a national literature in its formative period without considering translation. This becomes apparent when we examine the role of translation in the formation of modern Korean literature.

The Historicity of Translation: The Division of Authorial Labor

Cicero and Horace were two of the earliest opponents of word-for-word translation in Western translation theory. They put forth the first theories of "sense-for-sense" translation. According to this theory, translation should aim beyond the merely linguistic or technical. This intellectual position, however, was inextricably tied to the fact that their work was part of an imperialist project. Lawrence Venuti explains that "the cultural functions of Roman translation stress the relative autonomy of the translated text, minimizing the importance of equivalence by defining it as a general semantic and stylistic correspondence."[25] After conquering Greece (beginning in the late third century and ending in the mid-first century B.C.E.), as a part of its post-colonial project, Rome needed to establish its own culture partially by appropriating Greek culture, while at the same time minimizing Rome's indebtedness to the "superiority" of Greece. This effort "to 'replicate' a Greek author in Latin in an inventive and original way was not founded on ideas of continuity or progress, but on an agenda of conquest."[26] From the beginning of the history of Western translation theory, translation and its theories have not been neutral but purposeful and manipulative, so that the meaning of the term "translation," the practice it denotes, and the judgment surrounding that practice have differed depending on the specific historical and political context in which the term was used. Ideas about translation are not ahistorical.

At the beginning of the twentieth century, the term "translation" (*pŏnyŏk*) in Korean denoted a much broader array of practices than those connected with the term nowadays. The term "literature" (*munhak*) was itself a translated word, and the writing that occurred under its sign had to be distinguished from the traditional formation of literature in Korea up to that time.[27] Moreover, while the definition of the new term "literature" was being constructed and recognized, Korean intellectuals practiced this new style of writing through the process of reading and translating foreign literary texts. Translation, for them, was not only the act of introducing foreign literatures but also the practice of writing in the new style, which itself came from that literature. One could say that translation, in the sense of going from one national literature to another, did not make sense yet at this point, because the translating literature itself was under construction. Translation was creating its own possibility.

Immanuel Wallerstein's discussion of the consolidation of the division of labor, and the correlative construction of relative value corresponding to different kinds of work, suggests a way to explain the relationship between the translator and writer in the formative period of modern literature in Korea and other East Asian countries. In his discussion of capitalism as a historical social system whose beginning is dated to the late fifteenth century, Wallerstein explains the reinforcement of the division of labor in the history of economy as follows: "a social distinction between productive and unproductive work began to be imposed on the working classes," and productive work started to be defined as money-earning work while nonproductive work was defined as merely subsistence activity.[28] Thus productive wage labor became primarily for the adult male, and nonproductive labor for females and children. He argues that although the division of labor by gender and age was not an invention of historical capitalism, it became clear and coercive under historical capitalism:

What was new under historical capitalism was the correlation of division of labor and valuation of work. Men may often have done different work from women (and adults different work from children and the elderly), but under historical capitalism there has been a steady devaluation of the work of women (and of the young and old), and a corresponding emphasis on the value of the adult male's work.[29]

Translation took place simultaneously with—or, more often, prior to—the creation of modern literary works in East Asian languages. At the very beginning of this process, only the translator was visible in most cases, while the author of the original was effaced. This is the opposite of the present situation, where translators are almost invisible. It was part of a common process that intellectuals started their careers as writers by translating and publishing translations of foreign literary works. Lu Xun, Futabatei Shimei, Yi Kwang-su, and Hyŏn Chin-gŏn, for instance, followed this path. The distinction between translation and creative writing was not clear, and translating was not considered a less important or degrading work. I argue that in early twentieth-century Korea, the division of labor between the writer and the translator was not absolute, and thus that the distinction between the original work and the translated work was far less clear than it is at present. The "correlation" of the division of labor between the writer and translator with a particular value hierarchy is therefore a historical event, and one that consolidated as the "national literature" stabilized.

The seemingly natural division and value-hierarchy between the author with originality and the translator as an imitator is again destabilized when we are reminded that the concepts of "author" and "authorship" are themselves recent historical constructs. Translation was degraded and stigmatized as secondary and imitative writing by being contrasted with the "original" writing, which in turn became an essential element in constructing the concept of authorship. The widespread concepts of authorship also validated the place of translation below "the original" in copyright law.[30] To make things more complicated, the very term "original" also began to acquire its modern meaning in the eighteenth century: "The term 'original' which in the Middle Ages had meant 'having existed from the first' came to mean 'underived, independent, first-hand'; and by the time that Edward Young in his epoch-making *Conjectures on*

Original Composition (1759) hailed Richardson as 'a genius as well moral as original', the word could be used as a term of praise meaning 'novel or fresh in character or style.' "[31]

Like the term "original," the word "author" also acquired its modern concept in eighteenth-century Europe. One of the elements of this change was economic, as a new class of writer began to seek economic viability from the sale of their work. In the process these writers began to redefine the essential characteristics of writing, and this process contributed to the conceptualization of authorship in its modern form.[32] This study of translation in the formative period of modern Korean literature, discloses that the division of the labor between the translator and the writer was incomplete, which reveals the very historicity of the term "translation" and the assumptions surrounding it.

The Politics in and of Translation

The devaluation of translation does not apply only to the degradation of translated texts themselves: more importantly, it implies the endorsement of essentialist cultural hierarchies and sustains the assumption of the cultural superiority of Western culture, which is always identified with the original.

Opposing the association of translation with derivative status, translation studies as a discipline started in the late 1970s, with the assertion that translation was not simply a branch of comparative literature but a field deserving study in its own right.[33] In the introduction to her 1980 book *Translation Studies*, Susan Bassnett also correctly points out the complexity and ramifications of translation studies as well as its importance as a field:

> The present book is an attempt to outline the scope of that discipline, to give more indication of the kind of work that has been done so far and to suggest directions in which further research is needed. Most importantly, it is an attempt to demonstrate that Translation Studies is indeed a discipline in its own right: not merely a minor branch of comparative literary study, nor yet a specific area of linguistics, but a vastly complex field with many far-reaching ramifications.[34]

The publication of Bassnett's book marked the consolidation of translation studies as an independent discipline, although studies on translation had been produced before.[35] The publication of the "Translation Studies" series in the 1990s, edited by Susan Bassnett and André Lefevere, shows the relative stabilization of translation studies as an independent discipline.[36]

Translation studies as a discipline endeavors to rethink translation as rewriting and refraction rather than as a mere reflection of the "original": "Translation is, of course, a rewriting of an original text. All rewritings, whatever their intention, reflect a certain ideology and a poetics, and as such manipulated literature to function in a given society in a given way."[37] The notion that translation is a rewriting entails a recognition of the role of power in the seemingly transparent process of translation. As Bassnett and Lefevere insightfully argue, "in an age of ever increasing manipulation of all kinds, the study of the manipulative processes of literature as exemplified by translation can help us towards a greater awareness of the world in which we live."[38] This perspective on translation as rewriting is the context in which I situate this study of translation in colonial Korea.

The development of translation studies was part of a reorientation of cultural studies in the mid-1970s that moved toward an emphasis on target cultures. Around the same time that Lefevere and Bassnett proclaimed the need for translation studies as an independent discipline, a number of other groups were producing work with a similar sensibility. One of them, which profoundly influenced Lefevere, was the polysystem theorist group, including Itamar Even-Zohar and Gideon Toury, whose studies are based on the assumption that literary translations are facts of the receiving culture.[39]

But Douglas Robinson rightly points to the inertia in intellectual assumptions about translation that still exists:

> It should be clear, however, that it is enormously difficult to displace intellectual assumptions that were first formulated by classical authorities like Cicero, Horace, Pliny and Quintilian two millennia ago; the classical ideas have widely been considered the only acceptable way of thinking about the practice of translation for three or four centuries. And indeed the old assumptions about translation, that it is a purely linguistic and largely impersonal process for achieving semantic equivalence between texts,

still dominate thinking about translation in many parts of the international translation-studies community.[40]

Robinson's concern about the continuing dominance of "the old assumptions" about translation might seem unnecessary in an environment where scholarship attending to social and cultural contexts has experienced significant growth since the 1990s and is currently an active field of inquiry and debate. But there is still a great distance between active fields and general assumptions, while the rapidly expanding field of machine translation and computer-aided translation, despite its association with the cutting edge of the digital age, reproduces and reinforces "the old assumptions" built into conventional translation methodologies, particularly the idea that translation is "a purely linguistic and largely impersonal process for achieving semantic equivalence between texts."

What needs to be emphasized is that it is not necessarily true that all scholars interested in translation (translation studies is truly broad and interdisciplinary, encompassing divergent academic orientations) are interested in historicity and politics, which are inherent in the translating process. This is not to say that translation studies that attend to linguistic elements are unnecessary. Instead, what I would like to bring to the fore are the assumptions and ramifications that it engenders. The *prevalence* of purely linguistic approaches within translation studies, which promote scientific models for research, have led to a prioritization of purportedly value-free and objective studies of translation. As a result, they deny consideration of the social engagement of translation, the creation and manipulation that are part of translation, and, more importantly, the politics surrounding the act and result of translation. The purely linguistic approaches toward translation, which ignore historical conditions under which the translation takes place, thus consciously and unconsciously admit and reinforce the value-hierarchy between the source and the target languages and cultures.

A critic's perspective on translation is inseparable from her approaches to questions such as the nature of modern literatures in non–Western European cultures. For instance, modern literary forms in Korea and East Asia developed through the process of translation and negotiation with Western European literatures. If one considers translation as a mere derivative form that is always secondary to "the original," then modern

Korean literature can never become more than a derivative imitation of European literatures. This value hierarchy is even repeated by Korean scholars of translation themselves.

Problematic Assumptions in Studies of Translation in Korea

Many studies of literary translation in Korea are problematic because they begin with the assumption that translation is a secondary writing in relation to the "original." One of the common conclusions, for instance, is that the translator or appropriator has not understood the "original" fully and properly. But translators' mistranslations cannot automatically be considered to be an unconscious misunderstanding of the source text. Even in the case of misunderstanding, it is sufficiently meaningful to investigate the patterns—and the literary or social connotations—of those misunderstandings, especially if they appear repeatedly in the receiving culture. Another inappropriate assumption is to understand the cultural difference embedded in languages as evidence of the target language's *lack*. This predetermined value judgment promotes the idea that the source language and culture are universal whereas the target language and culture are deficient.

The most comprehensive study of translation practices in modern Korean literature is Kim Pyŏng-ch'ŏl's *Han'guk kŭndae pŏnyŏk munhaksa yŏn'gu* (A history of literary translation in modern Korea), published in 1998.[41] It extensively catalogues Korean translations of Western literary works, annotates them, and outlines the general patterns of reception primarily based on statistical research. It both provides us with a list of Korean translations for further study and is a resource which we can use to discuss the prevalent assumption that translation demonstrates a lack.

Kim's study of translation is most valuable as an extensive database whose indispensability became evident once it was created. As he states in his preface, Kim started to collect only the titles of Korean translations of English and American literature, which was his specialty, but soon decided to expand the scope to include other major Western literatures, such as French, Russian, German, and occasionally some other literatures.

His annotated list is not as complete as its Japanese counterpart, *Meiji, Taishō, Shōwa hon'yaku bungaku mokuroku* (Index of translated literature in Meiji, Taishō, and Shōwa Japan), published in 1959, but still is an unprecedented and extremely valuable piece of research.[42] His study is also noteworthy because it attempts to search out the Japanese translations that served as the basis for Korean translations of work originally written in Western languages in the colonial period, providing an indication of the role of Japanese translation as a medium in the translating practice of modern Korea.[43]

One of the limitations of Kim's study, however, is his consistent division of "good" and "bad" translations. The criterion for "good" translation is unclear and unexplained, though it is apparent that for Kim a full and faithful translation is definitely a better translation than a partial and appropriative translation. The translator's social and literary situation is not a consideration for Kim, so he prioritizes faithfulness to the original. He also assumes that a translator's decision to translate noncanonical literary works is an indication of the translator's insufficient and immature understanding of the literature that he or she is going to translate.[44] But literary canons and aesthetic values as criteria in literature are neither natural nor permanent. They are constructed and legitimized by external literary conditions and interests. The aesthetic values deciding a "good" translation are also historically developed and arbitrary to a large extent. Ironically, certain translations are thus sometimes accepted as "better" translations not because they are more faithful to the translated texts or aesthetically accomplished but merely because they are familiar to the reader's literary taste.[45] These values become more problematic when applied to translations produced in literary and cultural situations different from our contemporary society.

Another of Kim's questionable assumptions is that translation follows a linear development. For him, Korean literary translations in the 1900s and 1910s were embryonic and premature, and 1920s Korea witnessed better translation than the previous period. Translation in the 1930s then became superior to that of the 1920s, and so on. This idea results from his prioritization of a full and faithful translation as the only desirable standard. Under this assumption, all the partial translations, unfaithful appropriations, and creative summarizations that were prevalent in early twentieth-century Korea become examples of improper and immature translating practices. This teleological perspective erases all the diverse experiments and accomplishments that do not correspond to the standard of translation current in our contemporary society. It essentially argues that early modern Korean literature is premature and transitional compared to the more "accomplished" literature of the later period, which is closer to the modern form of Western European literatures. This underlying assumption validates and reinforces the degradation of both Korean literature and translation as imitation, which is always only getting close to Western literature and "the original," respectively.[46]

The Ethics of Translation

Kim Pyŏng-ch'ŏl's value judgments of "good" and "bad" translations might be less arbitrary if he had incorporated the methodologies that Kim Young-hee uses to identify recommendable translations for different readerships. In 2002, Kim Young-hee and the Scholars of English Studies in Korea (SESK) launched a project to produce an annotated bibliography of Korean translations of English literature. Her team's primary goal was to recommend translations to serve various readers, for instance, "general readers, as school textbooks, or as texts that stand as literary works on their own."[47] For example, Kim and her team examined thirty-six Korean translations of Jane Austen's *Pride and Prejudice* published since 1945, and conclude that only two of them seem close to being recommendable translations. With this as their primary purpose, Kim and SESK set aside the historical and cultural context in which the translations were produced and judged them according to whether or not the translators had achieved the goals outlined in their prefaces. Although Kim Young-hee has intentionally excluded investigation of the specific cultural context in which a translation was produced, her approach itself demonstrates the impossibility of blanket applications of single linguistic norms to all translations.

Both Kim Pyŏng-ch'ŏl and Kim Young-hee "evaluate" the quality of translation and emphasize literal translation. But whereas Kim Pyŏng-ch'ŏl implies that literal and faithful translation is the norm for a "good" translation, Kim Young-hee proposes that this is not a norm but an ethical choice. Taking a cue from Gayatri Spivak's belief in literal translation as resistance against Western Universalism and Orientalism, Kim Young-hee argues that "'literal' and 'faithful' translations have the potential of becoming a force of resistance against internal and external hierarchies of the linguistic community" in Korea as well.[48] For her, literal translations potentially provide general readers with access to the foreign text comparable to that of specialists, and so contribute to a narrowing of the gap between them. She also maintains that literal translation will let readers recognize that the English literary text they are reading is not a normative or "natural" but a "foreign" text.[49] But she does not elaborate her argument to answer specifically how Korean literal translations can function to resist the external hierarchy of different linguistic communities. In addition, as Kim is also aware, it is necessary to ask whether we can apply the same logic to all translating languages. I will return to this issue later.

This seemingly linguistic methodology in translation is intertwined with political and ethical issues. By incorporating a poststructuralist view of language into the discussion of the English translations of "Third World" texts, Spivak criticizes the translator who is not attentive to the specificity and "rhetoricity" of the language that she translates. For Spivak, rhetoric disrupts logic about the production of an agent, and thus, "without a sense of the rhetoricity of language, a species of neo-colonialist construction of the non-western scene is afoot."[50] She goes on to argue that "in the act of wholesale translation into English there can be a betrayal of the democratic ideal into the law of the strongest. This happens when all the literature of the Third World gets translated into a sort of with-it translatese, so that the literature by a woman in Palestine begins to resemble, in the feel of its prose, something by a man in Taiwan."[51] Thus the domestication of the translation of foreign texts, which erases the rhetoricity of the Third Word text, is, for Spivak, fundamentally imperialist and unethical.

Spivak is not the only person who stresses the ethics manifested in the literalism of translation. Following Antoine Berman, who takes up literalism as an ethics of translation in that it renders the translating text into a venue where a cultural otherness is manifested,[52] Lawrence Venuti discusses the foreignizing/literal translation as a form of resistance against the cultural imperialism implied in British and American translating practices. He writes:

I want to suggest that insofar as foreignizing translation seeks to restrain the ethnocentric violence of translation, it is highly desirable today, a strategic cultural intervention in the current state of world affairs, pitched against the hegemonic English-language nations and the unequal cultural exchanges in which they engage their global others. Foreignizing translation in English can be a form of resistance against ethnocentrism and racism, cultural narcissism and imperialism, in the interests of democratic geopolitical relations.[53]

As shown in Spivak and Venuti, domestication in the English translation of a "Third World" text, by ironing out its specificity through free and smoothly readable translation, means that the conflicts and ruptures inherent in translation become invisible to the reader. This smooth and domesticating translation reinforces the dominance and universality of English over the foreign language by minimizing the recognition of difference.

The studies discussed so far all problematize domestication (liberal translation) of the texts from peripheral languages. There is, however, almost no study that considers liberal, domesticating translation as a legitimate ethical choice. That risks giving the impression that literalism in translation should always be taken as morally correct, whereas liberal and appropriative translation is unethical. But ethics are not inherent in the practice of literalism or foreignizing translation; they are defined differently depending on the sociopolitical context in which the literalism is practiced. The specific philological methodology of translation can manifest its political function only when it is situated in and engaging with a specific sociopolitical context. This might be why Kim Young-hee's incorporation of Spivak's argument into the Korean context could not be elaborated. The sociopolitical dependence of ethical judgment about literal translation becomes obvious when we look at the translation practices of early twentieth-century Korea. In a situation where the Western form of literature was already dominant and exerted not a reciprocal but a unilateral impact on Korea, appropriative and domesticating translation practice may have been considered a manifestation of cultural resistance and part of the effort to develop an alternative form of literature. What, then, did translation mean, and what was its function in early twentieth-century Korea?

The Meaning and Function of Translation in Colonial Korea

Literary translation in Korean dates back to the mid-fifteenth century, when the Korean script was invented. Among the novels written in Korean during Chosŏn Korea (1392–1910), about 40 percent (thirty-five out of ninety-five novels) have been confirmed as translations.[54] There are more translations that scholars cannot identify, though it is surely safe to assume that translated literature was not a marginal but a main field of Korean literary text production for a long time. The category of "Korean translations" included works of Korean literature originally written in Chinese, but most were translations of Chinese vernacular literature.[55] According to Min Kwan-dong, there were fifty Korean translations of Chinese vernacular novels, and if we include adaptations, the number reaches almost one hundred.[56] Although the division between translations and adaptations is not rigorously grounded, he emphasizes that "if we consider translation to be only those texts that meet our contemporary standards for translation, there would be only one such translation, the translation of the Chinese novel *Dream of the Red Chamber*, to be found in Naksŏnjae library."[57] This means that the common translating practice was not faithful and full translation but adaptive translation.

During the Chosŏn dynasty, the term *pŏnyŏk* (translation) was used to refer to diverse types of translation in tandem with other various words, and *pŏnyŏk* does not seem to have been a single dominant term to refer to translation as it is today. The Chinese script "飜譯," the Korean script for the same Chinese characters "*pŏnyŏk*," and the individual characters, "飜" and "譯," were all used in a variety of contexts and were also further combined with different Chinese characters to make more specific terms such as *chinbŏn* (眞飜) and *pŏnŏn* (翻諺) both of which mean a translation from Korean vernacular to classical Chinese. According to Yi Hyŏn-hŭi, the use of these terms was ambiguous and layered. They were used to refer to 1) translation that would be similar to the use of the term today, 2) the annotation of sounds (音注, ŭmju), and 3) copy or print (謄寫, tŭngsa).[58]

In addition to the term *pŏnyŏk*, terms such as *ŏnhae* (諺解), *isŏk* (吏釋), *chinbŏn* (眞繙), and *chikhae* (直解) were used to refer to specific types of translations in premodern Korea. Translation took place in numerous directions among texts written in classical Chinese, vernacular Chinese, vernacular Korean, and Idu (clerk readings, which use existing Chinese characters phonetically to represent Korean sounds).[59] *Pŏnyŏk* was neither a privileged term to refer to a certain type of rendition as it is today, nor a term that represents only a limited activity of linguistic translation.

In contrast to the word *pŏnyŏk*, the term *pŏnan* (繙案, adaptation) was hardly used at all to refer to a form of rendering prior to the mid-1910s. The term *pŏnan* did not appear in *Maeil sinbo*, the only Korean newspaper that circulated nationwide in 1910s, until January 20, 1916.[60] Yi Sang-hyŏp, a prominent translator/editor/journalist in the 1910s, never used the term *pŏnan* to refer to an adaptation, but instead explained adaptation as "a *pŏnyŏk* (translation) that changes Western writers' novels to make them fit our feelings and customs."[61]

Japanese fiction in the Edo period (1603–1867) was also "replete with examples of adapted variations of Ming narratives, rather than literal translations, despite the relative contemporary transparency of Chinese."[62] Japanese usage of those terms in the Edo and early Meiji (1868–1912) periods provides us with another interesting example that runs counter to our contemporary assumptions about the terms:

> Two modern Japanese words used to describe textual translation reflect this dichotomy: *hon'yaku* and *hon'an*. Although the first term, *hon'yaku*, appears in some Heian period documents, it gained a new prominence and meaning during the Tokugawa period, when it was used to distinguish correspondent translation of imported Dutch and other European-language scientific and medical texts. . . . [T]he Tokugawa period usage of the term *hon'yaku* to denote a sense of correspondence between source text and translation contains a healthy measure of *rangaku* confidence in the Western scientific tools of dissection, observation, and identification. . . . Now glossed as "adaptation," the term *hon'an* originally referred to translation in general. Over time, particularly since *hon'yaku* began to be used to signify literal translation, *hon'an* has come to refer to the intentional alteration or rewriting of classical or foreign literature and drama . . . . In the Meiji period the dichotomy between these two words reflected

fundamentally different aims: *Hon'yaku* sought for efficiency and accuracy in the service of progress and enlightenment, while *hon'an* sought to tame and modify the foreign to fit domestic sensibilities, usually in the service of art or entertainment.[63]

Meiji writers considered adaptive translation (*hon'an*) not as an "incomplete" concept of faithful translation but as a creative alternative genre to literal translation (*hon'yaku*). The hierarchical and evolutionary perspective from adaptive/liberal to faithful/literal translation is itself a view that was constructed and validated in the modern era, and ignores the historical and cultural specifics in which translations were practiced.

In Korea as well, literalness and faithfulness were not the criteria with which to single out "better" translation. During the so-called Korean Enlightenment, roughly from the 1890s to 1910s, literal translation was neither a definite preference nor a desirable practice among Korean intellectuals. Specifically, after Korea became Japan's protectorate in 1905, Korean intellectuals had to face the dilemma that their discourse on nation-building was similar to that of the colonial authorities.[64] In this historical situation, literal translation of Western and Japanese texts became the venue where Koreans confronted that dilemma. One newspaper editorial in 1909 specifically urged Korean intellectuals not to translate foreign texts literally. The editorialist criticized the indiscretion of Korean translators who rendered foreign texts literally without consideration of their appropriateness to Korea.[65] A translator's "choices" and ensuing "differences"—and distortions—made in the translated text were ethical in a subjugated culture because indigenization itself was one way of demonstrating agency under cultural and political dominance.

There is another significant factor when we discuss literal translation in colonial Korea: indirect translation or "relay translation." What could literal and faithful translation have meant when most translations were indirect translations from Japanese? What does it imply, for instance, to translate Russian literature from Japanese into Korean? Translators assumed that they were translating Russian literature, but in reality they were translating not Russian but Japanese. This complicates Naoki Sakai's "regime of translation," in which the languages are articulated as two different entities: a configuration by the regime of translation thus works for Russian and Korean literature on the conceptual level, but functions for Japanese and Korean on the practical level. It is not two sequential, binary relationships (Russian:Japanese, Japanese:Korean), but a simultaneous tri-partite relationship. When Korean intellectuals translated "Russian" literature, it was Korean and Russian literature that were theoretically being articulated as closed entities through the translation process. However, since the texts that Koreans were translating were written in Japanese and were modified by Japanese literary intervention, in actual translating practice, the Korean language was being configured vis-à-vis the Japanese language. Thus the translation of Russian literature was a process that familiarized Korean intellectuals with Japanese language and, ironically, constructed the Korean language (considered *the* emblem of Korean sovereignty in the colonial period) as an equivalent linguistic entity vis-à-vis the colonizer's language.

Yet it is symptomatic that Korean intellectuals did not repress the Russian presence in such indirect translations but made efforts to erase the Japanese; perhaps they were tempted to leave out the fact of the relay translation from the Japanese language because it was the colonizer's language and was considered relatively inferior to Western languages and literature by Koreans. Thus the number of relay translations that included the name of the original text's author increased as time went on, whereas the Japanese translations, which the translators referred to and translated from, remained unacknowledged for much longer. The prevalence of indirect translation partly explains why literal translation and discussions of it were rare in the colonial period.

Unlike literary historians in the post-liberation period, some Korean writers in the early twentieth century did not hesitate to acknowledge and problematize the impact and mediation of Japanese language and literature on Korean literature. "Korean writers are made-in-Japan (*ilbonche*)."[66] This is Yi Ik-sang's 1921 paraphrase of what the writer and translator Yi Kwang-su wrote in an article published in January 1921.[67] Yi Ik-sang takes Yi Kwang-su's argument and rephrases it. He agrees with Yi Kwang-su by saying, "It is true. Because we've learned from Japan. . . . It is unavoidable to imitate what we saw and heard." While pointing out the Japanese impact on Korean writers and literature, he accuses Korean writers of being unaware of the sociopolitical condition of contemporary Korea, and emphasizes the ethical role of writers, who are supposed to lead their people in the right direction.[68] Whether or not Yi Kwang-su and Yi Ik-sang's essays were fair, one of their main purposes was to criticize imprudent

Korean writers, and in order to do that, they had to bring up the Japanese presence in Korean literature.

It may well be true that Korean intellectuals did not go to Japan in the 1910s with the explicit purpose of studying literature, yet they nevertheless studied literature because they went to Japan. Kim Tong-in, for instance, went to Japan to study law but encountered modern literature and ended up becoming a prominent short story writer. In his memoir, he remembers that he did not understand what it meant when his friend Chu Yo-han told him that he would study literature when they met in Japan. After reading a Japanese translation of several Western literary works, Kim began to be attracted to literature.[69] It is not the case that Korean intellectuals read literary works knowing what literature—specifically, the modern form of literature—was; rather, they came to know what literature was through reading Western and Japanese literatures. But reading took place mostly in Japanese. Korean intellectuals' reading/translating of Western literatures was therefore also a process of internalizing the modern Japanese language.

Translation from Japanese into Korean was not a process of rendition from one system to another, but the very process of writing a literary work. Kim Tong-in, for instance, confessed the difficulty of writing fiction in Korean when he first began publishing his coterie magazine *Ch'angjo* (Creation) in 1919. As he writes in his memoir, "Japanese language and literature were quite useful [when I started writing my own stories]. Japanese literary language could be an example [for Korean literary language] because its mode of expression, and syntactic and grammatical changes, are similar to those of the Korean language. . . . But even though writing stories in my head was done in Japanese and so was not a problem at all, I had a hard time . . . writing them in the Korean language."[70] If this was the case for Korean writers, at least during the first two decades of the twentieth century, it is not surprising that some prominent Korean writers wrote their first works of fiction—whether officially published or not—in Japanese. For instance, Yi Kwang-su's first attempt at writing in the modern form was his Japanese short story "Ai ka" (Is it love?), and Kim Tong-in remembered that he wrote his first short story in Japanese during his stay in Japan, although he did not remember the details of the story.[71]

What should be highlighted here is that although they admitted the mediation of Japanese language and literature in the formation of Korean literature, these Korean writers simultaneously estranged them-selves from Japanese mediation, which resembles the very process of translation: the translator first succumbs to the text she is translating, but should then distance and estrange herself from it to translate it with her own words. Similarly, although most Korean intellectuals recognized the impact of Japanese literature on Korean literature, they did not en-thusiastically promote Japanese literature as a model. They admitted Ja-pan as a mediator, but not as one of the models they should ultimately emulate.[72] Thus it may seem ironic that in reality they actively used and communicated with Japanese literature possibly more than any other for-eign literature throughout the colonial period.[73] They described Japanese literature as derivative and second-grade, and excluded it from the op-tions of models for their literature. This hierarchical way of thinking was problematic in the global scope because it validated the West as universal yet at the same time served to reject the colonizer's cultural dominance. Korean writers had to deal with a doubly complex situation in the pro-cess of making their modern literature: on the one hand, they had West-ern literature as the literature they thought they should both compete with and emulate, and on the other hand, they had Japanese literature as a window into Western literature that they wanted, ultimately, to do without. This social context legitimizes liberal and unfaithful translation as a disruptive, if not subversive, practice, and complicates the judgment about the ethics of literal translation in colonial Korea.

At the very birth of modern Korean literature, none of the conven-tions of translation that we assume today had yet been established. Korean translators were more visible in several ways than were the "au-thors" of the texts they translated. First, the names of translators were materially more visible on printed texts than were the names of the writers of the source texts. Until 1919, foreign writers' names were more likely to be omitted than were translators' names. Among the transla-tions published between 1895 and 1909, sixty-one out of ninety-five omit-ted the foreign writer's name, whereas only twenty failed to include the translator's name. During 1911–19, fewer names were left out, but the prevalence of translators' names continued.[74] Second, liberal and adap-tive translations, which manifest the translator's presence in the translat-ing texts, were common. This included selective partial translation, re-structuring, and creative summaries.[75] For instance, among the Korean translations of Western texts produced between 1895 and 1909, only eighteen out of ninety-five were full and literal translations.[76] Third, translators were prominent writers and intellectuals, so their names in translating texts were recognized by readers. Korean writers such as Kim Ŏk, Ch'oe Nam-sŏn, Yi Kwang-su, Yŏm Sang-sŏp, and Hyŏn Chin-gŏn, to name only a few, were all translators before or while they wrote fiction or poetry themselves.

In early twentieth-century Korea, translation did have a specific meaning and function, but the term denoted a range of activity considerably wider than that associated with the term today. Here I use "translation" to refer to two things. First, it denotes a broad spectrum of substantial practice and texts. It includes types of rendition as various as paraphrasing, partial translation, and adaptation.[77] This expanded definition of "translation" is useful because in the formative period of modern Korean literature, there was nothing that corresponded to the narrow contemporary definition of "translation" as something always literal, full, and faithful to the "original." Second, I use "translation" as a figurative term referring to the transference of cultural capital through the process of substantial translation and the intertextual practices among different cultural fields.

Translators in the formative period were always also prominent authors and intellectuals, and the emergent Korean literature was a pastiche of adaptations, translations, and other "nonliterary" forms of discourse. While the new definition of literature was being constructed, Korean intellectuals' practice of this new style of writing occurred through the process of reading and translating foreign literary texts.[78] Translation, for them, was not only the act of introducing foreign literatures but the practice of writing in a new idiom, or discipline, which was itself the defining characteristic of that literature as well.

Translation as Methodology and as Subject

Translation's Forgotten History is part of translation studies as a specific discipline within or beside the (very large) umbrella of comparative studies. The study of the interactions among Russian, Japanese, and Korean literatures has its own significance because it is crucial to understanding modern Korean literature but has rarely been addressed for a variety of reasons: Cold War lines that prevented the development of Russian studies in South Korea, the colonial legacy that hindered the study of Japanese-Korean relations, and the linguistic challenge that required proficiency in three languages. However, equally significant in this book is a new approach to the topic. The goal of *Translation's Forgotten History* is not simply to track the impact of certain ideas or literary forms on Korean literature. The larger goal is to take translation as a methodology, and thereby to trace the specific material and institutional structures—as well as individual interventions—that created "Korean literature" of various strands in the colonial period, and how that work of construction took place through a reciprocally constitutive process of translating (and in the same process, also building as a body of texts) "Russian literature" and "Japanese literature." It is in the thick imbrication of these processes that I ground my argument that translation is truly a radical and ineradicable element in the construction of national literatures. It is in this sense that this book differs from comparative studies in a broad sense, and this is what is at stake in its method: an attempt to show the meanings and functions that translation (as a practice, a body of translated texts, and constitutive force) generated for modern national literatures during their formative period. It is here that we might begin to see literature as part of a dynamic *process* of negotiating various foreign and local values.

Meanwhile, translation as a subject has not been given due attention as a constituent force in the formation of modern literature, and has been forgotten in accounts of Korean literature for many decades until the mid-2000s, when it began to garner renewed interest. Along with articles and essays discussing translation in various contexts published over the past decade, the first three dissertations on the role of translation in the formation of modern Korean literature all came out in 2010: Pak Chin-yŏng's and Ch'oe T'ae-wŏn's in Korea, and my own dissertation in the United States.[79] Pak's work provides a useful, extensive introduction to the production of translations in the early twentieth century, mapping trends and styles of translation, indexed to different publisher and period. He does not, however, offer in-depth analysis of texts or how individual authors maneuvered in the institutional environment, and focuses most closely on 1910s adaptive translations serialized in the Korean language newspaper published by the Japanese colonial government (*Maeil sinbo*). Ch'oe T'ae-wŏn's dissertation has a somewhat narrower scope, focusing on a single author, Cho Chung-hwan, who translated Japanese novels in the 1910s, also published in the *Maeil sinbo*. The dissertation provides a detailed comparison of the Japanese source texts and Korean translations, showing what changes were made in the Korean translations and why, which will be a useful resource for further studies of Cho Chung-hwan and his era.

Translation's Forgotten History differs from these two studies in that they consider translations—which they call "adaptations" (*pŏnan*), contrary to actual usage at the time—as a specific, short-lived genre that served as a bridge between the new novel and the first modern Korean novel, published in 1917. Their accounts thus reiterate the common teleological perspective that excludes translated texts from consideration as legitimate constituents of modern Korean literature. The framework subsequently limits their ability to explain the impact of translation (including adaptive translation) on Korean literature later than the mid-1910s. Pak and Ch'oe's view of adaptive translations as a transitional form on the road to mature literature is well within the standard paradigm of national literature, which this book argues against. Nonetheless their works are great achievements, considering the difficulty in obtaining primary materials and the lack of previous scholarship on the topic.[80]

Why Russian Literature?

During the first decades of the twentieth century, Korean intellectuals enthusiastically imported foreign literatures. Russian literature was the most favored among them. The process of introducing and translating foreign literature started in the 1900s and reached its most dynamic peak in the 1920s.[81] Korean writers' essays show that they eagerly sought out and read Russian literature. For instance, Yi Hyo-sŏk remembers in his essay that he and his friends "also read English and French literature such as Hardy and Zola but nothing could compete with the popularity of Russian literature" during high school (the early 1920s).[82] Why were Korean writers attracted to Russian literature? What elements did Korean writers take from Russian literature?

Russian literature was prominent not only in Korea but in other East Asian countries as well. In the late nineteenth and early twentieth centuries, intellectuals in East Asia strove to form their own modern,

Western-style literature. In China, Korea, and Japan, Russian was the most popular "Western" literature during the formative period. It is difficult to single out one explanation, but there are a few factors to take into consideration. The first is geographical proximity. The political and geographical contact among these countries created both the need and the opportunity to know each other's language, causing a boom in language education. Literary works were often used as language texts, and language learners became familiar with the other's literature, whether or not this was their primary goal.[83] This process necessitated translations of Russian literature. A more indirect reason for Russian literature's popularity is that in the late nineteenth century, Russian literature entered the realm of what then was known to Japanese and Koreans as world literature, an established canon of European masterpieces.

Russian literature as world literature existed in East Asia mostly through other European languages, and these translations often became the basis for further translations. In Japan, many English translations were imported through the Maruzen bookstore, while direct translations from the Russian were produced by the Orthodox Theological Seminary and the Tokyo School of Foreign Languages. Nobori Shomu and Futabatei Shimei are representative translators produced by these schools. In China, May Fourth writers relied on English, German, or Japanese translations.[84] In Korea, it is possible that some Korean writers read English translations, but most contact came through Japanese translations, or Korean translations based on the Japanese. Moreover, France, England, and other European countries' validation of Russian literature as "world literature" legitimated and accelerated the importation of Russian literature in East Asia.[85]

These considerations, however, cannot fully explain the primacy of Russian among Western literatures in East Asia. It is likely that writers in Japan, China, and Korea felt a strong sympathy with Russian writers or with the characters in their works. Literature takes on a power beyond its role as an aesthetic product in societies where the state controls political speech. The Tsarist regime in Russia, the strong state in modern Japan, the Japanese colonial government in Korea—all controlled public speech and blocked politically dangerous expression, and this had the effect of endowing literature with a marked sociopolitical importance. In countries that were half- or fully colonized, such as China and Korea, literature became an alternative instrument for social reform, and a space in which intellectuals could express their sociopolitical concerns indirectly. Liang Qichao held literature to be "the most effective instrument of social reform."[86] Lu Xun considered literature as the best tool for changing the Chinese national character, while Yi Kwang-su considered it "a fundamental force which determines the rise and fall of a nation."[87]

One of the most noted elements of Tolstoy's persona as it was introduced in Korea was the claim that the Tsarist regime could not punish him because he was a renowned figure.[88] The image of the writer that Korean intellectuals idealized and took as a model was thus not that of someone who wrote aesthetically excellent literary works, but that of a man who engaged with his contemporary society through literature. This, to a certain extent, reflects the ideal man of letters in Confucian society, which stressed the leader's social/moral duty and benevolence. But it also answers to a condition in which East Asian intellectuals found themselves—namely, one with precious little room for direct engagement in their present lives, as the forces of colonization and development swept the world. In China, the May Fourth writers Lu Xun, Yu Dafu, Mao Dun, and Ba Jin found a resemblance between themselves and the "superfluous and revolutionary Hamlet tradition," exemplified by the intellectual heroes of nineteenth-century Russian novels, whose idealism was so often frustrated by state power.[89]

Lu Xun, in particular, specified why Chinese intellectuals sympathized with Russian literature. He wrote:

> Stories of detectives, adventurers, English ladies and African savages can only titillate the surfeited senses of those who have eaten and drunk their fill. But some of our young people were already conscious of being oppressed and in pain. They wanted to struggle, not to be scratched on the back, and were seeking for genuine guidance.
> That was when they discovered Russian literature.
> That was when they learned that Russian literature was our guide and friend. For from it we can see the kindly soul of the oppressed, their sufferings and struggles. Hope blazed up in our hearts when we read the works of the forties [1840s], and sorrow flooded our souls when we read those of the sixties [1860s].[90]

The image of others is produced through the projection and reflection of self-identity onto others, while self-identity itself is constructed through the same process. The images of and desires for Russian literature, in this case, disclose the self-identity of Chinese literature, or one that Chinese intellectuals were hoping to claim.

For many Korean intellectuals, Russian literature fit most closely with an ideal type of modern literature that Korean writers developed during the 1910s and 1920s. An Hwak, Chu Yo-sŏp, Kim Ki-jin, and Pak Yŏng-hŭi argued that Russian literature was different from other European literatures, such as French and English, in that it publicly pursued reform of Russian society. This led them to consider Russian literature morally superior.[91] What they saw in Russian literature was "a literature for life," meaning that Russian literature was not art for art's sake but rather an art for life's sake. The term "literature for life" was ambiguous, but it emphasized that Russian literature was involved in its society more than other literatures were. Although each writer had a slightly different idea of what "literature for life" meant, we can look at the example of Il So (probably a pen name) as one specific instance. He explained that Russian society was suffering a dark period under an authoritarian regime: people did not have any freedom of publication, speech, or organization, and the power of the Russian police put every citizen under its surveillance. He went on to argue that because Tolstoy was a great human being, the Tsarist regime could not punish him even though he stood against it.[92] Kim Myŏng-sik argued that whereas the literatures from the past were all dead because they focused on poetic and emotional expression, Russian literature was alive because it brought social concerns into the literary realm. According to Kim, Russian literature was a "living" literature because it expressed the agony and sorrow of a society and worked for social reform. Kim concluded that Russian writers sacrificed themselves for justice and righteousness and so made a literature not of beauty and technique but that of thought and people.[93] Korean writers' passionate reception of Russian literature was related to their desire for an active role for literature in their specific sociopolitical situation.

Japanese Mediation and Its Colonial Legacy

The predilection for Russian literature in Japan certainly explains in part its popularity in Korea. As Mochizuki Tetsuo argues, "other literatures, French, German, and English in particular, also played an important role in the shaping of modern Japanese literature, but of those introduced during the period [the nineteenth and early twentieth centuries], Russian literature is rightly regarded as the most influential."[94] According to Peter Berton and Paul F. Langer, who counted the number of translations in *Meiji, Taishō, Shōwa hon'yaku bungaku mokuroku* (Index of translated literature of Meiji, Taishō, and Shōwa Japan) and compiled a table listing the foreign authors most frequently translated into Japanese during the first century after the opening of Japan, five Russian authors are in the top eleven.[95]

Japan was the most important mediator in both political and cultural relationships between Korea and Russia in the late nineteenth and early twentieth centuries. In the political sphere, Japan affected Koreans' conception of Russia as a threatening and comparatively less developed country in the late nineteenth century.[96] Russia's political influence over Korea was most prominent when King Kojong went into exile under the protection of the Russian legation from February 1896 to February 1897, and subsequently pursued a pro-Russian policy against Japan's expansion. But Russia's loss in the Russo-Japanese War led Korea to become a Japanese protectorate in 1905 and a colony in 1910. Beginning in 1910, the contact Koreans had with Russian and other Western literatures was mediated almost completely through Japan.

The reception and translation of Russian literature in colonial Korea was thoroughly unsystematic. In Japan, most major Russian writers' complete works (*zenshū* in Japanese and *chŏnjip* in Korean)—which were not in fact complete compilations, but selections—were translated and published during the 1910s and 1920s, or the 1930s at the latest. Similar collections in Korean were published only in the postliberation period. Up until that point, the selection, translation, and introduction of foreign writers and works depended on the translators' personal preference, specific aims, cultural needs, political needs, and what was available to them. The patterns of reception in any location or cultural environment can hardly be delineated in a simple way, but one thing is clear: the range of selection relied heavily on the Japanese introduction of Russian writers and works. This is not to say that Korean reception exactly followed the patterns established in Japan; there were refractions in the form of changes in translations and in the emphasis/exclusion of certain information. But we can often find reasons why a specific Russian work, writer, or interpretation was popular in Korea by looking at the Japanese cases. In other words, we cannot understand Koreans' reception without considering the Japanese case.

Nevertheless, the role of Japan's mediation has not received the attention it deserves. Quite the contrary, it has been erased and neglected by translators and scholars. Neglect of Japan's mediation goes beyond the boundaries of the autonomous development camp in Korean literature in the 1970s and 1980s, mentioned above. Most Korean scholars since the colonial period consciously or unconsciously avoid the fact that Japan's mediation was instrumental in the importation of Western literatures. Only a few literary histories written since the beginning of the modern period consider it seriously. Im Hwa is an exception in emphasizing that the role of Japan's mediation is unarguably important. He maintains that if a scholar wants to understand the formative period of Korean literature, she *must* examine both the reception of Western literatures and Japan's mediation because most Western literatures entered Korea through Japan.[97] In the postliberation era, Korea's hostility toward Japan hindered the institutionalization of the study of Japanese literature.[98] These emotional and institutional difficulties have prevented Korean scholars from fully investigating the impact of Japanese mediation.

How has this erasure and avoidance played out? First, Korean translators and critics neglected the fact of indirect translation. Up until the 1920s, most foreign literary works were translated from Japanese. In the 1920s, translations from the original appeared more than they had previously, but quite a few translations remained dependent on Japanese translations. English literature was more often translated from the original, while the translation of French and German literature relied heavily on Japanese translation. In the case of Russian literary works, most were retranslated from Japanese and were completely dependent on the Japanese selection of particular texts. Second, some Korean translators pretended to retranslate from English or another Western language even though their Japanese was more developed than their English or other Western language.[99] Third, Korean translators who knew Russian pretended to translate from the Russian, yet continued to refer to Japanese versions of the work, as evidenced by their use of Japanese pronunciation of Russian names. This practice continued to the mid-1980s among Russian scholars in Korea.[100] Finally, even though some contemporary comparative studies of Korean literature in the colonial period demonstrate an awareness of the importance of the role that Japan played, they do not go on to investigate how Japan's mediation affected Korea's reception of any particular piece of literature.

As seen in the Korean case, the two-part schema of the original and the receiving culture is not adequate in the *early* stage of reception: a third party, the mediator(s), usually engages in the process of receiving. But "the early stage of reception" does not mean only the first encounter with a foreign literature but also the period between the first introduction of a foreign literature and the time when complete translations from the original are widely available, most of the accepted canon of the foreign literature has been translated, and the receiving culture has developed its own body of criticism of the received literature. Until this point is reached, the vast majority of people in the receiving culture are likely to experience the foreign literature under the influence of mediating cultures.

The essential role of the mediator(s) in the early stage of reception becomes obvious when we examine the history of the reception of Russian literature. Russian literature came to the French and German literary worlds first because a few key Russian writers and intellectuals had close relationships with the intellectuals of those countries. But even in England, which later gave birth to Constance Garnett, one of the most celebrated translators of Russian literature, writers and scholars initially read Russian literature mostly in French or in German. The United States faced the same situation.[101] In the case of Japan, there were three major conduits for Russian literature's introduction: students at the Tokyo School of Foreign Languages, students at the Orthodox Theological Seminary, and Maruzen, a Japanese bookseller established in 1869. Although the role of the first two groups, whose members translated Russian literature directly from Russian, was significant, the most influential was Maruzen, which imported European translations—mostly in English. Maruzen also imported European criticism and essays on Russian literature. Therefore the main mediator affecting the early reception of Russian literature in Japan was England. In the case of Korea, mentioned above, Japan was an essential window onto Russian literature, and Korea's reception was prefigured by Japan to a great extent. Mediation was essential to some degree in the early stage of reception of a foreign literature, and it was crucial when the reception was taking place under colonization. The flow of Russian literature around the world through various layers of mediation is not a process that we can afford to overlook. The reception in Korea, in particular, because of the extremely heavy impact of Japan's mediation, provides a stark picture of the general process.

Despite the significance of Japanese mediation, the work of both translators and writers in the colonial period and of contemporary Korean scholars is characterized by neglect of Japan as the main path of reception of Western literatures. Because of the continued effects of the colonial legacy and the Cold War—which have steered scholars away from translation and the Russian language, respectively—there have been few detailed studies of this impact. Due to this systematic understudy, the reflections and refractions that occurred in the triadic process of Korean writers' importation and appropriation of Western literatures have been neglected. Erasing the Japanese mediation also means missing the different functions that Russian literature filled in Korea and Japan. I hope that this study will provide a way of looking at the encounter with foreign texts in the colonial period in terms of a cooperation of diverse formative forces, which cannot be simplified and flattened into the issue of transplantation or autonomy in literary development in Korea.

Russian Language and Literature in Japan and Korea

The import of Russian literature into Korea was more dependent on Japan's mediation than was that of any other Western literature because there were so few Koreans who could translate into Korean from the Russian source text. Some Korean intellectuals who knew Russian were An Mak, Ch'oe Sŭng-man, Yi Ch'an, Chin Hak-mun, and members of Foreign Literature Studies Organization such as Ham Tae-hun, Yi Sŏn-gŭn, Kim On, and Yi Hong-jong. It is unclear whether they were capable of rendering Russian texts directly from Russian, however. Kim On and Ham Tae-hun had graduated from the Russian Department of Tokyo Foreign Language University. But it was only Ham Tae-hun and Kim On who actively translated Russian literature and wrote articles on it. Their Russian-language education was undertaken in Japan because formal instruction in Korea was discontinued with the beginning of the Russo-Japanese War in 1904. Except for these Koreans, most translators of Russian literature did not know Russian.

Japan's study of the West dates back to the mid-sixteenth century, but Japanese concern with Russia did not begin until the second half of the eighteenth century, when Russia's eastward and southward advance brought confrontations between Russian and Japanese people. The main sources for the early Russian studies in the Tokugawa period were "Dutch and Chinese sources, reports of natives and fishermen, as well as the 'northern' information obtained directly from exploration and travel."[102] But the difference between Dutch-Western studies and Russian studies was that Russian studies had the added importance of being a way of learning about a potential enemy, rather than just curiosity. In 1808, the shogunate asked a scholar to learn Russian and Manchurian in order to read diplomatic documents, marking the official beginning of government study of Russian. The first Japanese-Russian dictionary (*Russko-Iaponskii Slavar'—Wa-ro Tsugen Hiko*) was published in 1857 by the Asiatic Department of the Russian Ministry of Foreign Affairs.[103]

A couple of schools were available for Russian-language study in the beginning of the Meiji period, but intensive study of Russian in Tokyo began after the Russian priest Nikolai arrived in 1861 for Russian Orthodox missionary work. The so-called Nikolai School changed its name in 1873 from the School of Foreign Languages (Gogakkō) to the Orthodox Theological Seminary (Seikyō Shingakkō).[104] In terms of the study of Russian language and literature, the three most important schools before World War II were the Orthodox Theological Seminary, the Tokyo School of Foreign Languages (Tōkyō Gaikokugo Gakkō), and Waseda University. The Orthodox Theological Seminary became less popular after Meiji, but Waseda, founded in the Taishō period, continued to make great contributions to Russian studies in its stead.

After changing its name in 1873, the Orthodox Theological Seminary opened a separate school for girls. Both schools were seven-year secondary schools, and students with elementary education (*kōtō shōgakkō*) were qualified to enter them.[105] Students learned a number of subjects in addition to the Bible, and the texts were almost all in the Russian language. There were fifty students in the school in 1881, the year Konishi Masutarō, who translated Lao-tzu into Russian with Tolstoy, entered. The first graduation took place in 1882, and it is estimated that there were two graduates.[106] The number of graduates was never large, fluctuating between five and twelve. The best graduates had a chance to study in Orthodox seminaries in Russia.[107] The four main graduates of Orthodox Theological Seminary who contributed to Russian literature and thought were Seki Takesaburō, Nobori Shomu, Senuma Kayō, and Konishi Masutarō.[108] The school went into decline after the Meiji era and finally closed in 1918, a year before the Russian Department of Waseda University opened.[109]

The Tokyo School of Foreign Languages was founded in 1873, and many students who were interested in Russian transferred there from the Orthodox Theological Seminary. In the beginning, the school offered language instruction in English, French, German, Russian, and Chinese. In 1874 the English department organized a separate school, and this school added Korean in 1880. The school was open to students aged fourteen to eighteen with elementary school education, and classes were conducted for twenty-four hours in total, four days a week. The program was five years long but was changed to six years in 1874. In 1876, it was revised again to five years—three years of lower level and two years of upper level.[110] The program consisted of composition and translation, logic, arithmetic, algebra, geometry, accounting, geography, history, physics, philosophy, and gymnastics, all of which were taught in foreign languages. Although Russian literature was not specifically taught, literary works were often used as texts for language classes.[111]

The Tokyo School of Foreign Languages was closed in 1885 by order of Minister of Education Mori Arinori but opened again in 1897.[112] When it reopened, the school had seven language programs: English, French, German, Russian, Spanish, Chinese, and Korean. Italian was added two years later. The earlier school had been a secondary school, but the newly opened one was a three-year junior college. The basic program was three years, but there was a two-year intensive course (*bekka*) as well. The name of this intensive course was changed later to special course (*senshūka*). In 1906, a one-year intensive course was designed in the Russian, Chinese, and Korean language departments.[113] The first chair of the Russian Language Department—serving from 1899 to 1902—was Futabatei Shimei, who was also a graduate of the school, and because of his personality and the popularity of Russian literature, language and literature were more emphasized than in other departments.[114]

The Department of Russian Literature in Waseda University opened in 1919. During World War I, Professor Katagami Noboru in the Department of English Literature went to Russia and studied at Moscow University for several years. When he came back to Waseda, he organized the Russian Department. The first class started with seven students, and between eight and thirteen students entered the department annually.[115] The whole program took three years. But in 1935 the school authorities decided to abolish the Department of Russian Literature, and they closed it in 1937. The reason for this is not clear, but it is presumed that Waseda University made the decision because, when the Japanese student movement intensified around the Manchurian Incident, quite a few students of the Russian Department were arrested for their involvement.[116] The curriculum placed a clear emphasis on literature and literary history and criticism, setting it apart from the Orthodox Theological Seminary and the Tokyo School of Foreign Languages. Students could select three mandatory courses selected from six possible courses, on Gogol, Chekhov, Dostoevsky, Turgenev, Tolstoy, and Modern Russian writers.[117]

Graduates of these three schools contributed to Japanese diplomacy with Russia and to developments in the Japanese literary world. Among them, two important translators during the first stage in the reception of Russian literature were Futabatei Shimei, a graduate of the Tokyo School of Foreign Languages, and Nobori Shomu, a graduate of the Orthodox Theological Seminary. Meanwhile, although the most frequently translated Western prose in 1920s Korea was Russian, the number of Korean intellectuals who knew Russian was quite small, and it was only in the mid-1920s that the first generation, who had studied Russian language and literature in Japan, appeared in the Korean literary world.

In Korea, the first Russian school opened in May 1896. It was a part of the National School of Foreign Languages (Kwallip Oegugŏ Hakkyo), which officially started in 1895, incorporating a Japanese language school founded in 1891 and an English school dating from 1894. It subsequently created programs for French (1895), Russian (1896), Chinese (1897), and German (1898). It was established to answer the need to educate interpreters and translators following the modern treaties signed with Japan in 1876, and later with other Western countries. N. N. Biriukov, a Russian military captain, was assigned to the Russian school as the first instructor in February 1896. When it opened, fifty-one students enrolled, growing to eighty-eight in 1898. The increase reflects the growing prominence of Russian power after King Kojong's escape to the Russian legation in 1896–97 when Queen Min was assassinated by Japan. Despite an increase in student enrollment, the number of graduates fell because they either lost interest, quit due to the hard work, or found jobs after just a few years of study. The total number of graduates of the Russian school is unknown. The Russian school closed in 1904 when the Russo-Japanese War broke out and did not reopen during the colonial period. Up to 1906, the Western-language programs took students five years to complete, and Eastern-language programs four years, but every program was shortened to three years thereafter.[118]

Koreans who learned Russian language and literature studied either in the Tokyo School of Foreign Languages or at Waseda University. As far as is known, four Korean men majored in Russian literature in Japan during the colonial period. All were members of the Foreign Literature School (Haeoe Munhakp'a) organized in 1926 by Korean students who were studying foreign literature in Japanese universities at the time. They published their own journal, *Foreign Literature* (*Haeoe munhak*), in January 1927. Although the journal closed after the second issue (July 1927), the group continued to be active in introducing foreign literature into the Korean literary world in the second half of the 1920s and in the 1930s. The most active member of the group was Ham Tae-hun, who studied Russian language and literature in the Tokyo School of Foreign Languages and graduated in 1931. He was particularly interested in Chekhov and wrote energetically about Russian literature for Korean newspapers and journals. Kim On also studied in the Department of Russian Language at the Tokyo School of Foreign Languages and majored in Chekhov. Yi Hong-jong was another member of the Foreign Literature School, but dropped out. Yi Sŏn-gŭn studied history and Russian literature at Waseda University and contributed to the introduction of Pushkin to Korea.[119]

Although only a small number of Koreans studied in Russian departments, this does not necessarily mean that other Korean intellectuals had no chance to study Russian literature in universities. For example, Chin Hak-mun did not major in Russian literature, but was interested in it and translated a number of Russian works.[120] He was a student in the English department at Waseda University in the 1910s. At this time Waseda students studied and wrote their theses on Russian literature in the Department of English Literature.[121] This was an important group in the introduction of Russian literature to the Japanese literary world. Because the Russian department was founded relatively late (1919), some

students in the English department studied English in order to read
Russian literature in English translation. In his 1963 essay "Nengetsu
no ashioto" (Footsteps of time), Hirotsu Kazuo, who was a famous Chekhov translator-scholar as well as a writer, wrote that "at the time we were
students of the English department but our interest was only in Russian
and French literature. We used our English skill not to read English and
American literature but to read Russian and French."[122] When Hirotsu
studied at Waseda from 1910 to 1913, the only foreign literature department was the English department. From this, it can be supposed that
Chin also, directly or indirectly, learned about Russian literature in the
English department.

Although the reception of Russian literature in Japan has various
subcurrents (from nineteenth-century realist novels to twentieth-century
modernist poetry), the most influential Russian writers were the
nineteenth-century realist novelists, whose early reception was accelerated by sociopolitical conditions. For instance, Turgenev was first received
as the creator of the neologisms "nihilist" and "nihilism" in his *Fathers and
Sons*,[123] and Tolstoy's antiwar philosophy and anarchist/socialist thought
resonated with debates surrounding the Russo-Japanese War.[124] Later,
most of the Russian writers would be dealt with in terms of humanism.[125]

Even though Japanese intellectuals referred to many English translations and essays on Russian literature, the Japanese context of reception shows significant differences from the European one. The stark
difference is illustrated by the case of Turgenev. In England and France,
Turgenev was the first among Russian writers to become popular because his writing style resembled a Victorian style and suited European
readers' taste.[126] However, it was the social aspects of Turgenev's novel
Fathers and Sons that first attracted Japanese intellectuals.[127] The social
involvement of Russian literature was a conspicuous feature in the Japanese reception, and this image exerted an impact on Korean intellectuals' predilection for Russian literature, especially in the 1920s.

In Korea, all Russian literature was amenable to description using one
adjective, "*Rosia-jök*" (*Roshia-teki* in Japanese), meaning "typically Russian,"
and Korean writers recognized and shared the various meanings of this
word. This category of "Russian" preceded contact with any Russian literary works, and it affected Koreans' understanding and interpretation
of individual Russian writers and their works. In the very beginning of
the reception of Russian literature in Western Europe, Russian literature
was often characterized as crude and unpleasant to readers with delicate

taste.[128] But this negative connotation never existed in Japan and Korea. André Lefevere also mentions the impact of the image of a certain literature on the reader: "In the past, as in the present, rewriters created images of a writer, a work, a period, a genre, sometimes even a whole literature. These images existed side by side with the realities they competed with, but the images always tended to reach more people than the corresponding realities did, and they most certainly do so now. Yet the creation of these images and the impact they made has not often been studied in the past, and is still not the object of detailed study."[129] Rather than individual literary works, the *image* of Russian literature and its authors, as entities that addressed social problems under a suppressive regime, motivated a consistent interest in Russian literature among Korean writers.

Though not without exception, the introduction of Russian writers and their works in Korea was generally influenced by the images of Russian literature created in Japan. But in the Korean reception we can see even greater emphasis on politics and social engagement. In the 1920s, the reception of Russian writers and literary works in Korea was politicized to a certain extent, and this is true even if we exclude the clear case of proletarian literature. Not only Gorky, for his involvement in proletarian literature, but nineteenth-century Russian writers such as Tolstoy, Turgenev, Chekhov, and Dostoevsky were considered socialist (an ambiguous term at the time) or resistant intellectuals.[130]

Reception was not always simultaneous in Japan and Korea. Korea's reception of strands introduced in Japan sometimes took place simultaneously and sometimes much later. The reception process could be refracted in the Korean case by political circumstances, censorship, and/or ideological differences between the translator and the Russian and Japanese sources. Russian writers were introduced as socially engaged writers in the 1900s and 1910s, and became more radical in Korea in the 1920s. As mentioned above, Tolstoy and Dostoevsky were even introduced as socialists in one essay because of their interest in society and the lives of the people around them. Chekhov was considered a writer who had deep sympathy for lower-class people, and who reflected the pessimistic atmosphere of the society around him in the late nineteenth century. Turgenev's novels and his characters were enthusiastically received by the early proletarian writers. It goes without saying that Gorky enjoyed great popularity among proletarian writers in the late 1920s, and especially in the early and mid-1930s.

In the selection and introduction of Russian literature, Korean intellectuals solidified an image of a certain literature, and this process was also an integral part of the formation of their own self-image as writers, and the construction of a place for literature in society. They identified with Russian writers' personal lives, along with the characters in Russian works, which were taken as role models for Korean writers and their own fictional characters.

Korean intellectuals' identification with Russian writers and their characters was not at all minor. The followers of Tolstoy as a great light are not hard to find: Ch'oe Nam-sŏn, Yi Kwang-su, Kim Tong-in, and pacifist anarchists of the 1920s. Gorky was another writer whose personal life sometimes eclipsed his literary works. When the writer's real life was not so notable, Korean writers identified not with the Russian writer but with his fictional characters. In Turgenev's case, the writer's personal life was not introduced and not popularly known (probably because of his weak and irresolute personal character and bourgeois lifestyle). Instead, writers like Kim Ki-jin identified with some of his fictional characters. The characters in Turgenev's novels fascinated other Korean writers as well, and their names often appear in Korean literary works and essays. Chekhov and Dostoevsky lie between the two cases. Their sympathy for lower-class people and episodes from their personal lives, their agony and despair, were popularly introduced as part of a humanist narrative. Although Soviet proletarian literature had an impact on all East Asian countries, the popularity of Russian literature in Korea began well before the importation of proletarian literature. In colonial Korea, nineteenth-century Russian writers were represented as having a connection to proletarian literature, notably by the early proletarian literature leaders such as Kim Ki-jin and Pak Yŏng-hŭi, as discussed in Chapter 3.

Because Korean writers often assumed that they did not have role models in their own modern literature due to its short history, they projected their ideal identity through Russian literature. The process of appropriating and rewriting Russian literature reflects a procedure in which writers constructed their own social identity and legitimized their literature during the colonial period. Examining Korean intellectuals' rewriting of Russian literature lets us focus on the ways in which translation functioned as a medium that helped Korean intellectuals re-form and explicate the world around them.

Introduction to Chapters

The following chapters employ both historical approaches and close literary readings to examine Korean writers' incorporation of Russian literature through Japanese mediation while they were in the process of forging their own modern literature. Korean intellectuals used literary translation as a way of actively engaging with the social and intellectual transformations of early colonial Korea.

Approaching the topic from several perspectives, this introduction providing theoretical and contextual explanation is followed by a discussion of the construction of the modern intellectual/writer and a modern literary theory, and then two chapters showing the actual process of translation and creation. Chapter 1 thus focuses on the building and deployment of discourses about the modern intellectual/writer and modern literary theory rather than on the creation of literary works. Chapters 2 and 3 demonstrate the concrete process of literary translation and appropriation in the creation of particular modern Korean stories.

The selection of writers covers the Russian authors most frequently translated into Korean in the early twentieth century (Tolstoy, Chekhov, and Turgenev), while covering some of Korean literature's canonical authors, including representatives of the Korean Enlightenment school, the school of national literature, and the proletarian literary movement.[131] This book ends with a short epilogue that deals with three major issues: Russian literature in postcolonial Korea, the shared sensibility in East Asia embodied in their engagement with Russian literature, and the possibility of writing an alternative literary history through translation as methodology.

Chapter 1, Manipulation of Fame and Anxiety: Construction of a Model Intellectual and a Theory of Literature, examines Korean writers' construction of Tolstoy as a towering moral authority in order to promote and legitimate their own ideas about modern intellectuals and a new literature. This chapter argues that translation of foreign texts, while serving to introduce the source literature, also fulfilled the translators' desire to authorize their own arguments. Ch'oe Nam-sŏn, the first Korean intellectual to publish modern-style poetry and literary journals, built up Tolstoy's fame in Korea while utilizing that authority to validate his own ideas about the need for young, engaged intellectuals.

Yi Kwang-su, recognized as having written the first modern novel, adopted parts of Tolstoy's writings on art to create his own theory of Korean national literature. In this process he revealed his complex anxiety as a colonial intellectual. He openly and proudly claimed himself as a student of Tolstoy and emphasized Tolstoy's influence on him, while giving little credit to the Japanese theorists (for instance, Tsubouchi Shōyō) whose work he used at least as much as he used Tolstoy. I argue that Yi's overemphasis on the Russian texts may be a symptom of a colonial ambivalence (or predicament) in which he tried to conceal the colonial influence in his own work and, by implication, the coloniality of modern Korean literature. Thus this chapter tries to show the complications of colonization that were imbedded in theories of modern Korean literature from the beginning.

Chapter 2, Rewriting Literature and Reality: Translation, Journalism, and Modern Literature, examines Hyŏn Chin-gŏn's adaptation of a Chekhov short story. This chapter both demonstrates the process of Hyŏn's creative engagement with Chekhov in the mid-1920s and shows the interpenetration of translation, creative writing, and journalistic discourse at the time. For instance, in Hyŏn's adaptation his female protagonist, Suni, who is a child bride, burns down her husband's house to escape her unendurable marriage to an older man. Through this character, Hyŏn was able to link female arson with resistance to the institution of young marriage, which was a hotly debated issue at the time. I argue that Hyŏn's portrayal of Suni as a sympathetic criminal commented on and eventually actually influenced journalistic discourse on early marriage and associated incidents of female arson in the late 1920s and early 1930s. This illustrates how translation, journalistic writing, and creative writing all influenced each other and how translation was one among many modes of intervening in ongoing public debates.

More broadly, this chapter analyzes three rewritings of Chekhov's text, by writers from Japan, New Zealand, and Korea. These three rewritten texts in different languages not only maximize the visibility of the social problem of child labor that is a main theme of Chekhov's story, but also introduce a theme that is not emphasized in the source text: gender. In the hands of the three writers, Chekov's original character is transformed into a boy working in a billiard room, a nursemaid whose femaleness is a central problem for the story, and a sexually abused young bride. In dialogue with the Chekhov story, each of the three writers created a figure who responded to his or her own society's pressing social issues, making it possible for the Chekhov character to be enriched by multifaceted afterlives. The travels and transformations of this literary character allow us to reconsider world literature; against the diffusion model that privileges the original forms at their origin, we can focus on the processes of literary relations that make up world literature. This perspective could become an alternative to influence studies that often reinforce cultural hierarchies invented in the modern era.

Chapter 3, Aspirations for a New Literature: Constructing Proletarian Literature from Nineteenth-Century Russian Literature, investigates Turgenev's place in the early phases of Korean proletarian literature. The argument here is that it was not Soviet proletarian writers but prerevolutionary Russian writers—particularly Turgenev, a prototypical bourgeois writer—who exerted a significant impact on Korean proletarian literature in its early stages. This was possible through a process of politically committed appropriation. Cho Myŏng-hŭi, one of the most prominent proletarian writers, translated Turgenev's *Nakanunie* (On the eve) and later wrote a seminal short story, "Naktonggang" (Naktong River), using similar characters and plot structure. Cho's appropriation provides us with a noteworthy example not only of how a translation is affected by the medium of publication—newspaper serialization in this case—but also of how a writer/translator creates through the process of translation.

Using this case study, which demonstrates that Korean proletarian literature tried to construct a connection with the tradition of nineteenth-century Russian literature (rather than with Soviet proletarian literature), I aim to rethink the international coalition of proletarian literature, and argue that writers had a different sense of the contemporaneity and internationality, which were key features of proletarian literature. Korean writers often associated the term "proletariat" with colonized Korea(ns) in a way that included the colonized intellectuals themselves. This may help explain the prevalence of Korean proletarian literature written by *and about* intellectuals. This understanding lets us better comprehend both proletarian literary writers' aspirations and their literary crystallization of those aspirations in different sociocultural contexts.

CHAPTER I

Manipulation of Fame and Anxiety

Construction of a Model Intellectual
and a Theory of Literature

Yi Kwang-su's historic 1916 article on literature, entitled "Munhak iran hao" (What is literature?), opens by drawing a distinction between the contemporary use of "*munhak*" (literature) and the traditional one:

> The word "*munhak*" is now different from the way it was used in the past. Now, *munhak* takes on a usage similar to that used by Westerners, so that we can say *munhak* is a translation of *Literatur* or *Literature* [foreign languages in the original]. Thus *munhak* is not traditional Korean literature but the denotation of *munhak* in Western languages.[1]

It may seem an unusual move to borrow an unknown Western phrase, "*Literatur* or *Literature*," to explain the meaning of a Korean word that was in common use at the time. This paradox goes to the heart of Yi's predicament of having to establish the concept of modern literature and simultaneously infuse it with new meaning and value. Modern Korean literature was formed in a dynamic interaction with Western literatures during the first half of the twentieth century, and during the process of this formation, Korean intellectuals used the term "*munhak*" as a translation for a western concept of "literature" before there were any substantial works of "literature" in Korean.[2]

Although Yi Kwang-su claims that "*munhak*" was no longer a word that contemporary Koreans could use to refer to their own literature, he was not advocating a simple transplantation of the institution from the West. On the contrary, he urged the creation of a new Korean literature, using Western literature as a mediator or medium. The "new Korean literature" that Yi promoted was developed as an ongoing practice, in a process of mediation and transformation of foreign concepts and literary works. But to establish modern literature, Korea would first need people to write, and to underwrite, the first modern literary works. Ch'oe Nam-sŏn and Yi Kwang-su's efforts to create a model of the writer/intellectual and a theory of literature are apparent in their translation and interpretation of the world-famous Russian writer Lev Tolstoy (1828–1910) and his works.

This chapter examines the appropriation of Tolstoy's ideas on life and literature through which Korean intellectuals, particularly Ch'oe Nam-sŏn (1890–1957) and Yi Kwang-su (1892–?), established a model for a modern Korean intellectual and developed a theory of literature for Korea and the Korean language, in the early twentieth century. Ch'oe was active as a publisher of influential journals such as *Sonyŏn* (The young, 1908–11), which is generally considered the first literary journal in Korea, and *Ch'ŏngch'un* (Youth, 1914–18). Yi is credited with having written what is usually considered the first modern Korean novel, *Mujŏng* (The heartless, 1917), and worked together with Ch'oe on the journals Ch'oe published. Both Ch'oe and Yi claimed Tolstoy as their intellectual model and employed Tolstoy's ideas to develop modern Korean literature. Tolstoy was the first Western writer to receive sustained attention among those who were endeavoring to create a modern Korean literature. Among Russian prose writers, Tolstoy was the one whose works were the most frequently translated, and during the early twentieth century Korean commentators wrote more articles on Tolstoy than on any other author.[3]

Through the examination of Ch'oe and Yi's writings, this chapter discusses Korean writers' creation and substantialization of Tolstoy as the epitome of incontestable moral authority in order to validate their own thoughts on modern intellectuals and a new literature. While seeming to serve merely to introduce the source literature, I would argue, translation of foreign texts also accomplished the translators' desire to legitimize their own opinions. As Ch'oe Nam-sŏn's case shows, he constructed Tolstoy's fame in Korea while using that authority to legitimize his own ideas about the need for young, engaged intellectuals in a new Korean society. In Yi Kwang-su's case, he took on parts of Tolstoy's theory of art to forge his own ideas of Korean literature but at the same time revealed his own complex anxiety as a colonial intellectual. Yi frequently declared that he was a follower of Tolstoy and stressed Tolstoy's influence on him, but was somewhat less enthusiastic about discussing the impact of Japanese theorists whose ideas he used at least as much as he used those of Tolstoy. Yi's overemphasis on the Russian texts, I would argue, may be an indication of a colonial incongruity and predicament in which he struggled to conceal the coloniality of his own literary theory and, by extension, the coloniality of modern Korean literature. I hope that this chapter will provide a better understanding of complications of colonization that were entrenched in theories of modern Korean literature from its foundation.

Contingency and Availability: The Tolstoy Boom in Japan

Why did Ch'oe and Yi select Tolstoy as a model for themselves and other Koreans? To answer that question, we need to acknowledge the role of contingency and accessibility in the rise of Tolstoy's popularity in Korea. As was standard for Korean intellectuals at the time, Ch'oe and Yi went to study in the country that had established itself as the most modern in East Asia—Japan. At exactly the time they happened to be there, an enormous Tolstoy boom was sweeping Japan. Had they instead studied there in the 1880s and 1890s, when Turgenev was in vogue, the pattern of importation might have been different.[4] Even though they had almost no direct exchange with the people involved in importing Russian literature to Japan, Ch'oe and Yi introduced Tolstoy to Koreans because he was revered by a significant number of Japanese intellectuals, much more so than were other Western writers. Contingency and availability were thus crucial factors in the introduction of Russian literature in Korea, and one of the factors that prefigured its patterns. Before looking at Ch'oe and Yi's opportunistic use of Tolstoy, we therefore need to examine the context of their encounter with Tolstoy in Japan.

Ch'oe Nam-sŏn was born into a *chung'in* family in Seoul in 1890. The *chung'in* was the middle class, between aristocrats and commoners, and made significant contributions to modernization in Korea; Choe's father, Ch'oe Hŏn-gyu, worked for the meteorological office.[5] At the age of twelve, in 1902, Ch'oe stopped learning Chinese characters and the Classics—he already knew enough Chinese characters to write—and entered Kyŏngsŏng Haktang (Kyŏngsŏng Private School). There, he studied Japanese language for three months and started to subscribe to the *Ōsaka asahi shinbun* (Ōsaka Asahi News) from its Korean branch office. The newspaper was one of the most important conduits of modernity, in form, institution, and language. Ch'oe also subscribed to Korean newspapers such as the *Cheguk sinmun* (Imperial News), *Hwangsŏng sinmun* (Capitol News), and *Taehan maeil sinbo* (Korean Daily News). Although he was only fourteen years old by this time, he probably had a reasonable understanding of the international situation from these Korean and Japanese newspapers.[6]

In October 1904, Ch'oe was one of the students selected by the Korean government to be sent to Japan to study. He took a special class in Tōkyō Furitsu Daiichi Chūgakkō (Tokyo First Public Middle School) as a Korean government fellowship student,[7] but he had to return to Korea in January 1905 because his parents fell ill.[8] A few months after his return, in August 1905, Korea became a protectorate of Japan, a development that caused him great distress. He decided to go to study in Japan again in the spring of 1906 at his own expense and entered Waseda University in September of the same year,[9] but again soon dropped out. According to Ch'oe's memoir, a student-led mock congress adopted a resolution that insulted Korean students, which led to Korean students' confrontation with the university that did not make a public apology regarding the incident, which was requested by Korean students, and some Korean students including Ch'oe dropped out as a result.[10] Though he quit school, he stayed in Tokyo and published a number of poems in *Taehan hakhoe wŏlbo* (Korean Society Monthly Report), a bulletin of the society of Korean students in Japan. In June 1908, he returned to Korea with many reference works for his writing and the newest printing equipment,[11] and published the first issue of *Sonyŏn* in November 1908, five months after his homecoming.

Yi Kwang-su and Ch'oe Nam-sŏn met for the first time in 1908, while they were in Japan. Yi first went to Japan to study in August 1905, around the time Theodore Roosevelt's negotiation around the Portsmouth Treaty was finding an end to the Russo-Japanese War. After learning Japanese in Tōkai Gijuku (Tōkai School) and studying at Taisei Chūgakkō (Taisei Middle School) for about a year in 1906, Yi was admitted into the second

year of the Meiji Gakuin *futsū gakubu* (Meiji Academy general education
course) in 1907, and graduated in March 1910. After graduation, Yi returned to Korea and found jobs teaching at Osan Hakkyo (Osan School)
and editing a number of journals in Seoul and Shanghai. His second period of study in Japan started at Waseda University in September 1916,
following one year of study in a preparation school (Waseda Daigaku
Kōtō Yoka), and he stayed in Japan until he was forced to flee to Shanghai after writing a draft manifesto for the Chosŏn ch'ŏngnyŏn tongnip-
tan (Korean liberation youth association) in January 1919.[12]

When Ch'oe Nam-sŏn and Yi Kwang-su first learned of Tolstoy's
work as young Koreans living in Japan, Tolstoy had already achieved great
fame, even before his well-known antiwar message during the Russo-
Japanese War. The introduction of Tolstoy's novels in Japan started in
the late 1880s, and the first translation into Japanese was a part of *War
and Peace*, done by Mori Tai in 1886.[13] Following this work, quite a few
translations of Tolstoy's philosophical and fictional works circulated in
the Japanese literary world. Around 1890 a substantial introduction to Tolstoy that included his literary works, philosophy, and biography was
published in several periodicals, and in the 1890s a number of Tolstoy's
novels were translated and numerous essays were written about him, including the important "A Biography of Tolstoy" by Tokutomi Roka.[14]

Tolstoy was received in different ways by different groups, but the
aspect of his persona that appealed most to Japanese readers was his humanist and pacifist social philosophy. This humanism and pacifism resonated with Japanese anarchists and early socialists around the time of the
Russo-Japanese War. It was Tolstoy's antiwar efforts that had the greatest influence on his reception in the Meiji period (1868–1912). Knowledge
of his antiwar philosophy caused a sensation throughout Japan and deeply
moved Japanese intellectuals. When Tolstoy's antiwar essay "Bethink
Yourselves!" was published in *The Times* in England on June 27, 1904,[15] it
created a sensation and was reprinted across Western countries. It was
soon translated into Japanese and printed in *Heimin shinbun* (The Common Man's Newspaper) in Japan on August 7 of the same year. Japanese
intellectuals' response to this essay was so enthusiastic that "the issue of
Heimin shinbun immediately sold out its print run of 8000."[16] The work
was also published as a single volume, and many other newspapers and
magazines published excerpts. Japanese intellectuals recognized the relationship between Tolstoy's ideas of philanthropy and pacifism and their

own antiwar anarchism, which manifested itself in a denial of the necessity of both class and the state. From this point on, the early socialist group Heiminsha (Common People's Society) continuously published essays on Tolstoy's philosophy. They also sent Tolstoy a letter with copies of their newspaper in September 1904 and received a reply from him, although his reply arrived after the newspaper had been discontinued.

It was not the case, however, that every Japanese intellectual accepted Tolstoy's ideas wholeheartedly. Japanese intellectuals' nationalism often conflicted with Tolstoy's antiwar opinions. They preferred to recognize that Tolstoy was a great person and a Russian prophet, but also to point out that he was not Japanese.[17] In fact, this need to reconcile pacifism and nationalism was not limited to Japanese intellectuals, but runs through Tolstoy's own ideas. Tolstoy's feelings about the war were ambivalent, and he himself suffered from patriotism, although he did try to resist it. When he heard about the fall of Port Arthur, he wrote in his diary, "The surrender of Port Arthur has distressed me. I suffer from it. This is patriotism. I was brought up on it and am not free from it, just as I am not free from personal egoism, family egoism, even aristocratic egoism."[18] But this ambivalence never appeared in print. Only his antiwar stance, which the essay "Bethink Yourselves!" expressed, publicly represented his ideas on the Russo-Japanese War.[19]

Even the Japanese intellectuals who supported Tolstoy's antiwar stance, such as the dedicated socialist Kōtoku Shūsui, did not endorse Tolstoy's analysis of the cause of war. Tolstoy argued that war resulted from individuals' estrangement from God and their forgetfulness of God's words.[20] In his article "Comments on Tolstoy's Anti-War Opinion," Kōtoku wrote, "Tolstoy indicts individuals' corruption as the cause of war, and so he wants to correct the situation by teaching them to repent. But we socialists argue that war results from economic competition, and thus we can prevent war only by stopping that competition. This is where we cannot agree with Tolstoy."[21]

By publishing his critique on Tolstoy, Kōtoku continued to distinguish himself from the Christians, who were having a profound impact on the Japanese socialist movement.[22] In the end, it was Tolstoy's grounding of his ideology in religion that triggered the destabilization and disintegration of the socialist group that formed the core of the *Heimin shinbun*.[23] In August 1905, the journal *Chokugen* (Straight talk) belatedly published Tolstoy's reply disapproving of socialism for its emphasis on materialism, and Christian-socialists such as Nakazato Kaizan decided to follow Tolstoy.[24]

This notwithstanding, Tolstoy's philosophy and ethics continued to profoundly influence many Japanese anarchists and early socialists, beginning with Kinoshita Naoe, the author of novels depicting sociopolitical problems. According to the literary scholar Sōma Taizō, Tolstoy was first introduced to Japan as a great thinker who could guide Japanese progressive Christians and early socialists in their search for truth and justice.[25]

The biggest difference between Japan and Korea in the early reception of Tolstoy is that whereas Japanese intellectuals were already bringing Tolstoy's ideas to bear on anarchism and socialism in the first decade of the 1900s, Ch'oe and Yi did not express any noticeable interest in that connection. Rather, they focused on his ideas about labor and humanistic love, and on his theory of art.[26] Ch'oe showed no enthusiasm for introducing Tolstoy's writings on sociopolitical issues, and even Yi Kwang-su, who introduced a wider range of Tolstoy's ideas, did not endorse Tolstoy's radical political ideas. In one of his articles, Yi does touch on the anarchistic strands in Tolstoy's writing, commenting, "Tolstoy's main theory of nations, societies, and economics is that you should follow your beliefs in life with free will, without submitting to power."[27] Yi went on to argue, however, that although Tolstoy's ideas seem to have something in common with anarchism and socialism, they are actually fundamentally different from those ideologies. For Yi, the main difference lay in the fact that socialism and anarchism necessitated violent revolution, whereas Tolstoy preached nonviolence and love.[28]

The impact of the Russo-Japanese War on cultural discourse was truly wide-ranging, and was not limited to Russia and Japan. One of those effects, although indirect, was to shape Korean intellectuals' future agenda: Tolstoy's antiwar theory swept Japan's intellectual world, and created a Tolstoy boom that continued throughout the 1910s in Japan. This is what created the conditions of exposure for Ch'oe and Yi's contact with Tolstoy. But as their selective adoption of Japan's reception of Tolstoy indicates, the content of this reception was not necessarily best suited to their intellectual needs (discussed later). If another author had been in the ascendancy in Japan during this period, it is quite possible that Ch'oe and Yi would have grappled with his intellectual tradition instead, and taken from it what they needed for their own purposes.

Ch'oe Nam-sŏn's Introduction of Tolstoy: A Contextual Overview

The introduction of Tolstoy in Korea was prefigured by the characteristics of Japan's reception to a large extent but the intellectuals who undertook the work of building a Tolstoy for the Korean context used the materials available to them with specific intentions in mind. For Ch'oe and Yi, introducing Tolstoy was part of at least two larger projects: for Ch'oe, constructing a model public intellectual and writer through the journal *Sonyŏn*, and for Yi, developing a theory of modern literature, which would become the first substantial theorization of literature in Korea.

Before going into further details about Ch'oe's introduction of Tolstoy in *Sonyŏn*, we need to understand the historical context and impact of *Sonyŏn* on Korean society when it was published. *Sonyŏn* was not only the first modern literary journal in Korea, but it was also connected with the early nationalist movement. Ch'oe was involved in the Sinminhoe (New People's Society) and Ch'ŏngnyŏn Haguhoe (Youth Association), which had been founded under the guidance of the famous nationalist An Ch'ang-ho. Ch'oe supported An's idea of gradualism, which advocated independence through education and the gradual elevation of the Korean people, rather than revolutionary action against Japan. *Sonyŏn* also worked as the public forum for the association. Beyond Ch'oe's personal involvement, the journal's title *Sonyŏn*, meaning "The young," also placed it within a wider tradition of nationalist intellectuals in colonized countries. Describing the characteristics of emerging colonial nationalism, Benedict Anderson argues that "almost invariably they [the emerging nationalist intelligentsia in the colonies] were very young and attached a complex political significance to their youth."[29] The connection of *Sonyŏn* to an international trend is clearer when we compare it with other East Asian countries under threat of colonization. In China, Liang Qichao proposed the theory of "Young China," and in Japan, a journal entitled *Shōnen sekai* (Youth world) began publishing in 1895.[30]

After Korea became a Japanese protectorate in 1905, the Korean liberation movement shifted its stance from maintaining Korea as an independent country to restoring its national autonomy. Two main streams of the liberation movement were the "righteous army" movement and gradualism (the Korean Enlightenment movement). The righteous army movement pursued immediate military action to recover national sovereignty, even though they had little hope of victory in a direct confrontation with imperial Japan. Gradualism's supporters argued that Koreans should acknowledge their impotence and foster their abilities and augment their power in every respect, until they gained enough strength to fight Japan. Gradualism's supporters' plan was to enlighten the Korean people and raise young Koreans as the center of the liberation movement inside Korea, while a military force based outside Korea would train for future engagement.[31] Two leading groups in the gradualism camp were the Taehan Chaganghoe (Korea Self-Strengthening Society, March 31, 1906–August 19, 1907), which was a legal organization, and the Sinminhoe (New People's Society, April 1907–September 1911), which was a secret organization. An Ch'ang-ho was the leader of the Sinminhoe, and Ch'oe himself was a member.[32]

The Sinminhoe did not publish its own bulletin, even though it emphasized the importance of newspapers and other publications. Instead, it utilized the *Taehan maeil sinbo* (Korean Daily), a nationalist newspaper that first appeared in July 1904. Yang Ki-tak was the chief editor and Earnest Thomas Bethell was the newspaper's president. Because the head of the newspaper was English, the *Taehan maeil sinbo* was able to avoid Japanese censorship. Yang Ki-tak became an executive director of the Sinminhoe; most editors and staff of the newspaper were also members of the group.[33]

Within the Sinminhoe, Ch'oe was in charge of publications. He started publishing *Sonyŏn* in 1908 as an organ of the gradualist movement, but *Sonyŏn* could never fully play this role in public because the Sinminhoe was a secret society. After the Sinminhoe organized a legal organization as part of the youth movement, called the Ch'ŏngnyŏn Haguhoe (Youth Association, September 1909), *Sonyŏn* served as a bulletin of that association.[34] It published the manifesto of the Ch'ŏngnyŏn Haguhoe, and a summary of the establishment committee meeting in the month the association was founded.[35]

Ch'oe himself was one of three chief organizers of the Ch'ŏngnyŏn Haguhoe,[36] and thus a brief account of the aims and characteristics of the Ch'ŏngnyŏn Haguhoe provides some insight into the character of the journal *Sonyŏn*. Ch'oe later recalled that the Ch'ŏngnyŏn Haguhoe aimed at restoring national sovereignty and modeled itself after some European youth political groups, including Young Italy, which had contributed to the unification of Italy.[37] Members of the Sinminhoe believed that the subject of their movement was the Korean people in general but that the vital core should be young people, the inheritors of a future Korea. They organized the youth movement as a separate entity to emphasize this. The youth movement focused on the education of young people on the one hand, and the organization of youth societies, such as the youth association and Ch'ŏngnyŏn Tongjihoe (Youth Fellow Group), on the other. The Ch'ŏngnyŏn Haguhoe was the leading group of the youth movement,[38] and the concept of gradualism as the path to a revival of the nation that the Ch'ŏngnyŏn Haguhoe manifested was briefly described in the first issue of *Sonyŏn*. On the front page of this issue, Ch'oe expressed the sentiment that Korean *sonyŏn* (young people) were duty-bound to enlighten Korea and contribute to the development of world culture, and claimed that *Sonyŏn* would help foster the growth of such people in Korea.[39]

According to Ch'oe's memoir, "*Sonyŏn* was used as a school textbook in Pyŏng'an and Hwanghae provinces, and some people even committed it to memory. . . . It was very influential and the only national journal at the time."[40] *Sonyŏn* published 1,000 copies in 1910, the year of Korea's colonization. Its print run may have decreased following a suspension of publication that year, which lasted for a few months. But considering that *Maeil sinbo* (Maeil Daily) published 2,646 copies every day around that time, the circulation of *Sonyŏn* was significant.[41] Whatever *Sonyŏn* introduced would have been accorded a degree of respect and influence in Korean intellectual society.

In his writing in *Sonyŏn*, Ch'oe never discusses his reasons for choosing Tolstoy, other than to say that "in Russia, there is a famous and sincere writer called Tolstoy, so I'll write soon about his life and work."[42] Why did Ch'oe choose Tolstoy as the figure who would take up more pages in *Sonyŏn* than any other foreign writer? We can assume that Ch'oe had discovered Tolstoy in Japanese translations during his period of study in Japan, but this does not explain why he placed Tolstoy at the top of his list of notable writers. It seems likely that Ch'oe's choice was anything but arbitrary, and that Tolstoy became the model intellectual in Korea as a result of Ch'oe's deliberate exclusion of other literary figures also well known in Japan at the time.

In an essay in 1955 in which he describes the literary circles of those early days, Ch'oe writes, "There were both direct and indirect reasons for publishing the special issue on Tolstoy. But the most important one was that we were fascinated with Ibsen, Hugo, and Tolstoy because we were opposed to the current tendency of the Japanese literary world, where popular novels were so prevalent."[43] Ch'oe's comment is somewhat misleading, in that the writers he mentions were extremely popular in Japan.[44] But we can guess what he is trying to convey. In explaining the reasoning behind his selections and translations of certain writers and works, Ch'oe reveals that he intentionally chose them to prevent the Korean literary world from becoming like the Japanese one, which, in Ch'oe's eyes, was obsessed with popular novels. We may also speculate that Ch'oe's selection of Tolstoy was part of his project of maintaining the dignity of the institution of intellectual leadership within the idiom of modern literature, and establishing his own position as a viable role model for his Korean readership.

Ch'oe translated and published six of Tolstoy's short stories in *Sonyŏn*, as well as ten articles on Tolstoy and a long poem lamenting his death. Ch'oe's articles mainly document Tolstoy's way of life, principles, and life lessons.[45] The stories that Ch'oe chose to translate were written in Tolstoy's later life, after he had turned to religion and rejected his former writings such as *War and Peace* and *Anna Karenina*.[46] During this period, Tolstoy mostly wrote didactic stories and novels, including *Resurrection*, which attained a level of popularity in Korea far surpassing that of any of Tolstoy's other masterpieces.

In the middle of his article "T'olssŭt'oi sŏnsaeng ŭi kyosi" (Tolstoy's teaching), laying out the principles of Tolstoysm, Ch'oe makes it clear that he is citing Tolstoy's principles not from Tolstoy's own writing but from Nakazato Yanosuke's: "This is not [the translation of what] Tolstoy himself wrote, but the summary of what the Japanese Nakazato Yanosuke wrote [about Tolstoy]. We also studied Tolstoy's philosophy, but it is still difficult to explain it systematically."[47] Although Ch'oe does not give the title of the book he used, it was Nakazato Kaizan's (1885–1944) *Torusutoi genkōroku* (Tolstoy's sayings and doings), published in Japan in November 1906.[48] Kaizan started writing the book in 1905, the year the war ended and Tolstoy's fame soared because of his antiwar campaign.[49] Kaizan contributed to *Heimin shinbun* and was deeply influenced by Tolstoy's antiwar messages and anarchistic ideas.[50] This is the context for the Japanese book that Ch'oe used for his introduction of Tolstoy's thought. The source Ch'oe used was the expanded edition of Kaizan's book, published in November 1906, four months after the first edition came out. From a comparison of the two texts, it is clear that almost all of Ch'oe's writings on Tolstoy came from this second edition, and that Ch'oe's various small articles on Tolstoy's sayings and doings were translated from the expanded part of the second edition.

The first edition of Kaizan's book consists of seventeen sections and a supplement. Another seven sections were added to the second, expanded edition, and the whole second edition consists of 251 pages. The first part (pp. 1–72) is about Tolstoy's life from his childhood to the time he began writing *Confession*, and includes a detailed explanation of his literary works. The second part (pp. 73–131) deals with his later life, after *Confession*. The third group of essays, a part of which was added for the second edition, is mostly Tolstoy's sayings and actions, his writing on various subjects, anecdotes about him, and descriptions of his relationships with other intellectuals (pp. 131–251). Ch'oe's biographical introduction of Tolstoy is a summary of the first and second parts of Kaizan's book, and his short articles on Tolstoy are mostly based on its third part.

Deification of a Foreign Writer: The Project of Self-Validation

Working from a basic premise that translation is one way of rewriting a text, André Lefevere argues that it is necessary to investigate what happens in the process of rewriting, and why.[51] If it is acceptable that even an apparently literal translation is a way of rewriting a so-called original, then a freer adaptation of a certain text could be considered a much more purposeful rewriting of the original. Examining the specific characteristics of Ch'oe's selection and subsequent representation of certain features of Tolstoy's life and writings can therefore tell us about Ch'oe's purposes and expectations in introducing Tolstoy to Korean society. The salient features of Ch'oe's particular representation of Tolstoy in the journal *Sonyŏn* can be grouped into three categories. First, Ch'oe views Tolstoy more as a prophet and mentor than as a writer. Second, he stresses the details of Tolstoy's daily practices and life principles. Third, Ch'oe consistently excludes Tolstoy's criticisms of modern nations and societies.

It is noteworthy that, from the outset, Ch'oe's deification of Tolstoy makes him almost comparable to Christ. This emphasis on the sacred characteristics of Tolstoy also helps Ch'oe justify his argument that people should know about Tolstoy and his writings and follow certain features of Tolstoy's life principles. At the beginning of his first article on Tolstoy, "T'olssŭt'oi sŏnsaeng ŭi kyosi" (Tolstoy's teaching), Ch'oe writes:

> About a week ago, the most astonishing and worrying news was printed in the newspaper. It was not news that a monster which can consume every human being has come to Earth from Mars. Nor was it the news that Halley's Comet will hit Earth and it will explode. The news was that the health of Tolstoy, the greatest man among his contemporaries and the holiest since Christ, is in serious condition.
>   Tolstoy! It is nothing more than an everyday combination of consonants and vowels. But if you know who he is, you will realize that he is so dignified and great that you will be moved beyond description even when you try to speak his name. What can account for this? I have to write about him for people who don't know about him in order to explain.[52]

Ch'oe's overblown description of Tolstoy as "the holiest since Christ" (*Kŭrisŭdo ihu ŭi ch'oedae inkkyŏk*) is not one that Ch'oe invented. Nakazato Kaizan, the author of Ch'oe's Japanese source text, used this very expression (*kitoku irai no dai jinkaku*) in the prefaces of both the first and second, expanded, editions of his book. Another expression about Tolstoy, which Kaizan used in his preface for the expanded edition, is "a holy human being, more important than the wealth of the world."[53] In this way, Tolstoy had already been deified before Ch'oe borrowed the expression to introduce him in Korea. Yet, Ch'oe's emphasis on Tolstoy's importance does not stop with Kaizan's phrase but goes well beyond it, elevating Tolstoy to an absurd status:

> Alas! How many persons in our country would have any reaction at hearing the news that Tolstoy—who is so great that losing him would be worse than human annihilation or seeing the world destroyed—is sick? I have translated things about Tolstoy, feeling pity for the people who do not know the existence of the Sun even while they live in it. Thinking that this humble writing is the first to introduce Tolstoy in Korea, I realized that it is charged with an important mission. How far can it hope to accomplish that mission?[54]

Why did Ch'oe keep deifying Tolstoy to such an extreme? Ch'oe was not a Christian, as Kaizan was, and never showed any interest in Tolstoy's religious beliefs. I would argue that this extreme idolization was undoubtedly purposeful, and that the aura and fame that Ch'oe created around Tolstoy in this introduction worked to legitimatize what Ch'oe then said in his articles about Tolstoy.

At first, Ch'oe ignores the fact that Tolstoy was a writer. In the body of the subsequent text, he devotes only half a page out of nine pages to Tolstoy's contribution to literature, explaining that "the time when the world knew Tolstoy as a writer has passed. Now he is revered as the greatest prophet and teacher since the nineteenth century, and he imparts to us the most invaluable teachings."[55] To support his argument, he provides some examples of European attitudes toward Tolstoy. Ch'oe claims that the opinions he gives are based on replies submitted to a questionnaire in a German newspaper, but as was the custom at the time, he does not give a citation. According to him, the result of the questionnaire established that Tolstoy was the greatest among all his contemporaries, a result that was later duplicated by a French newspaper.[56]

The deification of Tolstoy eventually functioned as an effective validation of the life principle that Ch'oe was advocating for the Korean people, especially the significance placed on labor. Ch'oe presents himself as merely enumerating the details of Tolstoy's life, his greatness and his lessons, yet his elevation of Tolstoy as an incontestably respected figure throughout the world adds enormous authority and credibility to the value of the lessons that Ch'oe proceeds to selectively represent. Tolstoy stands as an unimpeachable (and, at that time in Korea, almost unknown) absolute value, legitimatizing the ideas Ch'oe lists in his name. After explaining the change in Tolstoy's attitude toward religious life, Ch'oe introduces Tolstoy's teachings on labor, according to which the greatest virtue is to work with one's hands. He then relates anecdotes of how Tolstoy, despite his status as a wealthy aristocrat, did everyday chores himself rather than leaving them to his servants.[57]

The subtitle to the main article "T'olssŭt'oi sŏnsaeng ŭi kyosi" (Tolstoy's teaching), which summarizes Tolstoy's life from his childhood, is "Nodong yŏkchak ŭi pogŭm" (Preaching on labor). This subtitle indicates that Ch'oe was most interested in introducing the Korean people to Tolstoy's teaching on labor. Ch'oe's first use of the word "labor" (*nodong yŏkchak*) appears in the middle of the article, when he introduces the context of Tolstoy's change of heart in middle age:

> He became despondent again and decided to kill himself. But at that moment he turned his attention to the peasants, who follow mandates from Heaven (*ch'ŏnmyŏng*), and labor (*nodong yŏkchak*) as far as their physical strength (*kŭnryŏk*) allows. Looking at them, he realized that these peasants are the people who understand the meaning of life.[58]

The subtitle, along with the entire emphasis on labor in the middle of the story, is not Kaizan's but Ch'oe's own creation. The story that Ch'oe's article introduces is based on Tolstoy's autobiographical writing, *Confession* (*Ispoved* in Russian). But Ch'oe's emphasis on the importance of labor is unique when we compare it with Tolstoy's actual writing.

The emphasis in Tolstoy's *Confession* is somewhat different from Ch'oe's. The protagonist, the young Tolstoy, pursues physical pleasure and a cruel war as a young soldier, and later enjoys fame and money as a writer. He gets married and has a family but suffers ceaselessly from the emptiness of his life, especially the meaninglessness of his existence in upper-class society, with nothing to hold it together but Epicurean amusement. He is often tempted to commit suicide but at the same time is afraid of death. He sincerely questions himself about his identity and the meaning of life, but neither natural science nor philosophy affords him an answer. Meanwhile, he finds out that there are simple folk and peasants who have real faith and know the meaning of life. In contrast to the people of his circle, "where all life passes in idleness, amusement, and the tedium of life," Tolstoy sees that "the whole life of these people [peasants] is passed in *hard work*, and that they are satisfied with life" (emphasis added) and live without vanity and fear.[59] Observing that their lives are based on their religious faith rather than on any kind of knowledge, he tries to understand the teachings of Orthodox Church, but all he finds is that it is founded on a lie and does not follow God's true words. Instead, Tolstoy is attracted to the sincere and honest Christianity of the peasants, and concludes that the Orthodox Church is incompatible with true Christianity. He decides to practice true Christianity in his life as well.[60]

Although the value of labor is undeniably mentioned in *Confession*, the core of the story is Tolstoy's discovery of a "true" Christianity from his observation of peasants, which he experienced as a fundamental change in his life. For Tolstoy, true Christianity (not the peasants' toil) was the ultimate end to his long wandering. Kaizan, in his introduction, primarily followed the content of Tolstoy's book and summarized it in the section "Mr. Tolstoy's Confession" (pp. 73–88). But what matters for Ch'oe is not Tolstoy's belief in Christianity but the fact that Tolstoy found a meaningful life in peasant routine and, in following the peasants' lifestyle, engaged in physical work himself despite his aristocratic status.

Ch'oe's short articles that introduce Tolstoy clearly focus on Tolstoy's ideas on labor and his practice of certain life principles. In "Uridŭl ŭi ŭimu" (Our duty), Ch'oe relates the following anecdote about Tolstoy:[61]

> One day a visitor said to Tolstoy, "I hope you take good care of yourself so that you may propagate your beliefs for a long time." But Tolstoy answered this way: "You talking about propagation? It is the devil's test. Our first duty is to live a true life. Teaching other people is not our duty. Our duty is to *work* by ourselves." (Emphasis added)

Following this article, Ch'oe describes in "Sŏnsaeng ŭi soŏn silhaeng" (Tolstoy's practice) how Tolstoy did every household chore by himself without letting other people do them for him.[62] The introduction of Tolstoy's daily plan comes next in the same issue of *Sonyŏn*, and describes Tolstoy's diligence and persistent practice of his principles:

> After finishing *Confession*, Tolstoy gave up his life as a writer and became a farmer. He made a daily plan and spent four hours a day working on the farm and four hours making shoes. He worked on the farm in Yasnaia Poliana from April to December, and he read books and wrote in Moscow in winter. The daily plan changed a little bit according to his changing health as he got older, but he never stopped living up to the plan.[63]

It is no exaggeration to say that Ch'oe's sole interest in introducing Tolstoy lay in Tolstoy's thought on labor, and his principles and practice of everyday living. The most pressing issue for Ch'oe in his representation of Tolstoy's thought may have been Ch'oe's own conviction that Korean youths had to rely on their own effort and diligence to obtain the necessities of life and to educate themselves in order to improve their society. This emphasis resonated strongly with the idea of gradualism in the Sinminhoe and Ch'ŏngnyŏn Haguhoe, mentioned above.

The principles of the Sinminhoe and Ch'ŏngnyŏn Haguhoe were summed up in the phrase *musil-yŏkhaeng* (務實力行, making strenuous effort through practice rather than words).[64] It was imperative, Ch'oe believed, that young people live up to the liberation of Korea in their actions, instead of simply expressing their sorrowful indignation and deploring the current situation. In his essay "Youth Association," Ch'oe writes, "The Youth Association was organized. Why? In order to unite young people who build up their lives with *musil* and *yŏkhaeng*. In order to build up people with sound mind."[65] In another article, "The Aims of the Youth Association," Ch'oe more specifically clarifies the meaning of *musil-yŏkhaeng*:

> The Youth Association was organized to answer the demands of enlightened young people. Young people today do not believe that leisurely amusement is their calling and that laziness is their moral virtue. They have become conscious of their situation. They have become conscious of their historical duty and ambition. . . . We stand at a crossroads, surviving or falling, working or being at leisure. We choose the way that will lead us to do good work, so that we may survive and prosper. . . . Therefore, the Youth Association, where truly awakened young people gather, proudly plants the flag of *musil-yŏkhaeng* in the world.[66]

For Ch'oe, *musil-yŏkhaeng* was the indispensable touchstone for Korean youth. Laziness and a leisurely life were to be condemned, while work, diligence, and action were the most important moral values. Ch'oe's emphasis on labor and diligence, bolstered by his introduction of Tolstoy's life principles, can be understood in the same vein.

If we go further, we can infer that, in addition to providing a role model for Korean youth, Ch'oe's anecdote about Tolstoy was a criticism of *yangban* (Korean aristocrats) who regarded physical work as improper for themselves and who enjoyed a leisurely life insofar as their economic situation allowed. As an intellectual from the *chung'in* (middle class), Ch'oe had been submitting articles to nationalist newspapers such as *Hwangsŏng sinmun* and *Tongnip sinmun* since the age of twelve, to publicly criticize the impotence of the Korean government.[67] The *chung'in* were customarily in charge of administrative and technical work. They would correspond to today's doctors, translators/interpreters, accountants, financial managers, and so forth. Their social status was between *yang-ban* (aristocrats) and *sangmin* (commoners). The name *chung'in* (middle) originated not from their position in the hierarchy, however, but from the fact that they resided in the middle of old Seoul. Their knowledge, skill, and status were passed on to their offspring. When Korea opened to Western countries, the *chung'in* class adapted to and coped with the situation quickly, something that was much more difficult for members of the *yang-ban* class, who were more deeply bound by and dependent on Confucian ideas. The *chung'in* class played a critical role in the modernization of Korea due to their practical knowledge and rationalism.[68] Korean intellectuals from this class viewed the corruption of a self-interested aristocracy as one of the main reasons for the tragic loss of Korean sovereignty to Japanese protectorship in 1905. Representation of Tolstoy as an aristocrat who nevertheless worked to educate himself about life's realities can thus be interpreted as a criticism of the Korean aristocracy.

Selections and Exclusions: Mediated and Censored

While emphasizing Tolstoy's writings and episodes about labor, Ch'oe deliberately excluded Tolstoy's criticism of modern societies and endorsement of revolutionary political movements. Tolstoy rejected the authority of the Church because it legitimized the State and sanctioned violence against the people. He condemned every form of compulsion, and his ideas could thus be considered anarchist.[69] Before Ch'oe explained Tolstoy's lessons on labor, he wrote, "I won't introduce Tolstoy's criticisms of modern civilization and modern societies and nations because I don't think that these issues are necessary yet for our young people. Instead I'll select only his great writings on the value of labor, and present them to everyone."[70]

Comparison of Ch'oe's translation with the Japanese source text clearly shows what Ch'oe meant to convey to the reader when he introduced Tolstoy. In his article "T'olsŭt'oi sŏnsaeng ŭi kyosi" (Tolstoy's teaching), Ch'oe translates Tolstoy's principles on labor. As discussed above, he mentions that he translated them from Nakazato Yanosuke (Nakazato Kaizan). The portion Ch'oe translated is entitled "Torusu-toizumu kōryō" (The Principles of Tolstoysm) in the expanded edition of Kaizan's book (November 1906). Kaizan's "The Principles of Tol-stoysm" consists of eight short sections, but Ch'oe translated only five of them. The three sections that Ch'oe left out are entitled "False Civiliza-tion," "The True Meaning of Revolution," and "Repent!" All three con-tain radical ideas on civilization and the state. For instance, in "False Civilization" Tolstoy holds that "the current civilization is false because most people are starving and being killed for only a few people's pleasure and vanity. . . . The state forces people to kill other people and, if they do not follow the order, they are punished."[71] For the five sections that Ch'oe did translate, his rendition is extremely faithful to Kaizan, with the exception of one sentence in the seventh section that he chose to omit. This sentence criticizes "the state that supports the exploiters of many workers."[72]

Ch'oe's emphasis on labor continues in "Tolstoy's Teaching" and is even more conspicuous here than in other articles. Half of Kaizan's "The Principles of Tolstoysm"—four out of eight sections—handle labor (労働, rōdō in Japanese), and Ch'oe translated these word for word, meaning that the translation has the same word order and same Chinese char-acters. It is close to literal translation. But there is one exception, and that is the word "labor" (rōdō). The Korean pronunciation of the Chi-nese characters of the Japanese word rōdō is nodong. But Ch'oe changed "rōdō," which might have connoted the Japanese socialist movement, to "nodong yŏkchak" (勞動力作), which emphasizes a strenuous physical effort to produce/create something. One sentence that Kaizan empha-sizes using side dots is "without labor (rōdō), without life (jinsei)" in section five. Ch'oe also emphasizes three more phrases: "Nodong yŏkchak is the best and first virtue" in section five, "[Nodong yŏkchak refers to] the hard work (noryŏk) of two arms and two legs" in section six, and "Let everyone do nodong yŏkchak" in section eight.[73] Ch'oe's interest in promoting his ideas through translation is obvious in light of the fact that, even though he seems to render Kaizan's writing literally, Ch'oe purposely selected the sections on labor, substituted the word "labor" with his own invented term, and added marks to emphasize those spe-cific phrases.

Yet, there may be one other reason Ch'oe erased Tolstoy's anarchistic ideas about the state: he may have been wary of censorship by Japan and have thus omitted the politically radical content as an act of preemptive self-censorship. Japan promulgated the Newspaper Law in July 24, 1907, but punitive suspension of Korean newspapers had been occurring since August 13, 1904, when the *Taedong sinbo* (Taedong News) was suspended.[74] Japan consolidated censorship in February 23, 1909 with the *ch'ulp'an pŏp* (Publication Law), which enacted a system of prepublication censorship. The number of Korean journals had increased from two in 1907 to fourteen in 1908, but two political journals among them were forced to cease publication in 1909.[75] The full introduction of Tolstoy was published in *Sonyŏn* on July 1, 1909, about four months after the Publication Law was promulgated.

In relation to the discussion of censorship, Ch'oe's unusual remarks on his translation of Nakazato Kaizan's writing are also worth pointing out. Not only did he mention his Japanese source by name, but he noted the fact that he had deliberately omitted something from it and specified the omitted sections, writing, "[Section] I, II, III erased" before starting in with Section IV. It is remarkable that he mentioned the source text and left a trace of the omission. Even though Ch'oe translated and summarized Kaizan's book in other places, he did not mention it in these other articles and sections. It had been five years since the first suspension of a Korean newspaper when Ch'oe was introducing Tolstoy, and he was surely aware of what he should avoid in order to prevent suspension of his journal. In any case, the facts that Ch'oe's essays left their erased traces and changed the term for labor into another term that had no connection to Japanese socialists demonstrate that Ch'oe's texts may have undergone either official censorship or self-censorship. Still, taking into account Ch'oe's situation as an intellectual under censorship, his interest in promoting labor through Tolstoy is persistent and conspicuous.

Kaizan prefaces his own introduction of Tolstoy by briefly stating, "I did my best to crystallize Tolstoysm, and readers will understand it if they peruse my summary."[76] As he says, his is not a literal translation of Tolstoy's writing, but instead focused on the kernel of Tolstoy's thought that Kaizan wanted to single out. It is not clear whether or not Ch'oe agreed with Kaizan's representation of Tolstoy's thought, though he decided that it was not necessary to translate the first three sections for young Korean people. As a result of Ch'oe's introduction, these thoughts and practices constituted the core of Tolstoysm in Korea at the time.

Metonymic Displacement: The Death of Tolstoy and the Loss of Korean Sovereignty

Publication of *Sonyŏn* was suspended around the time of the Japanese annexation of Korea. *Sonyŏn*'s August 1910 issue was seized, and the journal was suspended for four months. It was allowed to publish again in December 1910, but the issue of January 1911 was confiscated again. It published one more issue, its last, in May 1911. Four months after the first suspension of the journal, on December 15, 1910, Ch'oe published the special issue dedicated to Tolstoy, who had died in November of that year. Under the title "T'olssŭt'oi sŏnsaeng hase kinyŏm" (Remembering Tolstoy), Ch'oe explains the reason for the special issue: "After passing through the dark valley of the past four months, I hold a pen again and humbly publish this issue because I feel that I should express our condolences just as other nations have."[77] Clearly the expression "the dark valley of the past four months" has a double meaning, being both the period of suspended publication and the time since the Japanese annexation of Korea.

The most obvious reason for the special issue on Tolstoy was Tolstoy's death. But I argue that by using Tolstoy's death as a metonym, Ch'oe was simultaneously able to express his agony and sorrow as a newly colonized intellectual.[78] Ch'oe's internal censorship was surely related to his experience with the suspension of publication ordered by the Japanese authorities in 1910. In his reminiscences about Tolstoy's influence on Korea, Ch'oe Myŏng-ik writes:

> Even though his [Tolstoy's] death caused shock and sadness for everyone in the world who knew him, it was not the case in Korea. At that time Koreans were experiencing too much tragedy of their own to mourn Tolstoy's death: a few months before Tolstoy's death we lost our country, and about forty righteous intellectuals, such as Hwang Hyŏn and Ch'oe U-sun, committed suicide immediately following the annexation.[79]

Given these circumstances, Ch'oe Nam-sŏn's attention to Tolstoy's death becomes understandable only when we consider the overlap between his mourning for the death of Korean sovereignty and for the death of Tolstoy.

In the special issue of *Sonyŏn*, Ch'oe expresses his feelings and thoughts on Tolstoy's life and death in a long poem entitled "T'olsŭt'oi sŏnsaeng ŭl kokham" (Lamentation on Tolstoy's death).[80] It is comprised of seventy-two stanzas, each with four lines. The first four stanzas express the narrator's sorrow over Tolstoy's death. The next ten stanzas sing about the biographical Tolstoy's conflict between a selfish self and an altruistic self, which any human being is doomed to possess, however great he is. The description of Tolstoy's agony caused by his inner conflict continues until stanza thirty-eight. The next ten stanzas eulogize his strength of will and the virtue by which he overcame the temptation to pursue success, wealth, and fame even though he could have acquired them had he wanted to.

Up until stanza forty-eight, the narrator describes Tolstoy's life without surfacing himself, but he steps forward in stanza forty-nine to describe Tolstoy's greatness. In the last part of poem, the narrator overlaps his own condition with Tolstoy's by changing the distance between the protagonist and the narrator. The pronoun the narrator uses to indicate the protagonist changes from "he" [Tolstoy] into "I" [supposedly Ch'oe] and back again into "him," which refers to the narrator. Stanza sixty-nine reads, "When an ordinary person [presumably Ch'oe] in the big world/ being pressed down by a rock/ became flat and broken/ what a great consolation Tolstoy's existence gave him!"[81] The reader can assume that if "the ordinary person" is a colonized intellectual, then "a rock" is Japanese imperialism or the colonization itself. The topic of this poem changes from Tolstoy's death to Ch'oe's oppression. In the next stanza, it becomes clearer that the poem is a lamentation about Ch'oe's current situation: "As a widow bursts into tears/ whatever she sees,/ [I am] not crying/ over Tolstoy for his sake./ Thinking of my circumstances in the future to come,/ I cannot help crying."[82] Interestingly, this stanza has three pairs of metonymic displacement: a widow's lament over the loss of her husband, Ch'oe mourning over Tolstoy, and the colonized weeping over his country. The genre of poetry itself gives Ch'oe enough room to change the position of the narrator without difficulty, and so he is freer to express not only sorrow over the loss of Tolstoy but his own agony as an intellectual in a colonized country.

Tolstoy was not just an object of knowledge, a foreign writer to introduce, but, more significantly, a symbol, a flexible and half-empty signifier that Korean writers could fill up with their desires and expectations in order to find ways to cope with their precarious social condition in a rapidly changing and soon colonized country. Tolstoy's case shows that flattening but absolutizing a foreign figure/value may be accelerated in a colony when it seems to serve the interests of the colonized. In this process, the Japanese introduction and interpretation of Russian literature—which was also affected by its Western reception and understanding (particularly as expressed in materials written in English)—did prefigure the characteristics of Russian literature that Korean intellectuals understood. But again, another highly selective process and practice took place when Russian literature came to Korea and was utilized to operate in more or less unpredictable and highly appropriative ways, as we will also see in Yi Kwang-su's case in the following sections.

Yi Kwang-su's Tolstoy and Humanism in 1910s Japan

Although Ch'oe Nam-sŏn and Yi Kwang-su both came into contact with Tolstoy's writings while residing in Japan in the early 1900s, their fundamental interest in Tolstoy's ideas and writings evolved in two different directions. Ch'oe placed primary stress on Tolstoy's idea and practice of labor, whereas Yi was particularly affected by Tolstoy's humanism and theory of art in constructing his own theory for Korean literature.

Yi discovered Tolstoy through his Japanese schoolmate Yamazaki Toshio, while he was in the Meiji Academy toward the end of his first stay in Japan, around 1909:

> I guess I was eighteen when I read Tolstoy for the first time. When I was in the fourth year [of the Meiji school in 1909], I had a friend, Yamazaki Toshio, who was very puritanical. One day, he lent me a book called *Waga shūkyō* (My Religion), the Japanese translation of Tolstoy, from his elder brother's study. After I read it, I was truly moved and thought that the idea contained in this book indeed was true, that we could make a peaceful world if we were to practice what it said, and that Tolstoy was a real teacher and I would live up to his principles.[83]

Yamazaki Toshio was a religious Christian and was often bullied by schoolmates because he had delivered a speech against war.[84] From this point on, humanism began to affect all aspects of Yi's life and ideas, and the impact may have been consolidated by the huge popularity of Tolstoy's humanism among Japanese intellectuals during his second stay in Japan.

As stated above, Yi was in Japan during the high tide of Tolstoy's popularity there: Yi first went to Japan in 1905 and graduated from the Meiji Academy in Tokyo in 1910. He returned to Korea in 1910 and taught at the Osan School. In 1915, he returned to Japan and stayed until 1919. The coincidence of Yi's contact with the Tolstoy boom in Japan when he was in his teens and twenties may have resulted in his becoming a Tolstoyan. He was deeply moved by Tolstoy's humanism, and this permeated his thoughts on literature in general. Yi thought that humanism was the end goal toward which all arts should aim, and praised Tolstoy's *Resurrection* for its humanism, love for people, moving story, and didactic impact.[85] Although the humanistic art that Yi Kwang-su pursued is hard to define, one of its clear central themes is altruistic love.[86]

In the 1910s, at the time of Yi's second sojourn in Japan, Tolstoy had become a symbol of humanism in Japanese intellectual society. This can be seen in the introduction of Tolstoy by the Shirakaba (White Birch) school and in a journal devoted to him and his work, *Torusutoi kenkyū* (Tolstoy studies). Humanism also affected the reception of other Russian writers at this time. Humanism, which became closely associated with Tolstoy and Tolstoysm in Japan, came to characterize the Japanese literary world in the early twentieth century.

The meaning of "humanism" is too broad to define in a few words, and changes according to time, location, and specific field of study. In Japan, the word "humanism" was translated into roughly three terms: *jindōshugi* (ethics-centered humanitarianism), *jinbunshugi* (humanities-centered knowledge), and *jinponshugi* (human-centered systems of value).[87] The humanism that was popular in the Taishō period (1912–26) is best captured by the term *jindōshugi*—humanitarianism or "ethical humanism."[88] As described by literary historian Honda Shūgo, the Shirakaba school existed at the center of a humanism boom in the Taishō period, and the popularity of Tolstoy was a part of this phenomenon. The Japanese word *jindōshugi*, ethical humanism, was closely tied to the introduction of Tolstoy's thought and its ardent reception by the Shirakaba group.[89] In Korea, the humanism associated with Tolstoy was also translated into *indojuūi* (ethical humanism) directly from the Japanese word.

A group of young Japanese men, graduates of the Gakushūin (Peers school), founded the journal *Shirakaba* (White birch) in April 1910. Mushanokōji Saneatsu, Shiga Naoya, Arishima Takeo, Satomi Ton, Nagayo Yoshirō, and other young writers were members of the Shirakaba group. Among them, Mushanokōji Saneatsu was so moved by Tolstoy that he imitated his way of life and was often called "Tolstoy" by his classmates.[90] In 1918 he even founded a village to embody Tolstoy's philosophy, aiming at building a utopian community there.[91]

The Shirakaba group did not share any single style of writing, but they had in common a dislike of naturalism and an admiration of Tolstoy and Western art.[92] On the whole, they were attracted to his humanism, and one can see the profound impact that Tolstoy's humanistic philosophy had on the writings of this group.[93] This can be clearly observed in one of Nagayo Yoshirō's essays. He wrote in 1917, "No one in present society is in a position to look down upon humanism. It must be respected. It will lose its importance only when justice (*seigi*) has become a much greater force in this world. Humanism has justice as its aim."[94] This stance attracted many writers in the 1910s, when the group was at the height of its influence.

The surging popularity of humanism and its distinctive connection with Tolstoy in Japan in the 1910s also appear in the monthly journal *Torusutoi kenkyū* (Tolstoy studies). The journal was published every month without fail from September 1916 to January 1919. Each of the twenty-nine issues comprises about seventy-two pages. The Shinchōsha publishing company, which published *Tolstoy Studies*, also ran the Torusutoi Kai (Tolstoy Club), which issued *Tolstoy Studies*, published *Torusutoi gyōsho* (Tolstoy's works), and organized lectures on Tolstoy.[95]

The editors' comments in the first issue of *Tolstoy Studies* establish the goal of the journal and the degree of their admiration for Tolstoy:

> The name Tolstoy suggests something that this small journal cannot accommodate. Tolstoy is a cosmos. Half of the spiritual world is possessed by this name. Some people think that [because of the name itself] *Tolstoy Studies* is confined to a narrow area, but the name Tolstoy is something that includes everything. This journal does not necessarily intend to study only Tolstoy. We aim to pursue humanism in a broad sense.[96]

According to the editors' note in the second issue, the popularity of the journal was greater than expected: "The journal sold out the day after its release. They printed more copies, but these also sold out in three or four days." It seems that the readers' interest in Tolstoy surprised the editors of the journal as well.[97] The publication of the journal also triggered wider interest in Tolstoy among regular readers. Probably thanks to the journal, "all newspapers and journals enthusiastically took up Tolstoy, with one journal publishing a special issue on Tolstoy. In addition, people started Tolstoy study groups around Japan."[98] The Shirakaba school's admiration of Tolstoy throughout the 1910s, and the publication of *Tolstoy Studies* from 1916 to 1919, demonstrate Japanese writers' deep immersion in Tolstoy's humanism. They also show, as the editors write, that the name Tolstoy was not only about the great Tolstoy himself, but also a symbol of what Japanese intellectuals sought within their society.

Tensions and Collisions in Yi Kwang-su's Theory of Literature

Yi Kwang-su was greatly inspired not only by Tolstoy's humanism in general but also specifically by his idea of art based on humanism, and Yi's theory of literature shares important features with those expressed in Tolstoy's *What Is Art?*[99] In his article "Tolstoy and I," Yi recollects that "since that time [around 1910], it has been Tolstoy who has been most influential on my thought on art."[100] In terms of both literature and life as a whole, Tolstoy served as a beacon for Yi Kwang-su throughout the 1910s. In his article "Tolstoy's Ideas on Life—His Religion and Art," Yi eulogizes Tolstoy's greatness in terms that remind us of Ch'oe Nam-sŏn's representation of Tolstoy in his journal *Sonyŏn*: "Tolstoy is one of the great figures to have been born on this earth. He might be the most important since Jesus Christ. Wherein lies his greatness? It is in his great love for mankind, which he shares with Buddha and Christ."[101] Yi's connections with Tolstoy eventually led to his excommunication from Korean Christianity[102] because Tolstoyan religion contained heretical tenets such as a rejection of the fall of Adam, the Trinity, and the scheme of the Redemption, claiming that truth existed only in Jesus Christ's words.[103] In deifying Tolstoy, Yi Kwang-su situated Tolstoy as a light leading himself and the Korean people through the dark colonial period.

Along with his comments directly about Tolstoy, Yi's articles and fiction also bear a resemblance to Tolstoy's ideas on religion and literature. In addition to comparing the two, in what follows I investigate Yi's transformation and manipulation of Tolstoy's ideas and his creation of a new theory of literature that went beyond the theories being shared by other Korean intellectuals at the time. I would argue that Yi creatively intertwined the literary theory being adopted and circulated among Korean intellectuals with Tolstoy's theory of art, thereby creating his own theory of modern Korean literature, which is credited as being the first modern theory of literature in general and of Korean national literature in particular.

But unlike Yi's exclusive emphasis on Tolstoy's influence on his theory, significant parts of Yi's writings on literature in fact strongly resonate with Japanese literary theories around the turn of the century, particularly when it comes to Yi's ideas on national literature. How Yi built his theory of literature is rather complicated and sometimes hard to explain systematically, but we can discern a few distinctive components that forged his theory through their interaction with various ideas that were available to him at the time. An examination of these complex interactions and Yi's approaches to them will help us understand some of the quandaries that the theorization of a new literature in colonial Korea entailed. What did "literature" and "writer" mean to a belated modernity, and how were they expected to function in a colonized country? What complexity and challenges may the incorporation of the metropole's aesthetic theories into a colony have revealed? How did the colony compensate for the lack of political sovereignty (absence of the state) in the construction of a national literature?

As a way to answer these questions, we need to focus on a few elements related to the construction of Yi's theory of literature:

- The ideas that Yi shared with Tolstoy, and the features of Yi's theories that are not compatible with Tolstoy's
- The theories that Yi had in common with contemporary Korean intellectuals
- The writings of Japanese literary theorists and historians that Yi may have encountered, mostly during his second sojourn in Japan in the 1910s

- The process by which Yi transformed these strands, and the product and implications of that transformation

Tolstoy's theory of art was first introduced to Japan by Saikaishi Shizuka, a graduate of the Seikyō Shingakkō (Orthodox Theological Seminary) in Tokyo, who summarized Tolstoy's *What Is Art?* in the journal *Teikoku Bungaku* (Imperial literature) in 1898.[104] A more detailed introduction appeared in Hasegawa Tenkei's essay in the Waseda school bulletin in 1902,[105] and the first book form of the work was published in 1906.[106] Tolstoy's theory of art was already well known in the Meiji period, and Japanese writers showed both sympathy and antipathy toward it. The antipathy may have been caused by the religious concepts contained in the fundamental premise of the theory.[107] In his essay "Shackled Art," for instance, Shimamura Hōgetsu criticized Tolstoy's theory of art for being bound to religion, specifically Christianity, and for degenerating into a sermon about religious doctrines.[108]

In Korea, there was no openly expressed antipathy toward Tolstoy's theory of art, but Korean writers did not all accept Tolstoy's thought uncritically. The ambivalence of Yi Kwang-su, the first importer of Tolstoy's ideas on art, is revealed in the fact that he consciously or unconsciously significantly toned down the religious aspects of Tolstoy's theory of art when writing about Tolstoy. This occurred notwithstanding the fact that Yi was a disciple of Tolstoy and was himself a Christian. Specifically, Yi replaced Tolstoy's universal Christianity, as the fundamental value that literature should serve, with the Korean nation. It is not the case that Yi did not understand the core of Tolstoy's theory of art; according to his essay, Yi clearly understood its religious basis: "Tolstoy is a writer, but it is necessary to understand his religious philosophy in order to grasp the essence of his thoughts on art. This is so because for Tolstoy, life means religion and art is the expression of this."[109] Nevertheless, by minimizing the religious aspect of Tolstoy's writings of art in the discussion of his own theory of literature, Yi may well have avoided palpable conflict between Tolstoy's Christian universalism and his own patriotism before it could even surface.

Though Yi himself was adamant about Tolstoy's influence on him, we can find a number of crucial differences. To begin, we can compare Yi's thoughts on literature with Tolstoy's by referring to Yi's most important articles on literature, his 1910 "Munhak ŭi kach'i" (The value of literature) and 1916 "Munhak iran hao" (What is literature?), which arguably established the first theoretic foundation of modern literature and Korean national literature in the twentieth century. For a richer analysis, we can look at Yi's writings on Tolstoy and literature published in the 1920s and 1930s.

The most important and basic principle of literature, which Yi holds in common with Tolstoy, is that literature, as one form of art, is based on a person's capacity to experience the emotions that another person expresses. Literature's aim is to transmit those emotions and thus unite people. For Yi, "literature comes into being when, after experiencing something, regardless of whether it arises inside or outside the mind, a person tries to describe and convey it to other people in a written form and to move other people's emotions."[110] Both Yi and Tolstoy consider the communication of emotion to be literature's main raison d'etre. The idea is clearer in Tolstoy's formulation, which proposes that the "activity of art is based on the fact that a man, receiving through his sense of hearing or sight, another man's expression of feeling, is capable of experiencing the emotion which moved the man who expressed it."[111] The activity of art, then, is successful when the expression of emotion allows other people to feel similar things, and to experience the communication of emotions. This becomes the condition of people being united.

Emotion, of course, is one of the key elements in Romanticism. Hwang Chong-yŏn, a prominent scholar of modern Korean literature, points out in his 1997 article that Yi's literature and thought in the 1910s are close to Romanticism, which complicates the conventional view that Yi's 1910s ideas belong to the Korean Enlightenment school. Hwang explains that "Yi Kwang-su's idea that underlines emotion (chujŏngjuŭi) is romantic in that he considers the new contact with human inner nature more urgent than any other rational knowledge or moral demand, and that he emphasizes the life's special satisfaction that such contact with the inner nature brings."[112] Although Hwang does not discuss any specific connections that Yi's thought on emotion itself had with that of Western Romanticism, as in most other modern literatures, the discussion of emotion in modern Korean literarture intersected with ideas generated by Romanticism. Without doubt, Tolstoy and the Japanese intellectuals' ideas about emotion that Yi incorporated also aligned with Romanticism or the discursive environment where it grew and prospered.[113]

Yi also adopts Tolstoy's idea that art functions in the same way that words transmit knowledge and experience—words convey knowledge, and art transmits emotions. In one of his articles on literature, Yi explains this idea of Tolstoy's and declares that he completely agrees with it. Yi's explanation of Tolstoy's book *What Is Art?* is one of the rare cases where Yi explicates Tolstoy's theory of literature in detail and asserts his fundamental agreement. Yi explains that "in his theory of art, Tolstoy said, 'Art is a kind of language and so it functions as a means of conveying what a person feels to his or her people (*tongp'o*).'"[114] He continues: "What is interesting to me is the idea that art is a kind of language. We transfer what we think to people through words. In a more sophisticated formulation, this means that we convey our ideas, which are products of intellectual activity, through our words, but we transmit emotion, impressions, and feelings through special words that are known as art."[115] Yi's explanation closely echoes specific sentences of Tolstoy's:

> Speech, transmitting the thoughts and experiences of men, serves as a means of union among them, and art acts in a similar manner. The peculiarity of this latter means of intercourse, distinguishing it from intercourse by means of words, consists in this: that whereas by words a man transmits his thoughts to another, by means of art he transmits his feelings. (English, 47–48; Russian, 64)

Yi also shares with Tolstoy the idea that the emotional transmission can be categorized on various axes. Tolstoy argues that there is a wide spectrum of emotion transmitted by artistic activities: "The feelings with which the artist infects others are most various—very strong or very weak, very important or very insignificant, very bad or very good" (49; 65). Yi also suggests three categories of emotional transmission: "strength and weakness, profundity and shallowness, and nobility and vulgarity. The issue of nobility and vulgarity is related to the writer's personality."[116] The vocabulary used here by Tolstoy and Yi is almost identical. The difference between them, however, is Yi's emphasis on a writer's personality determining the quality of transmitted emotions. This idea is connected to Yi's claim that a writer is supposed to be "a thinker, a leader, and reformer of a society: and a model for young people as well as a writer."[117] The emphasis on a writer's role is discussed later in relation to the colonial reality of Korea.

In terms of how literature comes into being and functions, the two men also have some ideas in common. But Yi's ideas also include features that oppose Tolstoy's ideas and thus contradict those aspects that Yi takes from Tolstoy. Tolstoy criticizes any art that separates people, including "all patriotic art" (163; 157), whereas Yi's religious belief in a universal Christianity intermingled with his nationalist loyalties.[118] Yi's concern for the Korean nation and his belief in a universal Christianity coexisted despite the contradiction. Yi's concern for the nation is present from the beginning in his theory of literature, and he never says that literature should serve only a universal Christianity, in spite of his own religious beliefs.

Yi also had an ambivalent attitude toward humanism. He depicts Tolstoy as the most humanistic intellectual and his literature as a fulfillment of that humanism.[119] At the same time, Yi expresses humanism only as it relates to his own nation, ending up with a kind of social Darwinist perspective. Yi's humanism thus differs from Tolstoy's humanism, which Tolstoy says cannot be used in the service of a sect or nation.[120] Yi used the terms "people" (*saram*), "mankind" (*illyu*), and "compatriots" (*tongp'o*) interchangeably. But *tongp'o* clearly conveys a nationalistic bias because he uses it more often when he talks about the Korean people. In more extreme formulations, Yi sounds distinctly antihumanist in his later period, although this does not directly relate to his formulation of a literary theory. When discussing a writer's proper attitude in wartime, Yi argues that "war is evil. But a person who has the courage to confront war is virtuous. A people loses a war when its sense of morality has been debased."[121] Putting aside his later, rather contradictory and ironic development of humanistic ideas, it is obvious that Yi oscillates between a humanism that concerns every human being and a patriotism, exposing this ambivalence in his discussion of Korea's colonial situation. It is not surprising that his interpretation of and approaches toward the sociopolitical environment were reflected in his theory of literature, which was for him an emblem of cultural and political civilization.

Yi's belief in a universal Christianity combined with his nationalist loyalties to form a basic contradiction that infuses many of his conceptions of literature, including literature serving the world of universal Christianity yet serving a specific people; his support of humanism and his emphasis on a moral hierarchy based on power; and, finally, the tension between literature as morality but also as pleasure.

According to Tolstoy, art should be universal, uniting people in the same way that people are joined in union with God—specifically, the Christian God. He then criticizes categorically any art that separates people, and associates this kind of art with the non-Christian. For him, "non Christian art, while uniting some people together, makes that very union a cause of separation between these united people and others; so that union of this kind is often a source, not only of division, but even of enmity towards others." Tolstoy then gives examples: "Such is all patriotic art, with its anthems, poems, and monuments; such is all Church art, i.e. the art of certain cults, with their images, statues, processions, and other local ceremonies" (163; 157).

Yi's concern for the Korean nation and his belief in a universal Christianity were not sequential but coexisted, notwithstanding the ambivalence this entailed. From Tolstoy's perspective, Yi might be the very sort of person who misuses Tolstoy's concept of art. Warning against a misunderstanding of the concept of uniting people, Tolstoy writes:[122]

> The expression *unite men with God and with one another* may seem obscure to people accustomed to the misuse of these words which is so customary, but the words have a perfectly clear meaning nevertheless. They indicate that the Christian union of man (in contradiction to the partial, exclusive union of only some men) is that which unites all without exception. (163; 157)

Explaining Tolstoy's novel *Resurrection*, Yi praises Tolstoy's humanistic literature as it embodies his noble personality, his love for mankind, and his literature's potential to move and enlighten people.[123] Yi sees Tolstoy's humanism as the pinnacle of his achievement, even going so far as to say that his literature takes a back seat to it.[124] When Tolstoy's Christian humanism comes into contact with Yi's thinking, however, it often changes into patriotic idealism. Explaining this new idealism in relation to art, Yi argues:

> Every activity in our lives should serve life, and this idea also applies to art—in other words, art should imbue life with the energy to live. To give a fuller explanation, art should be something that makes life stronger, more beautiful, and more virtuous, but also something that makes people love each other more and become less selfish so that they may

sacrifice themselves for *the people* [compatriots]. From this line of thinking, the humanism of art emerges and new idealism comes into being.[125]
(Emphasis added)

In his later writing, where patriotic idealism goes further to boost the patriotism of the Korean people, Yi asserts that the power of a people is
based in the morality of the people. In his 1936 article about wartime literature, quoted above, it is not surprising that Yi ends up arguing that
"when I look at the current situation of Korea, I feel like we need a kind
of literature that takes the solemnity and heroism of war as its material.
Life is war. . . . War is evil, but victory is only possible for the man of
truth."[126]

Another dynamic at work in Yi's literary theory is the tension between
literature as morality and literature as pleasure. Yi's bases his theory on
the idea of freeing literature from moralistic dogmatism, yet he nevertheless persists in holding literature up as a vehicle for moral values. Yi faults
the Korean tradition for demanding that literature contain moral themes,
and argues that literature was not able to prosper in Korea because of
this.[127] He forthrightly declares that literature must aim at satisfying
emotional need and that such fulfillment is the source of literature's
appeal.[128] At the same time, he rejects the idea of literature as serving
pleasure and writes that "the literature of the present is different from
that of the past, which only served pleasure. . . . It is deplorable that
most of our Korean people think that literature of the present is only
amusement." Rather, according to Yi, poetry and fictional narratives
"discover and develop the truth of life and the universe, examine life,
and strive to represent human psychology and the process of its change."[129]
Not satisfied with this, he goes on to argue that "ethics and art are one—
if art is not moral, then it is not true art and also if ethics is not artistic,
then it is not true ethics."[130] His emphasis on the ethics of literature
echoes Tolstoy, who argues, "[art] is not pleasure; but it is a means of
union among men, joining them together in the same feelings, and indispensable for life and progress towards the well-being of individuals
and of humanity" (50; 66).

Emphasizing pleasure and morality at the same time sounds self-
contradictory, but is nonetheless valuable because it reflects Yi's two urgent desires for the future direction of Korean literature. For Yi, modern

Korean literature had to move away from a literature permeated with moral instruction. This goes hand in hand with his criticism of those Korean intellectuals who thought that literature should be nothing more than a means of moral education. At the same time, Yi demanded that literature not pander to vulgar interests. Yi's conviction that the Korean literary world needed to compensate for its late development may have contributed to the urgency of his sometimes contradictory suggestions for Korean literature's proper direction.

Yet this paradox does not appear only in Korean theorization of literature. The aestheticization process of art in the West, which endowed art with an autonomous space separate from political and religious realms, also entailed a contradictory request that art be socially functional. Art thus "aspired to both aesthetic autonomy and social consequences."[131] Tolstoy's theory of art does not engage this paradox because he did not have to prove that literature is an art form and that art has its autonomy and, thus, was able to focus on the function and effect of literature that would serve lofty purposes. Yi, in contrast, had to create a new concept of literature as an art independent of political and other cultural spheres— autonomous from premodern moral disciplines and didacticism, for instance—and simultaneously had to prove its social relevance, which, for Yi, may have been more significant than its autonomous aesthetics. This paradoxical coexistence of aesthetic autonomy and social relevance of art seems particularly prominent because Yi was seeking to establish a discourse on a new literature by condensing aesthetic autonomy and social relevance—which were more loosely connected over the significantly prolonged period of time in national literatures elsewhere, including Russia—within only a few pages of his theory of literature.

To understand Yi's further appropriation of Tolstoy for the production of his own ideas on literature, we can examine how Yi combined Tolstoy's ideas with ongoing discourses on literature in Korea, which also demonstrated close relationships with literary theories produced and circulated in Japan, and how he adapted those ideas to the pressing issues within the formation of Korean literature. The most conspicuous features shared among Korean intellectuals were an emphasis on the Korean language (*Chosŏn mal, Chosŏn mun, han'gŭl, kugŏ,* and *kungmun*) and the discourse of emotion (*chŏng*). These features clearly reflected Japanese intellectuals' theories on Japanese literature with rough but important distinctions, as though Korean literary theory was the other side of an imperfect decalcomania of the discourse of the metropole. I would argue that what took place was a paradigmatic transference—in both the linguistic and the figurative sense—that involved replacing the Japanese language with the Korean language and the Japanese nation with the Korean nation, although this also created a dissimilar, if not subversive, social meaning in a different context.

Discourses on Korean Language and Emotion

Although it apparently takes up the general question of literature, Yi's 1916 article "What Is Literature?" also addresses Korean literature specifically. It shows how the fundamental elements of literature become concretized in Korean written language, forming an emotional apprehension of the nation. In his first article on literature, written in 1910, Yi defines literature as "a written text, such as poetry and fictional narrative, that possesses the element of emotion."[132] Later, in 1916, he defines literature in more detail: "Literature is that which expresses the thoughts and emotions of human beings in certain forms."[133] By "certain forms," he means written language on the one hand, and literary genres, such as poetry, novels, drama, and criticism, on the other.[134] This focus on "written language" and "emotion" was shared by his contemporaries who were interested in defining and promoting Korean language and literature.

Concern about the Korean language, for example, comes through in Chu Si-kyŏng's article "Kugŏ wa kungmun ŭi p'iryo" (The necessity of the Korean language and Korean writing), written in 1907. At a time when Korean sovereignty was threatened, the emphasis among intellectuals on the Korean language came to be an expression of national sentiment because language was considered essential to the identity of a people. For Chu, "the fact that a country has a specific language and writing system means that the country is independent, and attests that a people that uses its language belongs to and makes up the nation."[135] The Korean language thus served as a symbol of spiritual independence that might compensate for the loss of sovereignty in politics. Although he maintained that Korean was inferior to other languages, Chu argued that people should "revere and develop it" because ignoring or shunning the Korean language amounted to a loss of independence.[136]

Yi's concern for Korean was similar to Chu's. He considered Korean a vessel for the essence of Korean-ness and, therefore, as warranting protection from the encroachments of colonization. After Korea's formal annexation by Japan, Korean literature seemed to him even more essential to realizing a Korean people because, through Korean fiction, people would be able to learn "the Korean language, which lately hardly shows up any more in the curricula of colonial education."[137]

The emphasis on Korean also involved a criticism of Chinese, which, Korean intellectuals held, prevented the development of a unique Korean language. Yi Kwang-su follows this trend in his arguments on the value of the Korean language, attacking Korean intellectuals who revered the Chinese language. He then goes on to advocate a restriction of the concept of Korean literature to include only those works written in Korean. Any other way of trying to distinguish the original Korean literary tradition from Chinese would have become too difficult. Emphasizing Korean national consciousness through the Korean language entailed criticizing the Chinese language and setting it up as an "other" against and through which the identity of Korean could be constructed. Yi argues that "written language is a container for a material called literature. Koreans have long thought that literary Chinese is the only written language, and this is the reason that literature could not develop in Korea. . . . That tendency remains even now, as some people still try to use the style of literary Chinese."[138]

Yi's efforts to separate literary Chinese from Korean allowed him to argue that "Korean literature designates only something written in Korean." According to him, "it is not an issue of who writes what"[139] of the language. Though this argument seems unsatisfactory from the standpoint of the present, it is important to realize what the redefinition authorized at the time. After defining Korean literature based on the language in which it was written, Yi gave a new origin to Korean literature, dating it to King Sejong's creation of the Korean written language in the mid-fifteenth century. This swept away all literature before that time except for that written in *idu*, a transcription system of the Three Kingdoms era.

But since there would not be a sustainable tradition if Yi excluded all literary Chinese writings in premodern Korea, Yi brought in another

tradition: translated literature written in the Korean language. The boundary of Korean literature that Yi drew touches on the question of the mem-
bership of translated texts in Korean literature. Yi considered Korean
translations of Chinese literary works to be works of Korean literature,
and argued that for the Korean people, a translation into Korean of a
Chinese text held more value than did its original. For instance, he did
not consider *Kuunmong*, one of the masterpieces of Korean literature,
written by Kim Man-jung in literary Chinese, to be an example of true
Korean literature. He argued that the anonymous translation of this work
into Korean had a far stronger impact on the development of Korean literature.[140] Yi believed that translators' contributions to the prosperity of
Korean literature, whether or not they themselves were conscious of it,
could not be overemphasized.[141] His inclusion of Chinese works that had
been translated into Korean and his exclusion of Korean authors' works
written in Chinese reflect Yi's efforts to stress the value of the Korean written language and the otherness of Chinese.[142] This stance also elevated his
own position as an introducer of foreign-language literatures into Korea.
This discourse on the uniqueness and independence of the Korean language thus worked in concert with the concept of emotion to validate
the argument that the literature of a people embodies its nationhood.

Korean intellectuals in the 1910s considered the concept of emotion
to be one of the fundamental elements of literature. For Yi, emotion was
not only an essential element of literature but essential to the creation of
literature. The discourse on emotion as it relates to the theory of literature began with Yi's definition of literature as "writings with the element
of emotion" in his article "The Value of Literature," written in 1910.

Yi's concept of emotion benefitted from Tsubouchi Shōyō's theory
of the novel. After Shōyō had written *Shōsetsu shinzui* (The essence of the
novel, 1885–86), a historic book on the concept of *shōsetsu* (fiction), emotion had come to be considered a prerequisite of *shōsetsu* in Japan.[143] Yi
pointed to Shōyō as one of three Japanese writers who had influenced
him.[144] In the section "Shōsetsu no shugan" (The Principle Object of Fiction), Shōyō stresses that "the principle object of fiction is *ninjō* (emotion, human feelings). Sociohistorical circumstances (*setai*) and customs
(*fūzoku*) are subsequent to this."[145] The word "*ninjō*" (in Korean *injŏng*)
is a compound of "human" (*nin*) and "emotion, feelings, or affection" (*jō*);
the *jō* is the same Chinese character, *chŏng* (emotion), that Yi used for
his conceptualization of literature. Shōyō went on to emphasize "the

'imitation' or 'mimetic depiction' (*mosha* or *mogi*) of 'human feelings' (*ninjō*) as the key to making the novel the 'most advanced form of literary art.'"[146] In *Shōsetsu shinzui*, he uses the term "*ninjō*" to refer to human feelings and psychology in a broad way, which includes both negative and positive aspects.[147] Shōyō included fiction in the realm of art (*bijutsu* is Shōyō's term)[148] and unshackled it from its role as a vehicle for political ideals and morals, or *kanzen chōaku* (encouraging virtue and chastising vice, *kwŏnsŏn ching'ak* in Korean).[149]

Yi Kwang-su adopted Shōyō's idea not only for fiction but for literature in general, and argued that "[writers] should not write literature for the effect of *kwŏnsŏn ching'ak*, they should represent real thought, emotion, and life before the reader without moral criteria."[150] But it is important to note that, separately from this concept of emotion as an object of description, Yi's idea about *the readers' emotions as objects of artistic infection* and their capacity to be infected with the feelings of others relies heavily on Tolstoy's theory.

Yi developed the concept of emotion further through the mid-1910s, along with intellectuals such as Ch'oe Tu-sŏn and An Hwak. In an article in 1914, Ch'oe Tu-sŏn argues that "although something might provide us with knowledge, although something might possess the form of poetry or a novel, although something might deal with the imagination, we cannot call these things literature. What allows a thing to become literature is the factor of vitality, in other words, the elements of *chŏng-ŭi* (emotion and will)."[151] Carrying the concept of emotion further, An Hwak gives a more detailed definition of literature. For him, "literature is that which expresses the impression of beauty in written language." Comparing literature with politics, he explains that "politics is that which controls the external world of people, while literature controls their inner emotions."[152]

The discourse on emotion as it relates to the definition of literature is fully fleshed out in Yi's famous 1916 article "What Is Literature?" For Yi, emotion serves as a means of expressing individuality, and thus emotion can also serve as a source for the emergence of modern literature. Yi argues:

> Literature has come to be based on emotion, and so the question of the importance of literature depends on how seriously we consider the relations between emotion and human beings. In the past, everyone looked down

on emotion and respected only reason and knowledge because they were not conscious of individuality.[153]

He claims that emotion enables a person to act independently of social restraints and to behave without deceiving himself or herself.[154]

Yi utilizes the categorization that divides human mind into the three realms of *chi* (intellect), *chŏng* (emotion), and *ŭi* (will) in order to emphasize the independent standing of emotion and that its value is equivalent to that of the two other realms:

> Recently people have come to know that the human mind operates based on the three elements of intellect, emotion, and will, and that these three all exist in our mind equally, without a hierarchical relationship. The status of emotion therefore was elevated. Emotion, which used to be a mere slave of intellect and will, now has acquired the power equal to that of intellect and will, and seeks its satisfaction through literature, music, fine art, etc., as intellect does through all fields of science. Given that the ancient times witnessed such art, emotion was not completely ignored. And yet it was not entirely for the satisfaction of emotion, and emotion was always combined with intellectual, moral, and religious significance, and had existed as supplement and accessary to morals and religion until the social upheaval of the Renaissance about five hundred years ago. After this, emotion was finally endowed with independent status and treated equally with intellect and will.[155]

For Yi, the success of literature results from the understanding that emotion is one of the three fundamental elements that enable human psychology to function. This elevation of emotion to the level of intellect and will also authorizes a revaluation of the role of literature.

The discourse of intellect, emotion, and will that Yi incorporated in order to build a theory of a new literature in Korea was not unique—it was prevalent in Japanese literary and social discourses. According to *Shinri hakuwa* (A story of psychology), written in 1912 by the child education expert Takashima Heizaburō, the distinction of the intellect, emotion, and will was commonly accepted, in that "anyone would now answer *chi, jō*, and *i* (intellect, emotion, and will) without hesitation when asked about the distinction of mental phenomenon (*seishin genshō*)."[156]

This description of the human mind in terms of intellect, emotion, and will can also be found in Natsume Sōseki's theory of literature, published in 1907. Explaining that technique and the precise description of an object do not necessarily mean the proper expression of ideals, he writes: "To put this in more easily understood terms, in depicting an object, even when we produce something very like the actual thing, the result at times fails to express the workings of our intellect, emotion, and will."[157] Sōseki's essay includes no detailed explanation as to what these three elements mean in relation to the function of the human mind and literature. But this very lack tells us that this distinction and the way of explaining human mind with these elements were already commonly used and understood. More specific usage of these three elements in relation to the explanation of literary writings can be found in earlier essays published by the intellectuals affiliated with Waseda University and its journals in the 1890s and 1900s, namely, the group of scholars and writers who developed *bijigaku* (the study of rhetoric).[158]

Manipulation of Tolstoy's Theory of Art: Literature as the Preserver of Nationhood

Yi's conception of emotion shares certain elements with the conceptions of his Korean contemporaries, in the sense that literature is that which contains emotion. However, Yi also elevates emotion by characterizing it as a means toward the manifestation of individuality and as a holder of the national essence. More than other writers in the 1910s concerned with the relationship between emotion and literature, Yi went beyond the simple claim that literature includes elements of emotion, to give a detailed picture of how literature works for and with emotion. What I would like to point out here is that Yi elaborated his theory of literature by combining the ongoing literary theorizing in Korea and Japan with Tolstoy's claims about the function of art. This did not include Tolstoy's claims as to the fundamental Christian aim of art; Yi consciously selected only the parts of the theory that served his purposes. This combination allowed Yi to show how literature could serve as a means of uniting a people and conveying its nationhood or national character (*minjoksŏng*).

But it should not be forgotten that the formulation of this theory is also a problematic borrowing of theories from the metropole, despite the absence of the writer's specific acknowledgment of this.

Yi makes a connection between literature and nationhood by arguing that it is the literature of a people that can most effectively convey "the spiritual civilization of that people, and this is the source of its nationhood."[159] For him, Korea had lost her valuable cultural heritage because she had lost her literature. Criticizing the importation of Chinese language and thought systems as a block to Korea's own self-realization, he argued that Korea had to construct a new literature, following a new Western conception of culture, in order to pass on the original Korean thoughts and emotions to later generations.[160] Yi's emphasis on the importance of a new Korean literature that foregrounds the Korean language does not concern only literature itself. According to his logic, the absence of literature among a people indicates a weakness of that people's nationhood and spiritual civilization, while the greatness of nationhood depends on its literature.

Yi was not the only person to emphasize the relationship between the literature of a people and its national consciousness. An Hwak, a Korean literary historian, also argued that "the so-called competition among races and peoples seems to be a political phenomenon, but in fact it is fundamentally a competition of the strength of their nationhood. Powerful countries try to spread their national ideas and assimilate other peoples," and thus "a person who concerns himself or herself with literature should make every effort to bring a new Korean literature to great success."[161] An's argument about the connection of literature with nationhood, however, stops at this point and does not describe exactly how literature works for the nation.

Yi does not explicitly take up the role of literature in preserving nationhood, but the way his arguments unfold in his article "What Is Literature?" gives a sufficiently robust picture. The literature of a people evokes emotion, which is the essence of its nationhood. Literature transmits this emotion through a people and unites them. If literature is the vehicle that transmits the "spiritual civilization of a nation as the source of the nationhood of a people,"[162] then it can be said that emotion is that which feeds the source of nationhood. Although Yi may not have been fully conscious of the ramifications of his claim, he nevertheless held that emotion can be considered as a basis of communication among people from different times and places, and as a medium of transmission of the national character of a people. His claim also suggests that literature is something that contains this kind of emotion, and so serves to preserve the nationhood of a people. Emotion is therefore elevated beyond a means of manifesting individuality, to the point of becoming the essence and source of the nationhood of a people.

The central idea that the literature of a people can "convey and transmit" emotions was borrowed from Tolstoy. But here, Yi successfully manipulates Tolstoy's idea to support his own theory for a national literature the concept of which Tolstoy would have disapproved. Tolstoy argues that "thanks to man's capacity to be infected with the feelings of others by means of art, all that is being lived through by his contemporaries is accessible to him, as well as the feelings experienced by men thousands of years ago, and he has also the possibility of transmitting his own feelings to others" (50; 66). Yi shares Tolstoy's idea that literature's ability to transmit emotions to others allows a people to understand their past and present and to convey it to the next generation. But Yi refracts this idea through the needs of Korean literature by arguing that Korean literature preserves and transmits the "spiritual civilization" of the Korean people as a basis for its "nationhood."[163]

From Kokubungaku *to* Chosŏn munhak: *Coloniality in Modern Korean Literature*

While the theory of emotional "infection" in Tolstoy's writings is a core element in Yi's theory of literature, the similarity between Yi's theory and Japanese discourses on literature is at least equally prominent, particularly in its explanation of national literature. Yi explains two material forms that define literature as follows:

> Literature is something that expresses human thoughts and emotions in specific forms. I mean two things by "specific forms." First, it refers to written texts. Oral folk tales therefore are not literature, and can be considered literature only after they are recorded in written language. Second,

literature has various literary forms, such as poetry, prose, drama, and essay. If something does not have a specific form, even though it is written, it
is hard to refer to it as literature.[164]

After providing the general concept of a new literature, Yi defines a
national literature as "something that can transmit most effectively a
nation's spiritual civilization,"[165] and Korean literature as "literature
written in the Korean language by Korean people,"[166] as discussed above.
He argues that there is nothing that we can call Korean literature from
the Koryŏ dynasty until King Sejong invented Korean script except for
the small number of writings that were written in *idu*, a Korean variation
of classical Chinese.[167]

Yi's definition of literature, particularly national literature, echoes the
writings of a group of Japanese literary scholars who were trained in Japanese literature and history at Tokyo University in the 1880s. Alarmed by
the fact that the university's Department of Japanese and Chinese Literature (Wakan bungaku-ka) had been declining since its establishment
in 1877, probably due to Japanese intellectuals' attraction to Western culture, the president of the university, Katō Hiroyuki, requested in 1879 that
the Ministry of Education permit the creation of the Classical Training
Program (Koten kōshū-ka) for the formal education of Japanese literature and history as a part of a College of Letters (Bungaku-bu). After some
struggle the program was established in 1882, although it closed in 1888,
three years after the Department of Japanese and Chinese Literature was
divided into two individual entities. The short-lived Classical Training
Program and the Department of Japanese Literature turned out a group
of scholars who significantly affected the field of literary studies in the
1890s.[168] Among these Japanese literary historians were Mikami Sanji
(1865–1939) and Haga Yaichi (1867–1927), whose work is particularly ger-
mane to the theory of Korean literature articulated by Yi some twenty to
thirty years later.

In 1890 Mikami Sanji and Takasu Kuwasabuō coauthored *Nihon
bungakushi* (History of Japanese literature), a two-volume pioneering
study of Japanese literature that became a model for later histories. In their
forty-page introduction, Mikami and Takasu define a national literature
as "something through which the country's people (*kokumin*) express the
nation's unique thought (*shisō*), emotion (*kanjō*), and imagination (*sōzō*)
in the written form of its national language (*kokugo*)."[169] Mikami and

Takasu also state in their preface that they will almost exclusively handle writings composed in the Japanese language: "According to the definition stated in our introduction, we do not deal with writings written in Classical Chinese (*kanbun*). Yet we clarify the parts that are connected to Japanese national literature (*kokubungaku*)."[170]

Similar explanations can be found in other Japanese literary histories. In *Kokubungakushi jikkō* (Ten lectures on the history of national literature), published in 1899, nine years after Mikami and Takasu's *History of Japanese Literature*, Haga Yaichi also emphasizes literature as the expression of a nation's thought and emotion: "What is interesting in a literary history is that the spirit (*kifū*), thought (*shisō*), and emotion (*kanjō*) of a nation (*kokumin*) are naturally expressed in literature."[171] In addition to his explanation about the object that literature describes and contains, Haga also briefly expresses his opinion on translation at the end of his book, which reminds us of Yi's inclusion of translation as part of Korea's national literature:

> Nowadays writers and artists are extremely eager to receive new elements of Western culture. Simultaneously, they study [the] literature and art of their own tradition. The immature translation era (*yōchina hon'yaku jidai*) has already passed, and we have to some extent entered an era of adaptation (*hon'an*). But this does not mean that the translation (*hon'yaku*) of our era is working out without any problem. A great translation is a great national literature (*kokubungaku*).[172]

Yi's theory of literature shared both Haga's approach to translation and other distinctive elements of these Japanese literary theories. First, Yi shared the emphasis on a nation's native (in his case Korean) language, though he was also obsessed with "written" language and excluded all oral literary tradition. Second, he applied the absolute principle of language in defining a national literature, and so excluded all Korean people's literature written in Classical Chinese (as Mikami and Takasu proposed for Japanese literature). Third, he included Korean translations as Korean literature (as Haga included great Japanese translations). These three elements, which distinguish Yi's theory not only from today's literary theories but also from those of his Korean contemporaries, are easily understood when we refer to the Japanese literary historians' writings discussed above. However, Yi's theory was less flexible than were the Japanese literary historians' definitions of Japanese national literature. Yi excluded oral tradition and Chinese writings without exception and included all Korean translations, whereas Mikami and Takasu were willing to deal with Chinese writings if necessary and Haga included only great translations as Japanese national literature (and did not define "great" in this context).

Despite these subtle yet radical moves that Yi made in his theory of literature, his mechanism for defining and explaining Korean national literature demonstrates the paradigmatic switch between Japan and Korea within the same syntactic structure. In other words, in Yi's theory "Japanese" language, nation, and literature change into "Korean" within the same explanatory linguistic composition. Thus when Yi was introducing "literature" as a translated term and emphasizing Korean literature's uniqueness and authenticity, he was doing that by "translating" the discursive structure of the metropole in order to create its new meaning and function in and for the Korean language and its cultural context.

In this process of translation, however, there was a series of terms that Yi could not directly render from the Japanese—namely, *kungmun* (*kokubun* in Japanese; a national language), *kungmin* (*kokumin*; people of a nation) and *kungmunhak* (*kokubungaku*; national literature). In Korea these terms became *Chosŏnmun* (Korean language), *Chosŏnin* (Korean people), and *Chosŏn munhak* (Korean literature) twenty to thirty years after the term "national literature" (Japanese *kokubungaku*) had been naturalized and commonly used in 1890s Japan to refer to Japan's national literature.[173] When Yi refers to national literature in general, he uses the term "*minjok munhak*," which, unlike *kungmunhak*, does not convey the meaning of a literature of a nation-state.

Korean terms such as *Chosŏnmun* and *Chosŏn munhak*, I would argue, already connote Korean literature's coloniality, in that they indicate the language and literature of Korea as a colony vis-à-vis *kungmun* as the language of imperial Japan. In other words, the terms "*Chosŏnmun*" and "*Chosŏn munhak*" implicitly referenced the words "*kungmun*" and "*kungmunhak*"—which were untranslatable into the Korean language and Korean literature—as an imperial Other in a configuring relationship of each other's identity. Therefore, modern Korean language and literature were endowed with the label "colonial" simultaneously with the label "national" from the beginning. In fact, Yi uses *kungmun* a few times in his essay, but only when explaining it in relation to King Sejong's invention of it and referring to a group of stories written in vernacular Korean, in specific contrast to Chinese written language.[174] Interestingly, Yi never uses "*kungmun*" and "*kungmunhak*" when he defines Korean literature or refers to Korean national literature as a whole. Rather, symptomatically enough, Yi uses *kungmunhak* (or *kungmin munhak*; national literature) and *kungmun hakcha* (a writer/scholar of national literature) to refer to the entity of "Japanese" literature and "Japanese" writers in the same article.[175] Possibly Yi had already adopted the idea that Korea's national language was the language of the colonizer (Japan) and the Korean language was simply a local language. This distinction—of the metropole and colony literatures, and the colonial intellectuals' internalization of this distinction—were embodied in even the first attempts to theorize Korean literature.

In Japan, histories of Japanese literature, including those written by Mikami, Takasu, and Haga, had been published consecutively since the 1890s as textbooks for the education of future Japanese leaders and were expected to function as a means to construct the cultural identity of Japan as a nation-state.[176] It is worth pointing out that Japanese literary historians began to compile and publish Japan's national literary history "in the months between the promulgation of the Meiji Constitution in February 1889 and the publication of the Rescript on Education in October 1890, a period when the Emperor system of the Meiji state was formalized."[177] In Japan, aspirations for a national literature crystallized in the form of university education and the academic field of *kokubungaku*, but in colonial Korea, national literature was a concept without any substantial institution to promote it. The only visible, physical manifestation possible for the newly constructed Korean literature seems to have been the Korean script itself. Thus the intensity of colonial Korean intellectuals' attachment to Korean script differed from Japanese intellectuals' feelings about written Japanese.

Yi's obsession with "Korean" and "written language" led him to exclude all unrecorded Korean oral traditions and Korean people's writings in Classical Chinese from his concept of Korean literature, ironically highlighting his deep-seated anxiety about the identity of the literature of a colonized nation. Without institutional promotion of a national literature, Yi may have felt compelled to create an identity for Korean literature exclusively through the nonnegotiable criterion of the Korean script—a written language so distinctive that no one would be able to challenge either its ontological component or the visual boundary that it would create between Korean and other literatures.

Being a Munsa in Korea: The Colonial Predicament and Self-Empowered Agency

In tandem with Korean script, another significant element that Yi repeatedly emphasized about the new Korean literature was the agency of the *munsa* (man of letters, or writer). Yi discusses the general qualifications and social responsibility involved in being a *munsa*. He uses the vague phrase "art for life's sake," which Korean writers commonly used at the time to describe Russian literature, in order to describe the kind of literature that Korean writers were supposed to pursue.[178] In his 1921 article "Munsa wa suyang" (A writer and self-cultivation), he argues: "If anything does not contribute to life and, even more, causes harm, it is an evil. Even in the case of literature, if it harms any individual, particularly our nation, we absolutely need to destroy it. *Arts* [*sic*] *for life's sake* [English in original] is the motto that we should take for our literature."[179] Yi also deploys this vague expression about the expectations for a writer in Korea in a more substantial way in this same article:

> [When we only look at the cases of other countries,] we easily know how important self-cultivation is to a writer (*munsa*). If so, it goes without saying how important it is to writers of our country, where writers have a heavy responsibility to play various roles in their society as a thinker, social leader, a reformer of the society, and a model for young people, as well as [the responsibility of being] a writer. People who want to be a writer in our country truly need to be industrious and put a great deal of effort into studying hard and cultivating themselves.[180]

There is no explanation as to why writers in Korea are obligated to play all these social roles or why the Korean situation is different from that of the other countries Yi mentions (England, Germany, Russia, and Japan)—a difference implied in his argument that self-cultivation is particularly important for Korean writers. Yet for Yi, *munsa* are clearly supposed to make up for the lack of Korean political sovereignty, along with sustaining other symbolic cultural elements, such as the Korean language itself and print media written in that language.

If Yi's concept of writers less obviously claimed that writers needed to be an active sociopolitical agent in a colony, private Korean newspapers quite obviously proclaimed themselves a collective body that would play the role of a pseudo government of colonized Korea, in tandem with other diverse types of print media put out after the 1919 March First independence movement:

> Korean people still have no organization to supervise the politics of their country and no means to reprimand the government. Despite being insufficient, [a] handful of press media (*ŏllon kigwan*) are the only medium that expresses people's opinions (*minŭi*). Therefore the press media in contemporary Korean society, different from those of other societies, are a type of legislature (*ippŏp kigwan*) and supervisory institution (*kamdok kigwan*).[181]

Newspapers recognized that their anticolonial function in a confrontational relationship with the Japanese colonial government did not represent the Korean people and thus lacked the Korean people's moral support. This recognition legitimized newspapers' view of themselves as an alternative to, or deputy of, the absent Korean government in colonial Korea.[182] This context helps us understand the reasoning behind Yi's stress on writers' roles in society and the qualifications that they should achieve, which is arguably the most distinctive feature of his concept of writers in comparison to the concept of writers in the Japanese literary theories that he referred to.

Given that almost all Korean writers, including Yi Kwang-su himself, worked as journalists or were otherwise employed by newspapers at some point, the relationships between newspapers and writers were not simple at all.[183] Newspapers carried literature that those writers wrote, and writers worked as journalists for those newspapers. Moreover, Korean newspapers and writers shared a sense of duty, as an alternative public agency, to the lost sovereignty of colonial Korea. Ch'oe Nam-sŏn and Yi Kwang-su, who were both writers in a narrow sense and active social leaders, expanded the possible role of a writer/intellectual in a colony, and their emphasis on the agency of writers/intellectuals was interwoven with the newspapers' self-declared authority that aimed to substitute for Korea's lost political sovereignty.

Atsuko Ueda, a Japanese literary scholar, argues that in Japan "the establishment of emotions, customs, and manners as the main theme of the *shōsetsu* [novel] is inextricably linked to the defocalization of 'political' discourse. In the mid-1880s, emotions, customs, and manners appeared in direct opposition to a certain habitus that constituted the 'political' at that particular historical juncture."[184] She complicates this further by arguing that this repression of the political does not mean being apolitical but instead manifests different politicality in this very concealment of politics.[185]

But the establishment of literature in Korea shows a different deployment of the discourse on the literary and the political, even though the Japanese literary discourse based on "emotions, customs, and manners" affected Korean narrative on literature. In Korea, the colonization preceded the theorization of the concept of new literature. Because Korea had lost its political sovereignty before colonial Korean intellectuals began trying to conceptualize and understand a new literature of modern Korea, literature was reborn as a modern medium that carried and manifested both art as aesthetics (which is supposed to be independent of politics and religion) and art as political (which expresses politics in subtle and circumventing ways). In other words, I would argue, modern literature in colonial Korea was created simultaneously by *particularization* of its specific aesthetics and by the *expansion* of its sociopolitical function. The aspirations of this expanded social function of literature crystallized in the concept of *munsa* in Korea.

Yi's "What Is Literature?," credited as being the first substantial modern theory of literature in Korea, has a complex, lumpy texture in the places where its diverse conflicting ideas clash with each other and lay bare the paradoxical coexistence of aesthetic autonomy and the social relevance of art. In Yi's theory, Tolstoy's universalism, which is opposed to any patriotic and national literature, is manipulated to legitimize and promote the necessity of Korean national literature. Meanwhile, Yi explains the uniqueness and independence of Korean national literature by translating the colonizer's discursive structure and mechanism in order to create his own concept.[186] Yi's public emphasis on Tolstoy's influence on his theory and on every aspect of his life, while downplaying the apparent colonial influence (i.e., the immediate connection his theory had with Japanese discourse), paradoxically exposes his anxiety as a colonized intellectual who had voluntarily and involuntarily become a part of a colonial system, and demonstrates the complications and predicament that colonial knowledge production entailed.[187]

Conclusion

The modernization of Korean literature took place in a colonial situation, and one of the sites that bears the complexity of this intersection of modernity, colonialism, and nationalism is the process of the reception of foreign literature. Foreign literatures were introduced into Korea as part of the modernization project of national literature. However, as explained in detail in the introduction, this occurred mostly through Japan, and the case of Russian literature is more problematic than that of other foreign literatures because there were so few Koreans with a command of the language. Ch'oe Nam-sŏn and Yi Kwang-su, who enthusiastically introduced Tolstoy to Korea, did not know Russian, meaning that they had to read and translate texts of Tolstoy filtered through the interests of Japanese intellectuals. Tolstoy's "originals" were in Japanese for Ch'oe and Yi, and Japanese importation of Russian literature was therefore the opening premise for Korean translation.

Ch'oe and Yi nevertheless appropriated Tolstoy's thoughts and beliefs for their own purposes, and in that process further altered Tolstoy's profile in Korea. Ch'oe and Yi's representations of Tolstoy in their writings represent not only Tolstoy but their own concerns with Tolstoy. They eulogize and deify Tolstoy not merely to show their respect for him, but to manipulate his unassailable fame into a source of legitimation that can serve as a foundation for their own arguments. Ch'oe and Yi's essays reveal their own interests, ideas, ambivalence, hopes, and perceived reality. As leading intellectuals during the formation of modern Korean literature, Ch'oe and Yi consciously and unconsciously sensed the importance of their roles in a modern and colonized Korean society. Their project of modernizing Korean literature could not avoid importing Western literatures, but the process of importation did not involve the notion of Western literature *as it was*. Through Ch'oe, Yi, and others, works of Western literature were always undergoing translation and transformation.

What Ch'oe and Yi chose to adopt of Tolstoy's ideas tells us a lot about the pressing issues of colonial Korea. Ch'oe portrayed Tolstoy as a model intellectual whose way of life could provide an educational model for Korean youth, rather than as a religious pacifist or a radical idealist whose ideas might bring about drastic social change. Yi highlighted Tolstoy's theory of art, which Yi transformed to serve his own needs, combining it with ongoing discourses on literature in Korea and Japan. The exclusion of radical thought in both cases was perfectly in line with Ch'oe and Yi's respective ideas about sociopolitical change in colonial Korea, which were connected to gradualism or national enlightenment, emphasizing a long-term plan of empowering Koreans through education. It can also be inferred that because the Japanese enforced a harsh rule in Korea until the March First independence movement of 1919, the conditions in colonized Korea curtailed some forms of ideological importation. Literature, such as the works of Tolstoy, does not automatically have an impact on a society simply because it is available. It is ready to function in a new environment only when the agent perceives how it can fit into and endorse his or her ideas and purpose.

Yet, modern Korean literature was also being created under the Japanese colonial impact in a broad sense. More specifically, the new concept of literature and the theory of Korean national literature themselves were created by Korean intellectuals who learned in Japanese schools and read Japanese literary and art theory, or who at least were exposed to those discourses (which becomes even more complicated when we consider that Japanese literary theory was itself produced under the threat of Western imperialism and the impact of its discourse). Ch'oe and Yi's cases therefore show two connected strands of convoluted cultural appropriation: first, their building up of Tolstoy's fame eventually served as a means to promote their ideas and secure their unstable social status as new and young intellectuals/writers; and second, they redirected their anxiety in this process by repeatedly deifying Tolstoy while minimizing the exposure of Japanese intervention. This process is a sort of template for what happened in Korean relay translations of Russian texts from Japanese, which produced Korean translations that have Russian as a source text on a conceptual level but Japanese as the source language in reality, and that often neglect to acknowledge the impact and mediation of the Japanese language and culture. The coloniality (political and economic colonization and the diverse sociocultural impact that it entails), I would argue, was in a broad sense a constitutive force profoundly involved in the construction of modern Korean literature—and one that particularly affected its conceptualization and explanatory structure—rather than an external social condition that existed in parallel with, or intervened in, a separately constructed entity of modern Korean literature.

CHAPTER 2

Rewriting Literature and Reality

Translation, Journalism, and Modern Literature

Russian literature started to be brought to Korea in the late 1900s with Tolstoy, as discussed in Chapter 1, and its Korean translation was reaching a dynamic peak by the 1920s. One of the most prominent Russian writers introduced to Korea in the 1920s was Anton Pavlovich Chekhov (1860–1904). Chekhov's work is of particular importance to the history of translation in the building of Korean modern literature, because it became one of the touchstones for short story writing and the modern theater movements there. One of the people most responsible for establishing Chekhov's reputation in Korea was Hyŏn Chin-gŏn (1900–43). In the process, Hyŏn made profound contributions to the creation of the modern short story genre in Korea. As one of his contemporaries noted, "Mr. Hyŏn Chin-gŏn is so famous as a short story writer that he is considered Chosŏn's Chekhov (*Chosŏn ŭi Ch'ehop*)."[1] This shows that Hyŏn's style and status as a short story writer in Korean literature corresponded to Chekhov's style and status in Russian literature. Though Hyŏn rarely acknowledged it openly, a number of his most important short stories were fashioned from a "productive appropriation" of Chekhov's works.[2]

Hyŏn's contact with Chekhov's work came at a time of transition not only in Hyŏn's own style but within the Korean literary, intellectual, and political climate as a whole. Hyŏn's first story, "Hŭisaenghwa" (A flower of sacrifice), published in 1920, is a tragic love story. It was followed by a series of introspective autobiographical works depicting an intellectual in the throes of self-doubt. But by the mid-1920s, his subject matter had begun to turn to wider social issues—to the lives of the poor and disen-franchised. This shift in Hyŏn's own writing parallels a wider shift in co-lonial Korea. Decadent literature and "art for art's sake" had been in vogue in the early 1920s, partly in the wake of the failure of the March First independence movement of 1919, and partly in reaction to the as-sociated literature of nationalism and the Korean Enlightenment. By the mid-1920s, however, proletarian literature was beginning to develop in Korea, pioneered by authors such as Kim Ki-jin and Pak Yŏng-hŭi. Hyŏn kept a certain distance from the proletarian literature movement proper, but his growing interest in trying to represent the hard lives of common people can be seen against this background.[3]

It was in negotiating this shift, in finding a language to describe his new concerns, that Hyŏn's use of Chekhov's style and motifs became most prominent. Hyŏn's short story "Kkamakchapki" (Blindman's bluff, 1924) was modeled on Chekhov's "Potselui" (The kiss, 1887). "Unsu choŭn nal" (A lucky day, 1924) and "Pul" (Fire, 1925), which are regarded as represen-tative of Hyŏn's new direction, have noticeable similarities with Chekhov's "Toska" (Anguish, 1886) and "Spat' khochetsia" (Sleepy, 1888), respec-tively.[4] This chapter focuses on Hyŏn's 1925 short story, "Fire."

"Fire" provides a valuable case study because in it we can see transla-tion working as a relay between two different fields. First, as already men-tioned, Chekhov's story provided a fresh language for Hyŏn at the point when he was developing a new kind of vernacular, socially conscious literature. Specifically, in "Fire" Hyŏn used elements from Chekhov's "Sleepy" to create a new type of female character—one who rebels against her social position, in this case by burning down the house of the hus-band she has been forced to marry. Through this protagonist Hyŏn was able to dramatize the social-sexual quandary facing young brides and to comment on the topic of early marriage, which was a much-debated social problem at the time. I argue that Suni, the female arsonist in "Fire," was an unprecedented figure in the history of modern Korean literature, and it was translation as an act of "productive appropriation" that provided Hyŏn with a new way of addressing his lived reality through a modern literary form.

Second, "Fire" attests to how permeable the barrier between modern fiction and nonfiction writing was at this point in Korea. Literature not only *borrowed* themes from newspaper discourse but sometimes *con-tributed* a vocabulary of character and narrative to journalism, thereby

influencing accounts of reality written in newspapers. Hyŏn's story created the model of a sympathetic criminal—the criminal as victim—that
went on to become prevalent in later newspaper reports of actual female
arson. Though it is difficult to prove a cause-and-effect relationship,
"Fire" remains a text in which we can see the intersection of two different
moments of translation: one between Russian literature and Korean literature, the other between fiction and nonfiction. A close examination of
this intersection can show in detail how translation as productive appropriation creates new fiction and nonfiction possibilities for writers. Perhaps it even created *actual* possibilities for young women living in Korea
at the time.

In tandem with examining the entangled relationships among social discourse, journalism, translation, and creative writing of 1920s Korea, we can explore the ways in which Chekhov's story "Sleepy" was rewritten in three other languages (English, Japanese, and Korean), in
order to see how the movement of the Chekhov story into other cultures
affects the text. By going beyond national boundaries to discuss a fictional character's multidirectional travels from Russia to New Zealand,
Japan, and Korea, we may come to view world literature less as an entity
made up of literary works than as a process that emphasizes movement
and relationality—and that is constantly changing due to new produc-
tions and newly discovered relations. This reconceptualization of textual
connections will provide us with an alternate perspective to the influence studies and diffusionist theories of world literature, and will
highlight both the specific historical and literary context for the movement and the dynamic connections of a global text production.

The intent here is not to assess Chekov's impact on Korean literature,
but to show that reception is a multidirectional and involved process that
manifests in the formation of fictional narratives (not only in Korea, but
also in Japan and New Zealand), as well as journalistic narratives, legal
and social customs, and people's real lives. Multiple determinative factors and their complicated interactions were involved in creating a new
character type in Korean literary history, and that translation in this case
provided a Korean writer with a new way of perceiving his own lived reality and suggested a way for the writer to intervene (or try to intervene)
in that reality in a specific new form.

The idea that Korean literary history can be modeled as a simple
balance between such nationalist agency and foreign impact has been

pervasive in the field of modern Korean literary studies. Comparative studies of Western and Korean literature tend to be influence studies that emphasize the impact of Western literatures on Korean literature. On the other side, there is a body of work that excludes the process through which Korean literature interacted with foreign literatures to focus instead on authorial agency or national lineages, which are thereby designated nationalist.

Exploring the story "Fire" should demonstrate that there is no such binary or dichotomous structure in the historical processes themselves. As explained in the introduction, what has come to be known as national literature is so radically infiltrated by translation (indeed, it is made possible in the first place by translation, as discussed in the introduction), that there is simply no such thing as nationally locatable agency. Likewise, tracing how a foreign literary character interacted with diverse aspects of a local culture shows that there is no simple directionality of influence: the character not only transformed in relation to the context of 1920s Korean literature, it also proliferated across media, discourses, and social practices, continuing to transform as it did so. It is necessary to discuss Korean sociocultural factors in depth in order to show the case's complexity (a complexity which is constitutive of its significance), and thus to demonstrate the multifaceted and convoluted relationships among the constructive forces of modern Korean literature.

Chekhov in Japan and Korea

How was Chekhov understood and represented by Korean intellectuals? What were the sources for that representation? What impact did Japanese importation and description of Chekhov have on Korean contact with his work? What do translation and adaptation mean when Korean intellectuals translated Russian works from the Japanese rather than from the original Russian?

Both as a short story writer and as a playwright, Chekhov is unquestionably one of the most significant Russian writers. He was born in Taganrog, a port town on the Sea of Azov in the south of Russia, in 1860, one year before the abolition of serfdom. In 1879, he enrolled in the medical school at Moscow University and began submitting writing to various lowbrow publications to make extra money to support his family. With the support of Dmitry Grigorovich, an established novelist, and Suvorin, editor of the *Novoe Vremia* (New Times), the largest daily paper of the day, Chekhov was able to start developing "the style that is most characteristically his."[5] Chekhov's literary career can be roughly divided into two periods, with the turning point between them set in 1888, the year he wrote the novella *The Steppe*, a long and nearly plotless description of a boy's journey. Chekhov's earlier period is characterized by satirical and humorous pieces, whereas his later period is noted for its gloom and gray melancholy.

His subject matter is conspicuous for its lack of heroic characters and sensational events. The narratives focus on scenes of everyday life: Chekhov's characters include a wide range of regular Russian people, including landowners, civil servants of all levels, members of the intelligentsia, merchants, clergy, peasants, and a large body of the dispossessed.[6] His stories in the later period often examine states of mood, feeling, and psychology itself, rather than pivotal events or growth, so that his characters become part of a general landscape of melancholy. He does not display any ideological positions in his work, instead presenting reality in a flat, impressionistic style. This sets him apart from other great Russian writers such as Tolstoy and Dostoevsky, who sermonize through their novels. His stories rarely have identifiable plots, and when they do, the plots suddenly end at unexpected places. Many of Chekhov's stories do not have any formal denouement at all, which has become one of the characteristics of the modern short story genre. His main thematic interests reside in exposing hypocrisy and deception in his characters, portraying the impotence of human beings in the world, and emphasizing the lack of communication between people.

Chekhov was one of three most often translated Russian writers in Meiji and Taishō Japan, and in colonial Korea, the other two being Tolstoy and Turgenev. Chekhov was a popular writer throughout Meiji and Taishō Japan: in total, 232 translations of his stories came out in Japanese during this period. Chekhov's popularity in 1920s Korea is partly explained by this.[7] But rather than looking at how specific works of fiction were translated into each language, I focus below on essays and critical works about Chekhov to show how the literary, historical, and intellectual significance of this author and his work was constructed. This is the context for Hyŏn's contact with Chekhov's writings, and can help us understand the significance of his productive appropriation of "Sleepy" in the mid-1920s.

Like many Korean intellectuals, Hyŏn Chin-gŏn received his secondary education in Japan. From 1916 to 1918, between the ages of 16 and 18, he studied at the Seisoku Yobi Gakkō and Seijō Chūgakkō, in Tokyo. Since he began publishing his own stories and translations in 1920, he may already have been interested in literature when he was in Japan, though it is not known when he first read Chekhov. Hyŏn's initial contact with Chekhov's work may have occurred either in Japan or after he returned to Korea.

The early introduction of Chekhov into the Japanese intellectual environment was accompanied by the great popularity of anarcho-communist Pëtr A. Kropotkin's interpretation of Chekhov and his work. Although Chekhov's stories in the late 1880s established him as a major writer, they also stirred considerable controversy among Russian critics. Much of this revolved around the amorality implicit in Chekhov's narratives. Some criticized his work for lacking ideals and demonstrating moral indifference. V. G. Korolenko, Chekhov's contemporary, saw Chekhov's turning point in 1888 as consisting of a shift from youthful optimism to pessimism. D. S. Merezhkovsky considered Chekhov's message to be an indictment of the Russian intelligentsia and its progressive ideology. Lev Shestov condemned Chekhov as an abnormal person and a poet of hopelessness. Kropotkin's reading of Chekhov, however, held out the possibility of redemption in the Russian's works. Kropotkin wrote:

[Chekhov] is by no means a pessimist in the proper sense of the word; if he had come to despair, he would have taken the bankruptcy of the "intellectuals" as a necessary fatality. . . . He firmly believed that a better existence was possible—and would come.[8]

The popularity of this image persisted through Meiji and Taishō Japan. Kropotkin's *Russian Literature* (1905), which contained his essays on Chekhov, was widely read by Japanese intellectuals and was included in the private collections of well-known Japanese writers such as Natsume Sōseki and Akutagawa Ryūnosuke. It was translated into Japanese in 1920 and had been reprinted five times by 1922.[9] Even before the

Japanese translation of the entire volume, however, Kropotkin's essays on Chekhov had been translated individually, by Sōma Gyofū in "Che-hofu ron" (A study of Chekhov), published in 1909,[10] and by Maeda Akira in "Che-hofu shōden" (A short biography of Chekhov), written in 1913.[11] Kropotkin's view of Chekhov as an essentially positive author who allowed for the possibility of redemption was thus the basis for Hyŏn's first contact with Chekhov's work (regardless of whether this took place in the late 1910s in Japan or in the early 1920s in Korea, as mentioned earlier).

Two of the most important introductions to Chekhov in Korea in the early 1920s were Chu Yo-sŏp's "Nosŏa ŭi tae munho Ch'eekhop'ŭ" (The great Russian writer Chekhov), in 1920, and Pak Yŏng-hŭi's "Ch'ehop'ŭ hŭigok e nat'anan nosŏa hwanmyŏlgi ŭi kot'ong" (The agony of the disillusioned period of Russia described in Chekhov's dramas), in 1924.[12] The first of these, by Chu Yo-sŏp, a Korean short story writer, includes an analysis of Chekhov's works as well as a short biography. In opening, Chu points out that "Shakespeare and Tolstoy were introduced to the Korean literary world some time ago. But now I would like to provide the biography of a great Russian short story writer, Anton P. Chekhov, along with his short stories."[13] He outlines the changes in Chekhov's stories in terms of the two major periods: the early humorous style, and the later, more pessimistic one. He also emphasizes Chekhov's originality and keenness in grasping and describing the almost unnoticeable trivial details of everyday life.[14]

In his introduction, Chu Yo-sŏp compares Chekhov to Guy de Maupassant:

> Among all writers in the world Chekhov bears the greatest similarity to Maupassant. Their attitudes toward life are objective and sincere, and their writings are concise and lucid. Both like writing stories with trivial subject matter and try to suggest all of life through them. But when we compare these two writers' stories, they have a completely different sensibility. In other words, Maupassant's stories are *artistic* and *sensuous*, but those of Chekhov are *human-life-engaged* and *psychological*. Chekhov's are something like clear autumn weather but Maupassant's possess something like the energy emanating from the ripening of nature on a spring hill. Maupassant uses thick touches of colors and Chekhov uses only light touches. Chekhov is simple and plain but Maupassant splendid. Maupassant has the glittering light of a bright day but Chekhov is the dim light of twilight

and dawn. Chekhov calls people into meditation while Maupassant makes them sing a drunken song. In the final analysis, Maupassant has a *French style*, but Chekhov's color is *Russian in all respects*.[15] (Emphasis added)

Chu asserts that Maupassant and Chekhov are similar writers but then proceeds to elucidate all the differences between the two. His sensual and impressionistic assessment is fascinating, yet what is most important here is how he expands the differences between their individual styles into national characteristics, indicating that Russian and French literature must already have attained some stable set of associations prior to Chu's invocation of them.

The national characteristics that Chu refers to in fact come from Maeda Akira's essay "Chehofu shōden" (A short biography of Chekhov), written in 1913, which introduced Chekhov to Japan.[16] Chu's essay is essentially a translation of Maeda's, with a few additional sentences at the beginning. Chu not only rendered the content of the Maeda's essay into Korean but also borrowed many specific terms from Maeda, such as "human-life-engaged" (人生的), "psychological" (心理的), "artistic" (芸術的), and "sensuous" (官能的). Maeda's text had for its part relied greatly on Kropotkin's interpretation of Chekhov, as described above. Kropotkin's ideas about Chekhov were first broached in a series of lectures on nineteenth-century Russian literature he delivered at the Lowell Institute in Boston in March 1901, which were collected and published in his *Russian Literature* in London in 1905.[17] Kropotkin wrote:

> "The eighties" were perhaps the gloomiest period that Russia lived through for the last hundred years. . . . It was during those very years that Tchehoff [Chekhov] began to write; and, being a true poet, who feels and responds to the moods of the moment, he became the painter of that breakdown—of that failure of the "intellectuals" which hung as a nightmare above the civilized portion of Russian society. And again, being a great poet, he depicted that all-invading philistine meanness in such features that his picture will live. . . . With all that, Tchehoff . . . firmly believed that a better existence was possible—and would come.[18]

The social and intellectual background to Kropotkin's assessment was the 1880s, generally regarded as one of the darkest and most stagnant periods of the nineteenth century. In spite of this, Kropotkin argued,

Chekhov held strongly to the belief that Russian society could realize a better future. Though Maeda and Chu generally accepted this affirmative perspective, they did not completely share Kropotkin's view of the question of national character and its relation to Chekhov and Maupassant's work, which Kropotkin expressed as follows:

> [Chekhov/Tchehoff's] nearest relative is Guy de Maupassant, but a certain family resemblance between the two writers exists only in a few of their short stories. The manner of Tchehoff, and especially the mood in which all the sketches, the short novels, and the dramas of Tchehoff are written, are entirely his own. And then, there is all the difference between the two writers which exists between contemporary France and Russia at that special period of development through which our country has been passing lately.[19]

Kropotkin's main argument is that despite a certain similarity to Maupassant, Chekhov is unique. Moreover, in his account of the difference between the two writers, Kropotkin stresses the different socioeconomic situations facing France and Russia at specific points in their history, whereas Maeda's (and hence Chu's) rewriting of this difference transforms it into one between enduring national characters, with the distinctions between the two authors' works being taken as symptomatic of it.

The second major essay on Chekhov, published in 1924, was by Pak Yŏng-hŭi, a writer of proletarian literature, who noted:

> Since the nineteenth century, Russian literature has been in a truly close relationship to life, and has shown us a new world of existence and thought within our own human life. The majority of Russian literature is the confession of Russia, and embodies real and important lessons for human life. Russian literature is so close to life that we can say that while French literature is splendid and beautiful, Russian is gloomy, and while French is "thought" (*sasang*), Russian is "life" (*saenghwal*). If the former is the "truth" of this world, the latter is a cry for "the revolution of life" and "the reconstruction of life." Turgenev talked about it; Chekhov cried for it; Dostoevsky declared it; and Tolstoy yearned for it.[20]

Although this resonates with Kropotkin, Maeda, and Chu, we can see that the adjective "human-life-engaged" (*jinsei-teki* in Japanese; *insaeng-jŏk* in Korean), which Maeda and Chu used, becomes tinged with a proletarian literary perspective in Pak's term "the revolution of life" (*saengmyŏng ŭi hyŏngmyŏng*). "The revolution of life" should be thought of as something like "betterment of the future," for it does not denote actual revolution in the context of his article. Rather, Pak claims "a cry for 'the revolution of life'" as the defining characteristic of Russian literature as a whole, and then categorizes four of the best-known Russian writers according to how they relate to it. While the differences between individual writers are thus weakened, their commonalities are emphasized. For Pak, Chekhov is not gloomy or pessimistic but stands for the "revolution" and "reconstruction" of future existence, in tandem with other nineteenth-century Russian writers. Here a field of socially engaged literature is defined, and linked irrevocably to Russia. Though we may say that Kropotkin's understanding of Chekhov was more optimistic than some, we can also see that Pak has taken this optimism farther than Kropotkin ever did.

To sum up, the texts and discourses about Chekhov available in Japan were one determining factor in the reception of his works in Korea. This was characterized by a preference for Kropotkin's reading of Chekhov, in which Chekhov's dark and deflationary technique was read as a critique that still held out the possibility of redemption. In response to their own intellectual environment, Korean writers, especially Pak Yŏng-hǔi, also extended the possibility of redemption in Chekhov to the revolutionary aspiration that came into dialogue with the early proletarian literature movement. To this we should add the fact that Chekhov's reputation in Korea remained positive through the 1920s, while in Japan the negative appraisal of Lev Shestov came to have more influence.[21] Unremittingly critical of Chekhov, Shestov described him as a "poet of hopelessness": "Stubbornly, sadly, monotonously, during all the years of his literary activity, nearly a quarter of a century long, Tchekhov was doing one thing alone: by one means or another he was killing human hopes."[22] Whereas this view of Chekhov gained ground in Japan, it never established a foothold in Korea.[23] In speculating why this was the case, it can be said that, in general, few negative views of Western literature had been imported into Korea at this point. Korea had been colonized by Japan rather than by any of the Western powers, so it is understandable that the empowerment associated with Western literature was adopted in a primarily affirmative mode.

The overall image of Chekhov as a literary figure was fairly similar in Japan and Korea up to the mid-1920s, and this formed the intellectual background to Hyŏn's productive appropriation of Chekhov's "Sleepy." The following close examination of "Fire," Hyŏn's adaptation of "Sleepy," demonstrates one Korean writer's creative engagement with a foreign text and his own lived reality. The next two sections examine the unprecedented female character in "Fire" and then analyze the role of translation as the creative impetus that made its full elaboration possible.

The Place of Suni in the History of Modern Korean Literature

Hyŏn Chin-gŏn's "Fire" was published in *Kaebyŏk* (The creation) in January 1925. The story depicts the life of a fifteen-year-old girl, Suni, who has been married for a month when the story opens. During the day she suffers from overwork demanded by her mother-in-law, and at night sexual intercourse with her husband brings her only fear and pain. One night she decides to rid herself of the cause of this misery, and sets fire to the house while her husband and mother-in-law are asleep. Her logic is that if there were no house, she would not be forced to stay with her husband at night, and the final act brings her great happiness.

Suni's uniqueness among Hyŏn's female characters has been commented on by many present-day scholars. Kwŏn Yŏng-min considers Suni distinctive because she is an active female character, quite different from the passive heroines in Hyŏn's earlier stories.[24] Ku In-hwan and Sŏ Hyŏn-ju describe Suni's action as "resistance" against social customs and oppressive male behavior, and distinguish her from the passive and uncomplaining wives in Hyŏn's other stories.[25] Yun Pyŏng-ro takes the discussion a step farther, claiming that Suni demonstrates a strong subjectivity.[26] As Ch'oe Wŏn-sik points out, however, Suni has her limits, in that she does not recognize the fundamental causes of her difficult situation and her action does not solve any social problems.[27] What all agree on is that Suni is a unique female character in Hyŏn's literary works.

Suni is also an unprecedented female character for Korean literature as a whole in 1925. Taking stock of modern Korean literature from its generally recognized beginning with the publication of Yi Kwang-su's *Mujŏng* (The heartless), in 1917, up to Hyŏn's "Fire" in 1925, there is not a single female character who solves her problems by eliminating the cause of her misery or avenging herself upon it. Instead, self-destruction is the solution that female characters choose in male writers' stories from this period. In Yi Kwang-su's *Mujŏng* (1917) and *Chaesaeng* (Resurrection, 1924), and in Na To-hyang's *Hwanhŭi* (Joy, 1923), the female characters kill themselves (or attempt to) after being raped or trapped in an unhappy marriage. Most female characters in Kim Tong-in's stories of the 1920s also destroy themselves or are killed by male characters.[28]

While male writers' works offered fairly simple and limited solutions for female characters, female writers' works showed more diversity and described a more complicated psychology in their female characters. By 1925, there were three practicing Korean female writers: Kim Myŏng-sun, Na Hye-sŏk, and Kim Wŏn-ju. Most of their stories deal with forced marriage, the failure of love, and the miseries of married life, which, judging from how frequently they are described, must have been among the most pressing problems women faced at the time. The heroines in Kim Wŏn-ju's "Ŏnŭ sonyŏ ŭi chugŭm" (A girl's death, 1920) and Kim Myŏng-sun's "Ŭsim ŭi sonyŏ" (A suspicious girl, 1917) commit suicide because of unwanted but inescapable marriages. One character in Kim Myŏng-sun's "Torada pol ttae" (Looking back, 1924) resigns herself to a forced marriage. Some female characters choose to run away from home, as in Na Hye-sŏk's "Kyŏnghŭi" (Kyŏnghŭi, 1918) and Kim Myŏng-sun's "Ch'ŏnyŏ ŭi kanŭn kil" (The road a girl takes, 1920). Kim Wŏn-ju's "Hyewŏn" (Hyewŏn, 1921) ends with the protagonist's decision to start an independent life after being abandoned by her lover. Because these runaway stories end at the point where the protagonist leaves home, it is difficult to say what sort of life would have been imaginable for them after such an exit. But the decision itself is one form of imagining and representing resistance to the social customs that shackled women. But Hyŏn's protagonist, Suni, does not commit suicide or run away from the situation. She is unique in that she confronts the cause of her misery and destroys it. How and in what context did this unique female character come about? The next two sections analyze Hyŏn's appropriation of Chekhov's short story and his engagement with his own local environment.

Hyŏn's "Fire" and Chekhov's "Sleepy"

Hyŏn Chin-gŏn is a writer who left virtually no account of how his literary works were connected to other literature. In an interview in 1939,[29] he even refused to answer a direct question about which writers had influenced him, though when asked what advice he had for young Korean writers, he suggested that they "learn from Dumas and Hugo rather than trying to imitate Maupassant and Chekhov." He then added, "It's what I wish I had done, too."[30] His prioritizing of Dumas and Hugo may reflect the fact that Hyŏn had switched genres, from the short story to the historical novel, in the 1930s. The interview shows that modeling one's writing on a foreign author was considered an important step for young writers, and Hyŏn also belatedly admits the fact that he had been a disciple of Maupassant and Chekhov himself.

His reticence notwithstanding, Hyŏn's contemporaries recognized the resemblance between Hyŏn's and Chekhov's short stories. In March 1925, *Chosŏn mundan* (The Korean literary world), one of the main literary journals, started a writers' roundtable to discuss newly published literary works. Although "Fire" had appeared in January 1925, the panel discussed a story Hyŏn had published more recently, in February, "B sagam kwa lŏbŭletŏ" (Dormitory Supervisor Ms. B's love letters). Na To-hyang opened the discussion, however, with a comment on "Fire":

> If you take a look at Pinghŏ [Hyŏn]'s works, they look like Chekhov's short stories. For example, his "Fire," which was published in January, resembles one of Chekhov's stories where a young girl does hard work all day and kills a baby.[31]

Although Na did not specify the title of Chekhov's story, his comment provides enough clues. The Chekhov story is "Spat' khochetsia" (Sleepy), written in 1888.

This story was first translated into Japanese in 1905 by Osanai Kaoru, under the title "Inemuri" (Dozing; *Shichinin*, May 1905). It was retranslated with the titles "Suima" (Drowsiness; trans. Nishimura Shozan, *Taiyō*, September 1905), "Nemui" (Sleepy; trans. Kureno Chōon, *Kokoro no hana*, May 1912), and "Nebō" (Oversleeping; trans. Maeda Akira, in *Tanpen jisshu che-hofu shū*, Hakubunkan, 1913). Hirotsu Kazuo translated it as "Nemutai atama" (Sleepyhead; *Kiseki*, January 1913) and included it in his anthology of Chekhov's stories, *Seppun hoka hachihen* ("The Kiss" and eight other stories), in 1916. Kim Pyŏng-ch'ŏl writes that a Korean translation of "Sleepy" was published in 1924 under the title "Chollin mŏri" (Sleepyhead; trans. Kim Sŏk-song, *Sinyŏsŏng* 2:2, February 1924), but this text has not been found.[32] Since the literal translation of the Korean title is "Sleepyhead," it is possible that the Korean title "Chollin mŏri" was transliterated from the Japanese title of Hirotsu's translation. But whether or not a 1924 Korean translation was available, Hyŏn must have read Chekhov's stories in Japanese before any such translation came out—probably in Hirotsu's 1916 anthology, which includes "Sleepyhead" and "The Kiss," both of which Hyŏn reworked.

Varka, Chekhov's heroine in "Sleepy," is a thirteen-year-old nurse-maid who has to do household chores and run errands from morning until night, and then stay awake to watch over the family's baby. She suffers from constant lack of sleep, and the story culminates in her murder of the baby. Even this short summary demonstrates the overall affinity between the two stories.

In addition to the basic plotlines, the stories possess similar characters, settings, and time structures. The two female characters always feel tired and oppressed, and their nights are even more dreadful than their days. For Chekhov's Varka, daytime is bearable because everybody moves around and she is active doing things, so she feels less sleepy. But at night everyone is asleep except for Varka and the crying baby. For Hyŏn's Suni in "Fire," her husband's sexual approaches at night are the most terrifying and unbearable aspect of her existence, and this prevents her from sleeping. The beginnings of the two stories provide the reader with basic information about the protagonist and setting of each story. "Sleepy" starts as follows:

Night-time.
   Varka the nursemaid, a girl of about thirteen, rocks the cradle with the baby in [it] and croons very faintly:
   Bayu-bayushki-bayu
   I'll sing a song for you. . . .
   The baby is crying. It grew hoarse and wore itself out crying ages ago, but still it goes on screaming and goodness knows when it will stop. And Varka wants to sleep. Her eyes keep closing, her head droops, and her neck

aches. She can scarcely move her lips or eyelids, her face feels all parched and wooden, and her head seems to have become no bigger than a pin's.

"*Bayu-bayushki-bayu*," she croons, "I'll cook some groats for you. . . ."[33] (Chekhov, "Sleepy": English, 191; Russian, 12)

The opening of "Fire" reads:

The girl, Suni, only fifteen years old, had been married about a month ago, and felt that it was becoming hard for her to breathe even while asleep. She felt like a big rock was pressing her. If it were a rock, it would be cool at least, but what was pressing on her weak chest was as damp, wet, and muggy as the rainy season, and extremely heavy. He panted like a dog in the hottest period of summer. And then her body hurt, burned, and winced as if her back and hips had been split, broken apart, torn off and smashed into bits . . . .

"I might die; I might die if it continues! I have to wake up, wake up," Suni said this to herself but she couldn't open her eyes, stuck closed as if they had been glued. She couldn't drive the muddy sleep away.[34] (Hyŏn, "Fire," 145)

Both stories begin with a description of a young girl suffering at night, and unfold as night becomes day and the narrators describe the work of their busy daylight hours. Then night comes again. They commit their crimes on the second night, and with that both stories end.

The structural similarities are marked, but the most astonishing similarity appears at the end of the stories. First, Chekhov's:

And the baby screams and wears itself out screaming. Varka sees once more the muddy highway, the people with knapsacks, Pelageya, her father Yefim. She understands everything, she recognizes everyone, but through her half-sleep there is one thing that she simply cannot grasp: the nature of the force that binds her hand and foot, that oppresses her and makes life a misery. She looks all round the room, searching for this force in order to rid herself of it; but cannot find it. Worn out, she makes one last, supreme effort to concentrate her attention, looks up at the winking green patch, and, as she listens to the sound of the crying, finds it, this enemy that is making life a misery.

It is the baby.

She laughs in astonishment: how could she have failed to notice such a simple little thing before! The green patch, the shadows, and the cricket, also seem to be laughing in astonishment.

The delusion takes possession of Varka. She gets up from her stool, and walks up and down the room. There is a broad smile on her face and her eyes are unblinking. The thought that in a moment she will be rid of the baby that binds her hand and foot, tickles her with delight. . . . To kill the baby, then sleep, sleep, sleep. . . .

Laughing, winking at the green patch and wagging her finger at it, Varka creeps up to the cradle and bends over the baby. Having smothered it, she lies down quickly on the floor, laughs with joy that now she can sleep, and a minute later is sleeping the sleep of the dead. (Chekhov, "Sleepy": English, 195–96; Russian, 17)

Then Hyŏn's "Fire":

She became scared again upon seeing her husband. The rock which suffocated her by pressing her chest, the iron bar which broke her into bits. . . . She stopped weeping and started beating her brains to think about how to avoid the exhausting night. But no, it's not the night's fault. It's all the fault of this "enemy room." If the "enemy room" were gone, he might go away without doing anything to me but wiping my tears. If the "enemy room" were not here, there would be no place for him to give me such pain. The enemy room! Is there any possible way to be rid of it? She had not succeeded in escaping the room so far, so she began to think about removing it instead of escaping it.

The rice boiled and bubbled over. When she stood up to open the lid of the pot, a match on the kitchen stove caught her eyes. A wild idea flitted through her mind. She grabbed the match. The hand holding it trembled. She hid it inside her jacket quickly. "Why have I never discovered this until now?" she smiled.

On that night a fire suddenly started from the eaves of a room. With the help of the wind, the fire covered the whole roof in an instant and rose up. Suni, who was standing beside the wall of the neighbor's house, was so excited and happy that she leapt around with a bright smile on her face, something which had not visited her of late. (Hyŏn, "Fire," 151–52)

The endings portray a similar progress in the protagonists' thoughts and actions. Varka realizes that the thing which makes her life miserable is "the baby," while Suni discovers it is the "enemy room." Upon realizing this, "a delusion takes possession of Varka" and "a wild idea flit[s] through" Suni's mind. Finally, Varka smothers the baby and Suni sets fire to the room. Most significant, however, is the resemblance between the protagonists' feelings when they commit their crimes. Varka has "a broad smile on her face" before she kills the baby, and the very idea of killing "tickles her with delight." She laughs with joy after smothering the infant. In "Fire," Suni jumps around "with a bright smile on her face" after setting fire to the house. These finales depict the girls as having simple motivations for their crimes and as feeling no guilt but only release and jubilation. At the same time, the root cause of their oppressive situations involves complex issues of class, gender, age, labor, and sex. The endings of the stories thus perplex the reader and also maximize his or her awareness of the characters' innocence in the face of these forces.

From this examination of the two stories, it is clear that Hyŏn adopted Chekhov's Varka as a model when he brought such an unprecedented female character as Suni to life in a Korean short story. I argue that translation/appropriation functioned as an enabler for Hyŏn, both as a force and as an opening through which to create a new type of female character. Yet Hyŏn's local historical situation was also an indispensable factor in this moment of appropriation. Though not yet a part of Korean literature, discussions of miserable marriages, and even of arson, were part of journalistic writing in Korea at the time of Hyŏn's "Fire." Thus contact with a foreign text enabled this writer to find a form for a character that would speak to his own present social situation.

The Discourse of Early Marriage and Female Crime

In one of his later essays, Hyŏn Chin-gŏn lists of some of his short stories, which had coalesced around "hints" that had struck him from the outside world:

> I accidentally got some hints from somewhere for some of my stories—such as "Chosŏn ŭi ŏlgul," "Tarakcha," "Chisae nŭn an'gae," "P'iano," and "Pul" [Fire]—and created the story by developing the basic subject matter. But

the hints were extremely small and I altered them with literary elements so that in the end they are the products of imagination.[35]

The gist of Hyŏn's statement is that even though he found his subject matter in episodes in real life, there was no significant connection between real people and the specific details of his short stories. But what matters here is the "extremely small" hints for "Fire" that Hyŏn alludes to.

What might the hints have been that prompted Hyŏn's appropriation of Chekhov's "Sleepy" and eventually led to the story he tells in "Fire"? Considering the content of "Fire," the hints were probably discussions surrounding early marriage or young women crimes. At the time Hyŏn wrote "Fire," there were in fact contemporary discussions about the phenomenon of young women's crime, but let us first look at the history of and wider discourse on the custom of early marriage.[36]

In his study of the origin of early marriage in Korea, Kim Tu-hŏn enumerates four main causes for the prevalence of early marriage in the Koryŏ (918–1392) and Chosŏn (1392–1910) dynasties. First, during the Koryŏ dynasty Korean families married off their young daughters to avoid the Mongolian exaction of tribute in the form of young women. Second, during the Chosŏn dynasty, when a member of the royal family decided to marry and a search began for a spouse, everyone in the country, whether aristocrat or commoner, was forbidden to wed for the duration of the search. If such a search occurred when a young man or woman was at the proper age for marriage, it could jeopardize their chance of ever marrying, so people hastened their children's marriages whenever they could. Third, people thought early marriage would be more likely to ensure descendants for the family. Fourth, because Chosŏn people were not allowed to get married during periods of mourning and so forth, families sometimes made their children get married when they had the chance, even at young ages. Through these practices, early marriage developed as a custom in Korean society.[37]

Discussions of early marriage began in earnest during the Korean Enlightenment period (roughly the 1890s and 1900s). Some Korean intellectuals considered it the worst of Korean marriage customs and argued for its abolition.[38] The reasons for early marriage now differed from those in earlier periods: for example, with the deterioration of the economy, early marriage could be used to disguise the sale of a daughter to the groom's family.[39] In addition to discussions in the newspapers about abolishing early marriage, regulations on the minimum marriage age were reformed. A government of the Enlightenment group formed in 1894 and carried out the Kabo Reforms, which fixed the minimum age at twenty for men and sixteen for women. But this was not observed, and King Sunjong promulgated a new regulation in 1907, which set the minimum age at seventeen for men and fifteen for women.[40] Early marriage remained a popular practice, and discourses criticizing the custom appeared continuously in the newspapers.[41]

The criticisms enumerated the practice's many disadvantages. Often focusing on social hygiene problems, education of children, and new family ethics, the critics argued that early marriage led to weak families and that these would sow the seeds of a weaker nation. They also argued that when people married early, they could not pay attention to their own physical and mental education and so would not know how to raise their children. Children of physically immature parents would be weak, and this would lead to a population decline. If men married early, it would be difficult for them to tend to important affairs. Early marriage caused marital problems because people could not choose the right person for themselves, and the subsequent discord would affect society. Almost all the criticisms culminated in the reasoning that early marriage hindered the development of the nation and its people.[42]

As Chŏn Mi-gyŏng argues, Korean intellectuals' arguments for the abolition of early marriage at this time related to their project of introducing modern family ethics. The new ethics emphasized the bride and groom rather than the parents, and the wife-husband relationship was given at least as much importance as the parent-child relationship. There was also a new ethics for bringing up children, which claimed that children were not the parents' sole possession but were also of interest to the society at large. This argument became tied to a discourse that emphasized parents' duty vis-à-vis their children's education. Children began to be endowed with a "childhood," which included the right to be taken care of by their parents until they became adults.[43] Early marriage was also discussed in relation to the problems facing young widows, increases in divorce, health problems caused by early sexual relations, and, most important for this story, crimes triggered by early marriage.[44]

What, then, was the status of early marriage in the 1920s, when "Fire" was written? What were the solutions young women could choose when confronted by it? In 1915, the governor-general prohibited marriage registration for a man under seventeen and a woman under fifteen.[45] This age limit was renewed in 1921.[46] In real life, however, during the period from 1912 to 1915, 15 to 20 percent of women still got married before turning fifteen. By the 1920s, when Hyŏn wrote "Fire," this rate had dropped below 7 percent.[47] When we consider the possibility of common law and unregistered marriage, the proportion of early marriages may well have been higher than the statistics show. Girls who faced an early marriage had few choices. They could try to refuse to wed, but if this was not accepted, the only thing they could do was run away from their parents' house. Once a girl was already married, she could run away from her in-laws' house, commit suicide, get divorced if that was possible, kill her husband, or set fire to her in-laws' house.

Fictional and Journalistic Narratives, and Their Relation to Translation

Now let us investigate some of the journalistic discourse on actual cases of arson with circumstances similar to those in "Fire." Here I attempt to find the patterns of such crimes and the development of newspaper reports about them, and also speculate on the full cycle of intertextuality between the story "Fire" and journalistic writing.

The newspaper articles on young wives' arson in the 1920s and 1930s, discussed below, come from the databases of the *Tong'a, Chosŏn, Chung'ang, Chosŏn chung'ang, Chung'oe,* and *Sidae* daily newspapers. I isolated the articles dealing with young wives' arson after doing a keyword search for "arson." Among the cases of young wives' arson, I examined only the cases where women set fire to their in-laws' house due to an unhappy married life. This excludes cases where a girl or young woman committed arson out of jealousy or in order to elope with a lover. If the same incident was featured in more than one article, I prioritized the *Tong'a ilbo* (Tong'a Daily), which reported more cases than other newspapers. The increase in the number of newspaper reports on arson over time does not necessarily mean that the number of cases actually increased. But reports on a number of arson cases in *Tong'a Daily* show that arson eventually became a sort of stock subject for newspapers at the time, so the increase in the number of newspaper reports does probably correlate to some increase in the actual number of incidents.

The 1920s can be divided into the period before Hyŏn's "Fire" was published, in January 1925, and after. During the first half of the 1920s (1920–24), there were only two newspaper reports of arson corresponding to Suni's case. The first is from December 1921. According to the reporter, sixteen-year-old Sŏ Kan-nan had been married a few years earlier to a man ten years older than she.[48] She set fire to her husband's house thinking that if she burned it down, her husband would send her back to her parents. At the end of the article, the reporter adds briefly that the neighbors blamed Sŏ's parents for forcing her to marry. It is quite possible that the reporter interjected his own opinion into the article, attributing it to the "neighbors." But unlike reporters in the latter half of the 1920s, this reporter does not specifically cite *chohon* (early marriage) as the reason for the crime, nor does he express sympathy toward the arsonist straightforwardly. The second short article mentions an arson incident in October 1922, and includes no judgment on the event. A sixteen-year-old girl, Yun Sun-i, set fire to her husband's house because she had trouble with her husband.[49] It is interesting that the young girl's name in this report is the same as that of Hyŏn's female character Suni. The "hints" that Hyŏn mentioned in his essay may have come from this type of report.

In the latter half of the 1920s, the number of such arson cases increased rapidly, with seven being reported between 1925 and 1929.[50] According to the newspaper reports, the main causes of the incidents were a heavy workload, trouble with the husband, and longing for home. Two of the seven reports conclude that the crimes were the result of early marriage, and three of the remaining five exhibit some sympathy toward the criminal.[51] Five out of seven articles, therefore, express sympathy toward the young female arsonists rather than criticizing them. The reporters considered the arsonists not as criminals but as victims of social custom. In one instance, in 1928, seventeen-year-old An Ok-jin, who had been married at the age of fourteen, set fire to her husband's house. The reporter goes on to explain the reason for the crime:

> [The arsonist] was scared of her husband and desperately wanted to go back to her parents. . . . She set the fire *with the childlike idea (ŏrin saenggak ŭro)*

that she might be able to go back to her parents if her husband did not have the house. She repeated the act four times so the property loss was considerable. The fundamental cause of this crime is early marriage.[52] (Emphasis added)

This story is remarkably similar to "Fire," especially in terms of the young woman's unhappy situation and motive. This newspaper article carries the phrase "Crimes Caused by Early Marriage" as a part of its title, and the reporter implies that the young wife burned down the house only because she was too young to come up with a better solution. In so doing, the reporter vindicates her, morally speaking.

Even in the three articles that do not assert that the arson was caused by early marriage, the content and style of reporting convey the reporter's sympathy for the criminal. For instance, a reporter in 1928 describes the life of a young female arsonist. She is eighteen years old; when she was ten, her father sold her to a man twenty-five years her senior and she married him a few years later. She was married to him for three years before setting the fire when she was eighteen, and often stayed at her parents' house because she was scared of her husband. Upon the death of her mother a year before the arson, she did not want to go back to her frightening husband and so went to her uncle's house. But every time she fled to her uncle's, her husband would come and bring her back. She set fire to his house thinking that she could go back to her uncle's if her husband's house should disappear.[53] The detailed life story of this young female arsonist invites the reader to sympathize with her and makes her crime understandable. The emphasis on her miserable life and on her innocent motivation creates a narrative in which a criminal in the eyes of the law turns into a victim according to other standards of justice.

Such stories continued to increase in the early 1930s, rising to 13 reports between 1930 and 1935.[54] Beginning in the latter half of the 1920s, these reports often include phrases such as "crimes caused by early marriage" (*chohon i naŭn pŏmjoe*). Placing blame on the institution of early marriage thus became somewhat standard. The phrase appears in the titles for eleven of the thirteen newspaper reports on young wives' arson in the 1930s.[55] This reversal of guilt and innocence in the newspaper accounts is not unrelated to Hyŏn's rendition of Suni in "Fire." Though the relation might not be one of simple cause and effect, the figure of the innocent female arsonist had crystallized in both fiction and nonfiction in the mid- to late-1920s.

What does this increase of sympathy in newspaper reporting imply? How can we interpret it? Interestingly, there are a number of reports in which fictional characters are used to make sense of events in real life. The *Chung'oe ilbo* (Chung'oe Daily), for instance, carried a report of arson in January 1930, under the title " 'Kwang'yŏm sonata" (A sonata of mad flame).[56] This may have intrigued readers because it was the exact title of a recent work of short fiction. The newspaper article began, "The protagonist of Kim Tong-in's short story 'A Sonata of Mad Flame' has appeared in real life," and continued to tell the story of a twenty-four-year-old man, Kim Kwi-nam, who set fire to houses just to watch them burn. The short story that the reporter refers to features a struggling musician who sets fires and watches them to find inspiration for his music. Another use of fiction appears in a *Tong'a Daily* article in 1938.[57] A twenty-year-old woman in Yŏngbyŏn had been married a year earlier to a man fifteen years her senior. Unable to endure married life, she ran away, finally securing a divorce by repaying him 40 *won* of dowry. The reporter calls her "a contemporary Nora," referring to the central character in Henrik Ibsen's *A Doll's House*.

These stories suggest that the supposed barrier between modern fiction and journalistic writing is porous, and that the two can be interpenetrable. This porousness and interpenetrability would have been even more pronounced in the mid-1920s because most fiction writers (including well-known ones such as Yi Kwang-su, Kim Ŏk, Pak Yŏng-hŭi, Chu Yo-han, and Yŏm Sang-sŏp) worked as journalists to support themselves. The publication of Korean newspapers and magazines increased in the 1920s, when the Japanese colonial government changed its policy from *budan seiji* (military policy) to *bunka seiji* (cultural policy) after the 1919 nationwide mass protests known as the March First Movement. Private companies published newspapers, general magazines, and journals, while literary coteries put out their own magazines. Though censorship and publication restrictions continued, the post-1919 era marked a rapid increase in the number of Korean publications.

Thanks to this increase in newspapers and magazines where literary works could be printed, and to the growing number of literary coteries, professional writers started to form and to be recognized as a social group that could be distinguished from journalists per se.[58] Nevertheless, most fiction writers continued to work as journalists, for several reasons. First, they could not make ends meet solely by writing poems and novels. Second, coterie magazines tended to be unstable, ceasing publication after only a few issues due to financial problems, so writers needed to have other outlets for their work as well. Third, if a member from a certain literary coterie became a newspaper journalist, other members had a better chance of getting their work published in that newspaper, too.

There were also several reasons for newspaper owners to want to hire fiction writers as journalists. Because there had been only a single government-general organ since the Japanese annexation of Korea in 1910—namely, the *Maeil sinbo*—there was an undersupply of trained journalists in the early 1920s, so it was inevitable that private newspaper companies would hire writers of fiction. Another benefit was that such writers could fill the literary page at no extra cost.[59] Writers' double role thus expanded, with increased opportunities for publishing in both fiction and nonfiction. Hyŏn himself worked for the *Sidae Daily* from 1920 to 1923, and then for the *Chosŏn* and *Tong'a Daily* until 1936.[60] Korean intellectuals were almost always both fiction writers and journalists, and so had a deep familiarity with both the latest news and the latest literary works being created around them. It is therefore understandable that they might readily associate fictional events and events in real life, and sometimes blend the two sites of writing, to put words to people and events, and bring meaning to the world around them.

In addition to phrases like "crimes caused by early marriage" and reporters' general sympathy toward female arsonists, references to their "childlike" thoughts and feelings appear repeatedly in the newspaper reports after 1925, as a way to emphasize youth and innocence as factors in the crime. And as already seen, the first line of Hyŏn's story emphasizes that the female character is young: "The girl, Suni, *only* fifteen years old, had been married about a month ago and felt that it was becoming hard for her to breathe even while asleep" (emphasis added). Using the Western method for counting age, Suni would be only thirteen or fourteen—very close in age to Chekhov's thirteen-year-old Varka. Moreover, one of the differences between Chekhov's story and Hyŏn's is that Hyŏn's narrator sympathizes with his female character, whereas Chekhov's narrator keeps an emotional distance.

The author of the newspaper report about An Ok-jin, the young woman who committed arson in 1928, wrote that she set the fire with the "childlike idea" (*ŏrin saenggak ŭro*) that she might then be able to return to her parents' home.[61] Three other reports use similar language: Li Yŏ-du was married when she was fifteen but was always scared of her husband "because of her childlike heart" (*ŏrin maŭm e*);[62] Li Sun-ak set a fire "with a childlike heart" (*ŏrin maŭm e*), hoping that her husband might send her away;[63] and Pak Kŭm-sun set a fire "with a childlike heart" (*ŏrin mam [maŭm] e*), thinking she might be sent back to her parents.[64] The emphasis on each girl's naiveté, which serves as an explanation for and an exemption from what she has done, resonates so deeply with the description of the female character in Hyŏn's "Fire" that it seems quite possible that the reporters were conscious of Hyŏn's story and adopted its narrative and account of individual action. Interestingly, the reports that use the phrase "with a childlike heart" are all from the *Tong'a Daily*, where Hyŏn worked in the local news section from October 1927. It is even possible that he himself wrote or edited some of them.

Although it is unlikely that Hyŏn's story alone caused the development of sympathetic discourse surrounding female arson, it was on the leading edge of a general shift, partly symptomatic but also partially creating the possibility of this trope of the innocent female criminal. As we have seen in newspaper reports' references to "A Sonata of Mad Flame" and *A Doll's House*, journalists' writings sometimes interacted with existing fictional narrative and its characters when describing factual incidents. Hyŏn's description of Suni's innocence in her crime, as well as his account of her agony, may have had an effect on newspaper writing, creating *a form for a new way of perceiving lived reality*—in this case a mode of sympathy toward these young female criminals, whose numbers increased in the late 1920s and early 1930s, after Hyŏn's "Fire" was published.

Scholars have tended to assume that fiction had already acquired autonomous status as a discrete genre in 1920s Korea. Yi Kwang-su's theory of literature in 1916 and his writing of what is recognized as the first modern Korean novel in 1917 were watersheds in the modernizing project of Korean literature. Coterie literary journals, especially *Ch'angjo* (Creation), founded by Kim Tong-in in 1919, which promoted the concept of the pure novel and art for art's sake, demonstrated the autonomy of literature through their literary practice and publication. Korean literary histories explain that a whole variety of hybrid forms of writing—ranging from fragmented narrative and essay-like fiction to nonfiction writing with fictional elements—burgeoned in the 1890s and 1900s and continued to be produced in the 1910s, culminating in (or developing into) the form of the *sin-sosŏl* (new novel). The story of this development however, is also a story of the writing form of *sosŏl* (fictional narrative) settling down into a pure and autonomous form.[65] The notion that *sosŏl* is fiction whereas newspaper reports are nonfiction has become naturalized through this history. It is taken for granted that the 1920s witnessed the clear division of *sosŏl* from various kinds of nonfiction writing (such as newspaper articles and reports). But as we have seen, the boundary between *sosŏl* and newspaper reports was still permeable, and the two modes and fields of writing interpenetrated each other. The question of which is more truthful, fiction or journalism, was not settled, with the usual assumption that journalism trumps fiction perhaps even being reversed to some extent.[66]

What is visible and undeniable in Hyŏn's engagement with Chekhov's story is the fact that he actively employed its structure and characterization. As Hyŏn himself emphasizes, to get a hint from reality is one thing and to create a literary structure for it is another. Quite possibly, translating Chekhov's story provided Hyŏn with a new way of perceiving his own lived reality, and thus affected his way of interpreting, constructing, and shaping it. Translation as a "productive appropriation" creates new perceptions of the world and can thus become a way for the translator to shape his own reality into a specific new form.

This chapter has touched on two different types of translation in 1920s Korea: (1) translation between languages and cultures on the one hand, and (2) the translation between mediums or genres on the other. Whereas translation between two languages questions the division between imitation and originality, translation between two mediums—in this case, newspaper reports and works of fiction—questions the boundaries we use to define "truth" and "fiction." Which is more original, translation/adaptation or creation? Which are more truthful, works of fiction or newspaper reports in 1920s Korea? Translation as a practice of creative engagement and productive appropriation blurs the boundaries that culture and genre insist are clear.

A Traveling Character: Child Labor, Gender, Translation, and World Literature

In the early twentieth century, when copyright laws were looser than they are today, the fact that a literary text grew out of an appropriation or creative rewriting of a previously existing text in another language was seldom grounds for questioning its authenticity. Chekhov's heroine, a nursemaid who suffers from constant lack of sleep and finally murders the master's baby, was reborn not only in Korean in Hyŏn Chin-gŏn's story "Fire" but also in stories by the Japanese writer Masamune Hakuchō and New Zealander Katherine Mansfield in the early twentieth century.[67] The rewritten texts all maximize the visibility of the social problem of child labor, which is at the heart of Chekhov's story, but they also give us the chance to consider the importance of a relatively unstressed theme in the original story: gender. In the Japanese, English, and Korean rewritings, the main character transforms into a boy working in a billiard room, a nursemaid whose gender is made a central problem of the story, and a sexually abused young bride, respectively. In dialogue with the Chekhov story, each of the three writers created a figure who responded to his or her own society's social issues surrounding child labor and gender, making it possible for the Chekhov character to be enriched by multifaceted afterlives.

"Sleepy" was first translated into Japanese in 1905. In 1908 Masamune Hakuchō, a Japanese critic and writer, published "Tamatsukiya," or "A Billiard Room," his reworking of the story. Hakuchō's three-page story gives little detailed description of the situation and does not have the dramatic ending of Chekov's. Whereas Chekhov's story narrates the events of one day in the life of the nursemaid Varka, beginning the night before the murder and going through the day to the next night, Hakuchō's story spans only a few hours around midnight.

The story depicts three young men playing billiards and a teenaged boy counting their scores. This nameless child is called "boy" (*bo-i* in *katakana*). The boy feels extremely sleepy and hungry, but the three men decide to stay up all night because tomorrow is Sunday. They keep playing, and the boy keeps counting while dozing off. Their yelling often wakes him. The story winds up when one of the men gets tired and decides to end the game. The story ends with the narrator's commenting on the repetition the boy faces 10 or 100 years from now, still counting these scores. It is anticlimactic, without any significant change at the end of story. This anticlimactic ending, however, effectively draws the reader's attention to the repetition itself of the same never-ending dreadful day that the child will have to live in the future. The boy's miserable state is emphasized through a contrast with a brief dream he has about a happy moment he spent with his brother in his hometown, which is similar to the episodes in Chekhov story in which Varka sees her family in short dreams while rocking her master's crying baby through the night.

Hakuchō's story was published before the first factory laws regulating child labor in 1911.[68] He wrote it while he was working within the literary movement of naturalism, so it could be read as an effort to deliver a plausible (rather than an overtly fictional) character in order to expose a social problem. Hakuchō excises all of the most dramatic and shocking events in Chekov's story (the master's abuse of the nursemaid, her father's death, and finally the murder of the baby) and minimizes complex imagery (the lengthy descriptions of mixed images and moving light and shadow that represent the girl's consciousness in between sleep and waking). In so doing, he succeeds in foregrounding the issue of child labor itself and its hopeless continuation.

In 1910, two years after Hakuchō published his story "A Billiard Room," Katherine Mansfield, a New Zealand short story writer, published a story entitled "The Child-Who-Was-Tired" in England. Chekhov's "Sleepy" was translated into English in 1903, and we know that Mansfield admired Chekhov throughout her life, so it is likely that she had read it. Mansfield's story shares many features with Chekhov's: the protagonist is a nursemaid, the master and master's wife abuse her, she takes care of their baby at night and does chores during the daytime, and she kills the baby at the end of the story.

But there are also differences, the most salient of which is that the narrator in Mansfield's story is much closer to the protagonist than is the case in Chekhov's, and delivers free indirect speech that is assumed to belong to both the nursemaid and the narrator. Along with the narrator's subtle judgmental observations of the situation, the nursemaid's monologues, which objectively diagnose her sleepiness and inability to make the baby quiet, give voice to her self-reflection and manifest her subjectivity, unlike the case with Chekhov's nursemaid, whose voice the reader almost never hears.

The most significant difference, however, is that Mansfield's story centers on the issue of gender along with child labor. In Chekhov, the nursemaid happens to be a girl, but in Mansfield, the nursemaid's gender becomes important, in relation both to her own mother and to the mother of the baby she is caring for. In Chekhov's story, there is little difference between the master and his wife—they are both powerful people who exploit the nursemaid. But in Mansfield, there is a hierarchy between the "Man" and the "Frau" (his wife). The Frau is suffering from a fifth pregnancy, and her body has not had enough time to recover from the previous birth. Thus while being an oppressor of the nursemaid, the Frau is also described as oppressed herself. Moreover, the nursemaid's own mother, a waitress, gave birth to an illegitimate child—the nursemaid herself—and tried to kill her when she was an infant. The reader does not know anything about the nursemaid's father and is left to assume that her mother may have had to deal with the birth and the baby by herself, and felt so helpless that she tried to kill her offspring. Mansfield's story draws connections and parallels between the two mothers and the nursemaid, as all three suffer from child-bearing and child-rearing in one way or another. The unstressed theme of gender in Chekhov's story is thus brought to the surface in Mansfield's story. But gender would become an even more central theme in Hyŏn Chin-gŏn's "Fire," published in 1925.

As discussed above, Hyŏn's "Fire" depicts a young bride who suffers from overwork demanded by her mother-in-law during the day and sexual intercourse with her husband at night. This story shares with Chekhov's the fact that the protagonist is a young girl who is sleep-deprived because of all the labor that she has to do, though the focus shifts to her femaleness and the custom of early marriage in Korea. Hyŏn utilized elements from Chekhov's "Sleepy" to make visible young brides' social and sexual predicament and to create a new type of dissident female character that was sensational to the contemporary reader.

What the stories written by Mansfield and Hyŏn share is the narrator's relative proximity to the protagonist in contrast with the more neutral narrators in Chekhov and Hakuchō's stories. In Hakuchō's story, the narrator delivers the boy's desire and frustration in a dispassionate tone, although the narrator's perspective overlaps with the boy's in foreseeing an endless dreadful life at the end of the story. Meanwhile, as mentioned, we hear the female character's voice in Mansfield's story through free indirect speech more than in Chekhov's. When it comes to Hyŏn's, it is notable that the narrator is interested in sharing with the reader Suni's feelings and thought processes in the buildup to her setting the fire.

The sympathetic representation of protagonists in Mansfield and Hyŏn's stories has the effect of alleviating the shock that the ending of each story conveys to the reader. Unlike the relatively abrupt murder in the Chekhov story, the nursemaid's murder of the baby in Mansfield's story is foreshadowed to some extent through the distantly connected episodes that the nursemaid's own mother tried to kill her when she was an infant and that Frau, the mother of the baby who the nursemaid kills, suffers from continuing pregnancy and childbirth so much that she is indifferent to her own baby. These episodes present overlapping images of three female characters who suffer from child bearing/rearing, abandonment, and oppression, preparing the reader for some kind of catastrophic resolution. In Hyŏn's story, because the narrator follows Suni's feeling and thought so attentively, the reader more readily understands Suni's setting of the fire although her action would cause the deaths of her husband and mother-in-law. The proximity of the narrator and the female character in Hyŏn's story thus works to morally acquit her of her crime in coordination with the fictional description emphasizing her innocence and the sympathetic social discourse on young brides' arson at the time. Passing through this linguistic and social transformation and series of interventions, the Chekhov character was reborn in Japan, New Zealand, and Korea, creating shared concerns about the globally prevalent social issue of child labor and gender in modern society. This process accrued not only from the source text but also from other stories and ongoing sociocultural transformations.

In a 2011 article, Christopher Hill argues against "the diffusion model" of world literature, which assumes that literary forms remain unchanged in their movement into other cultures, and demonstrates the possibility of writing a global history of the novel that would focus on its transformation through movement across cultures.[69] He shows how the dense narrative discourse in Emile Zola's novel *Nana* is transposed into the features of the Nana character, and how in this transposition the character is flattened, yet this flattening does not simplify the character but rather opens the possibility of making the Nana figure more dynamic.

In the case of Chekhov, the short story genre itself, lacking the complex narrative discourse and characterization of a novel, already provides a more simplified literary narrative that can become highly mobile outside of its original social milieu. As we have seen in the case of this story, the core situation and character—that of a sleepy working child caught in a repetitive trap of exhaustion—is reborn in different social contexts.

How, then, can we understand these intercultural movements and connections in relation to the recent discussions of world literature? Despite their brilliant and inspiring explanations of the systems of world literature, Franco Moretti's and Pascale Casanova's world literature theories have been broadly criticized for their continuing Eurocentric perspectives.[70] Moretti's theorization is quite useful in the sense that it demystifies the apparently common-sense notion of the autonomous emergence of the literary form of the novel and development of literature in Western European countries and confirms that most literatures went through a process of compromise.[71] Applying Immanuel Wallerstein's socioeconomic theory of world systems, Moretti technically systemizes literatures of the world into those of a core and a periphery (and a semi-periphery), and oversimplifies the flow and process of the complicated encounters among cultures; he holds that the movement/flow takes place almost exclusively from the core (Spanish, French, and English literatures) to the periphery, and categorizes the textual production from these encounters into the three simple components of foreign form (foreign plot), local material (local characters), and local form (local narrative voice). Yet the most problematic implication of this schematization is its reaffirmation of a Eurocentric diffusionist model and avoidance of any possibility of relations and exchanges between "(semi-)peripheries."

This same criticism applies to another inspiring study of world literature, Pascale Casanova's *The World Republic of Letters*. The "Greenwich Meridian of Literature"—the term Casanova uses to indicate the relative autonomy of the literary field and literary modernity—is linked with the literary world and publishing industry in Paris. In Casanova's theory, every literary text is situated within competitive relations with other texts to join this literary modernity, and within hierarchical relations to this center of "the world republic of letters," which does not posit other diverse relationality, particularly among the literatures that exist remotely from the "Greenwich Meridian of Literature."

David Damrosch, in his book *What Is World Literature?*, defines a member of world literature as a work that is "actively present within a literary system beyond that of its original culture," which is indeed a compelling and reasonable explanation.[72] His definition, however, underestimates the impact that the geopolitical imbalance has on translation and circulation/recognition of a particular literature. It is certainly true that many literary works written in peripheral languages have been translated into other languages, which is a necessary process for a literature to be recognized as part of world literature, but there is still an enormous gap between, for instance, the number of Korean translations of English literature and the number of English translations of Korean literature. More important than the numbers is that scholars have not discussed these translations from peripheral languages as much as they have those from European languages. As a consequence the texts are not "actively present" in other languages. Thus, in reality, a work written in empowered Western languages, such as English and French, has a much greater chance of being "actively present" beyond its original literary system than does work written in a "periphery" language. Putting aside, for now, the political and economic inequality that intervenes within the cultural sphere, this unequal linguistic power structure becomes apparent when we consider the Nobel Prize in literature. One of the (albeit not primarily intended) effects of the prize is to disseminate a group of literary works internationally and, as a result, to make them "actively present" beyond their original literary systems. But this presence can be hardly attained by literary works from less empowered linguistic cultures, unless through translations into English or other European languages. While scholars like Damrosch seek to address historical imbalances in the composition of world literature, we might be better served by thinking of world literature less as an entity made up of certain literary works than as a totality of entangled literary and cultural relations. Even more importantly, we should consider "world literature" as a complex mode that constantly generates new meanings and implications through those entangled literary and cultural relations—relations that can be glimpsed in the travels of Chekhov's short story "Sleepy."

All three rewritings of "Sleepy" discussed above were at some point recognized by contemporaneous or later readers as adaptations of Chekhov's version. "Inspiration," "adaptation," "association," "copy," and "plagiarism" were all words used to describe the relations between the "original" and the later versions.[73] Particularly in Mansfield's case, the word "plagiarism" was often used to criticize her. My interest here is not in judging but rather in focusing on the fact that these writers' contemporary readers (mostly intellectuals) read the three stories in an intertextual condition that combined elements of the Chekhov story with existing social discourses, and with assumptions about the proper form and function of literature in and around social issues, to create unique meanings. In dialogue with the Chekhov story, the three writers created figures who responded to their societies' pressing social issues, making it possible for the Chekhov character to be enriched by multifaceted afterlives. A translation or adaptation is situated in reciprocal relations not only with the source text it utilizes but also in the further rewritings that have been, and are still yet to be, created.

As the travels of Chekhov's character show, compromise and negotiation occur in multidirectional and mediated ways—not necessarily from the center to the periphery and not unilaterally—and involve unexpected combinations and effects. A perspective that focuses on the movements and processes that create complicated multidimensional encounters could become an alternative to influence studies and diffusionist models that reinforce cultural hierarchies invented in the modern era.

CHAPTER 3

Aspirations for a New Literature

Constructing Proletarian Literature from Nineteenth-Century Russian Literature

In the early 1920s, after contact with socialist ideologies and the Russian revolution while working for Korea's independence, Korean socialist groups began to develop inside and outside Korea. These groups coalesced to become the foundation of the Communist Party of Korea, which formed in 1925.[1] This political movement brought significant change to the literary landscape in Korea. Manifestos and essays on proletarian literature began to appear in 1923. The first was written by Kim Ki-jin (1903–85), following his return to Korea from Japan with the ambition of establishing proletarian literature and thus changing the contemporary Korean literary field.

To understand this period in Korean literary history, we need to see it in context. After the Enlightenment period in the first two decades of the 1900s, and in the wake of the March First independence movement of 1919, Korean intellectuals experienced a mixture of simultaneous hope and despair. The March First Movement gave Korean intellectuals confidence that the energy of the Korean common people could be channeled into political achievement, but when the nationwide movement was squelched by the Japanese colonial regime they were driven to despair. Reflecting this disappointment, the early 1920s saw a sprouting of literary coterie groups that explored a decadent and defeated sensibility and advocated art for art's sake. But from 1923 on, a few members of those coterie groups began to take the path toward proletarian literature.[2] Kim Ki-jin and Pak Yŏng-hŭi, members of the *White Tide* (Paekcho) coterie, were two of the pioneers (as discussed in detail below).

Two other significant cultural groups were Yŏmgunsa (A Group of Flame) and PASKYULA, which were organized in Korea in 1922 and 1923, respectively. Yŏmgunsa was the first Korean cultural organization related to proletarian literature, and was founded by Song Yŏng, Yi Chŏk-hyo, Yi Ho, and Kim Yŏng-p'al, among others. They planned to publish two issues of their organ, *Yŏmgun*, but were banned before they could do that so the projected contents of these two issues are unknown. PASKYULA, a name derived from the members' initials, was organized by intellectuals of various backgrounds, including some former members of the *White Tide* coterie (Pak Yŏng-hŭi and Kim Ki-jin), poets with socialist leanings (Yi Ik-sang and Kim Sŏk-song), and a few members of the theater group T'owŏlhoe. These two groups were integrated to form KAPF (the acronym for Korea Artista Proletaria Federatio, or Korean Proletarian Artists' Federation) in 1925.[3] KAPF played a central role in the development of the proletarian literature and proletarian culture movement in Korea, until it had to be dismantled in 1935, following the arrest of the majority of its members by Japanese police in the early 1930s.[4]

Against this changing landscape of Korean literature, Korean intellectuals' overall interpretation of Russian literature also changed. The patterns that characterized the reception of nineteenth-century Russian writers and their works in Korea were constantly redefined and reworked depending on changes in the Korean context. The 1920s in Korea witnessed a radicalization of nineteenth-century Russian literature as socialist ideas and proletarian literature began to develop. Well-known Russian writers such as Tolstoy and Dostoevsky were interpreted as socialists, even though this misrepresented the authors' actual positions.

Similarly, although the first importation of the work of Ivan Turgenev (1818–83) to Korea in 1914 did not frame him in an overtly political light, interpretations of his works changed when politically committed literature became more dominant. Turgenev and some of his fictional characters from *On the Eve, Fathers and Sons,* and *Virgin Soil* became intellectual and literary role models for Korean proletarian writers. This appropriative representation of Russian writers raises two questions to consider about 1920s Korea: First, what did the terms "socialist" and "proletarian" mean at the time? And second, why did authors appropriate nineteenth-century Russian writers more enthusiastically than Soviet proletarian writers?

This chapter investigates Turgenev's place in the early phases of Korean proletarian literature, proposing that it was not Soviet proletarian writers but prerevolutionary Russian writers—particularly Turgenev, a prototypical bourgeois writer—who had the greatest effect on Korean proletarian literature in its early stages. This was possible through a process of politically committed appropriation.

Cho Myŏng-hŭi, one of Korea's most prominent proletarian writers, translated Turgenev's *Nakanunie* (On the eve) in 1924 and wrote a seminal short story, "Naktonggang" (Naktong River), in 1927 using similar characters and plot structure. Cho's serialization of his translation of *On the Eve* in a newspaper provides us with a noteworthy example of how a translated text can be just as affected by a negotiation with the medium of publication as by its negotiation with a foreign language. Cho's translation, which maximizes positive and progressive aspects of the story, foreshadows the characteristics of his later appropriation of the same novel. It was this process that transformed a classic of Russian bourgeois literature into one of the most significant works of Korean proletarian literature.

By examining the alignment of Korean proletarian literature with the tradition of nineteenth-century Russia and its literature, rather than with Soviet proletarian literature, I reconsider the international alliance of proletarian literature and argue that writers in colonial Korea had their own specific sense of the contemporaneity and internationality that characterized proletarian literature. For instance, the Korean intellectuals who led the proletarian literature movement often associated the term "proletariat" with colonized Korea and its people (or oppressed people in general), which included the colonized intellectuals themselves (and even the colonized Korean bourgeois class as the potential future proletariat). Their eclectic, if not ironic, concepts and ideas of the proletariat and proletarian literature thus rationalized the prevalence of Korean proletarian literature written by and about intellectuals. This comprehension of complexity that proletarian literature in colonial Korea displays will help us better understand proletarian literary writers' aspirations and their artistic substantialization of those aspirations in different sociocultural contexts.

Radicalizing Nineteenth-Century
Russian Literature

Korean intellectuals utilized most of the well-known prerevolutionary Russian writers and their works to promote their own radical social ideas in the 1920s. Tolstoy is one of the most significant examples of this phenomenon, and his case also gives us a chance to understand distinctions between his reception in the 1910s and the 1920s. I introduce below how his ideas on labor and art—the ideas that were the most prominently associated with him in the late 1900s and 1910s—were adapted and altered in the 1920s.

Some of the first attempts at readapting Tolstoy's ideas on labor to support a loosely defined socialism can be found in the bulletin of a labor organization in the early 1920s. The Chosŏn Nodong Kongje Hoe (Korean Labor Mutual Aid Association)—the first nationwide labor organization that studied the problem of labor and promoted the labor movement and the education of workers—was also one of the first radical labor organizations to utilize Tolstoy's fame to promote its legitimacy and importance. The organization was founded in 1920, after Japanese colonial rule changed from the military policy to the cultural policy, and launched its own journal, *Kongje* (Mutual aid), in September of the same year. It had come into being due to awareness both of the need to improve the conditions of the working classes and of the potential for workers to become a central force for social change and national independence.[5]

The first issue of *Kongje* includes two separate articles that introduce Tolstoy's thoughts on labor. First, in an essay celebrating the launch of the organization, Chŏng Se-yun, the head of the Pyongyang branch of the association, eulogizes the sanctity of labor. For him, the labor organization had a mission "to raise the twenty million heavenly people" (i.e., the Korean people) and "to build a small heaven." Chŏng argues that "only the person who believes in the sacred religion of labor can have a right to enter that heaven, and only the person who reaches the virtuous and beautiful tenets of mutual aid (*kongje pŏmmun*) can function as one of the heavenly people."[6] By employing religious terminology—including the Buddhist term *pŏmmun,* whose literal translation is "door to nirvana"—he elevates labor (*nodong*) and mutual aid (*kongje*) to the status of absolute virtue. He then cites two well-known thinkers to support his argument: Marx and Tolstoy. For Chŏng, "it is not coincidental that Mr. Marx foretold that we could acquire the accomplishment of world peace only through sincere laborers, and that Mr. Tolstoy also chose labor as something that could realize the demands of social peace."[7] The term "social peace," which for Chŏng can be accomplished only by "sincere laborers," might to some extent be used here as equivalent to the term "equality."

Considering the range of thinkers who might be cited to stress the importance of the launch of the labor association, we might ask: Why Tolstoy? This utilization of Tolstoy to validate the author's ideas on labor and the role of the labor association in Korean society reveals at least two interesting aspects of cultural appropriation. First, previously constructed images of Tolstoy in Korea continued to affect later representations. As explained in Chapter 1, Ch'oe Nam-sŏn's importation of Tolstoy in 1909–10 was the first introduction of a Russian writer to Korea. Ch'oe selectively introduced Tolstoy's thoughts on labor and his everyday practice of physical work despite his aristocratic status. Ch'oe's choices aimed at legitimizing his own ideal of a new type of modern intellectual who would act and work differently from premodern aristocrat-scholars. Thus it was labor that was most prominently associated with Tolstoy in Korea in the 1910s. Chŏng was therefore deploying the already-accepted figure of Tolstoy in his argument for the significance of labor.

Second, such cultural appropriation almost always serves the receiving culture's sociopolitical purposes. As seen in Chapter 1, Ch'oe Nam-sŏn intentionally and overtly excluded many of Tolstoy's more radical social ideas and changed the term "*nodong*" (labor) into "*nodong yŏkchak*," a phrase that emphasizes the strenuous physical effort required to produce/create something. But in Chŏng's article in *Kongje*, despite its use of the image of Tolstoy as initially constructed by Ch'oe, Tolstoy's ideas on labor acquire a political tinge when placed together with those of Marx, notwithstanding the fact that Tolstoy was opposed to Marxist ideas, which for Tolstoy were premised on violence and on the dictatorship of the proletariat.

The 1920s' reuse and alteration of the image of Tolstoy that Ch'oe had created around 1910 can be seen even more clearly in the second

Kongje article, written by Tongwŏn (probably a pen name) and published in the same issue. Tongwŏn employs the same word, "*yŏkchak*," that Ch'oe used, but situates it within the context of class struggle.

Tongwŏn begins his article by expressing his admiration for Tolstoy's greatness. He introduces Tolstoy as a person "who shed unprecedented light on the field of thought in the modern period and who enjoyed the greatest fame as a culture critic." Among the works of Tolstoy that Tongwŏn has read, he singles out Tolstoy's essay on social virtue and vice as having had an indescribable impact on him. In Tolstoy's preface to this essay, a traveler from elsewhere comes to Earth for the first time and observes human beings' lives. A human being asks the traveler what he thinks about life on Earth, and the traveler answers that there is one thing he has understood: the reality that a person who does not work (*yŏkchak*) lives richly, while a person who works without break cannot even afford clothes for himself. After citing this essay, Tongwŏn concludes that "it is natural in contemporary Russia that, if you do not work (*nodong*), you cannot eat."[8] Thus he uses the same term for physical labor that Ch'oe did, but by situating it within an argument about inequality between the classes, he makes it more radical.

There are other similar elements in this article—for example, Tongwŏn stresses that "the current labor movement must encompass laborers' resistance against capitalism and their demand for moral treatment that does not degrade them as machines."[9] It is noteworthy that he employs not Marx but Tolstoy to direct the reader's attention to the importance of labor and inequality, and, by extension, to what the labor movement in a capitalist society aims for. We can speculate that it was more effortless and persuasive for Tongwŏn to invoke Tolstoy, who was already well known to Korean intellectuals, than Marx, who was a relatively new name in Korea in 1920. Through Korean intellectuals' appropriation of Tolstoy in this labor journal, Tolstoy's ideas on labor, which were introduced as being relatively apolitical by Ch'oe in the 1910s, started being connected with socialism and the leftwing labor movement in 1920.

The second issue of *Kongje* was more radicalized, urging the necessity of incorporating socialism—which is used interchangeably with historical materialism—into the labor movement. In this issue Yu Chin-hŭi argues, in his article "A Socialist Study of the Labor Movement," that the aim of the labor movement is not only the satisfaction of laborers' material needs but, more fundamentally, "the liberation of laborers" from exploitation by the bourgeoisie and "the recovery of human rights."[10] He also asserts that the labor movement needs to become more militant and "aim for a revolution in the mode of production that will give everyone an equal right to use the means of production."[11] Yu's main argument is that it is necessary "to combine socialism [i.e., historical materialism] with the labor movement in order to obtain the highest possibility for the class struggle of the proletariat (*musanja*)."[12] This article does not mention Tolstoy in order to legitimize its ideas about labor, but brings in Dostoevsky, Tolstoy, Kropotkin, and Romain Rolland as pioneers of socialism.[13] Tolstoy thus becomes one of many Russian writers to be used in arguing for the importance of socialism.

In addition to Tolstoy's concept of labor, his literary theory was also radicalized in the 1920s. Yi Kwang-su introduced and incorporated Tolstoy's theory of art for the first time in Korea in order to forge his own theory of literature in the 1910s. As explored in Chapter 1, Yi successfully manipulated Tolstoy's theory of emotion, which for Tolstoy had served to realize true Christianity, but which for Yi became the basis for national literature. In this Yi ignored Tolstoy's fundamental claim about an art of true Christianity that would refute patriotism. Yi's ideas about what was proper subject matter also differed from Tolstoy's: whereas Tolstoy sought to describe peasants' lives and their wisdom and beauty when he wrote his theory of art, Yi's exemplary figures of literature are well-educated people from a high social class. He explains that, "for example, if we want to take the topic of love, it should be the love of highbred people, and that of the educated among highbred people, and that of the talented and attractive among the educated, and focus on the love forbidden by parents among the talented and attractive people."[14] Yi skillfully utilizes Tolstoy's idea of "infection"—art infects a person with another's feeling and thus unites them—in his nationalist view without any specific reference to the common people as a central force of culture. In the 1920s, however, the interpretation of Tolstoy's theory of art became imbued with populist and socialist ideas.

In his article "Tolstoy's Theory of Art," published in *Kaebyŏk* (The creation), a radical and widely circulated journal in 1920s Korea, Kim Yu-bang summarizes Tolstoy's arguments in his *Theory of Art*. As Kim writes in the preface to the article, he is aware that Tolstoy's theory is controversial and that some art theorists criticize Tolstoy for his hostility to art for art's sake. Kim writes that his goal is not to resolve the debate, though he thinks that "it would be significant to introduce Tolstoy's populist (*minjung-juŭi*) theory of art to Korean readers, who are just on the verge of inhaling a new air of democracy (*minbon-juŭi*),"[15] and also "to Korean society, where the concept of people (*minjung*) is about to come into existence."[16] Much of Kim's subsequent introduction is similar to Yi's. But the phrases he employs, such as "*minjung-juŭi*," "*minbon-juŭi*," and "*minjung*," frame Tolstoy as a populist, and connect this with a call for Korean intellectual attention to common people as a driving force for social change after the nationwide liberation movement of 1919.

A more intriguing appropriation of Tolstoy's theory of art is found in an article by the proletarian writer Pak Yŏng-hŭi in 1928. He examines the connection between Tolstoy's theory of art and Korean proletarian literature, in "Section IV: The Infection of Emotion" and "Section V: The Origin of Art" of his article:

> Some assert that art expresses thoughts (*sasang*), and others say that art expresses emotions (*kamjŏng*). To be specific, whereas some argue that art *structures (chojik hanŭn) the thoughts of the masses (taejung)*, others contend that art *infects the masses with [others'] emotion* and organizes (*chojik hanŭn*) their emotion. In his theory of art, *Tolstoy* explains that art is a means for people's emotional infection, and, in a true sense, his definition of art also applies to proletarian literature.[17] (Emphasis in original)

Though Pak's reading of Tolstoy seems uncontroversial, there are two significant distortions. The first is the incorporation of the word "masses." When Tolstoy explains that men are capable of being infected with other persons' emotion, and that art transmits and conveys emotion so that it unites people, he refers to all human beings being united. While Yi Kwang-su twists this into nationalism, with an emphasis on elite nationalism, with Pak, the term "human beings" becomes "the masses." The second is Pak's phrasing, "organizes their emotion." Pak's idea that art organizes people's emotion is entirely different from Tolstoy's idea that art unites people by transmitting and conveying emotion and infecting people with others' emotions.

Pak continues discussing the organization of emotion in the next section of his essay:

We can say that the emotional infection of art organizes people's emotion (*kamjŏng*) with an identical system (*tong'ilhan ch'egye*). When we listen to music, a person's expression of his or her feeling makes everyone's feeling (*kibun*) and emotion (*chŏngsŏ*) identical. In this way, art structures [people's emotion] into a shared system. . . . The systematic organization of the emotions [of people] can in the end form [their] thoughts identically.[18]

To structure human emotion systematically does not appear to be what Tolstoy's book on art advocates. In particular, the last sentence of the excerpt just quoted, which states that the organization of emotion ultimately brings about the identical formation of thoughts, goes beyond Tolstoy's theory of art to reveal Pak's own hopes. Pak uses such expressions as "identical emotion" and "identical thoughts," and this word "identical" presumably means not standardization/uniformity but empathy/collectivity/commonality. For Pak, identical emotions and thoughts evidently refer to the collectivity of the proletariat, or the oppressed.

If the case of Tolstoy shows us the stark difference between Korean intellectuals' reception of Russian literature in the 1910s and in the 1920s, then the case of Ivan Turgenev (1818–83) shows Korean proletarian writers' incorporation of a prerevolutionary writer as a model for themselves and their characters in 1920s Korea. Before investigating Korean proletarian writers' appropriation of Turgenev, let's examine the specificities of the reception of Turgenev in Japan and Korea, and the popularity of Turgenev's *On the Eve* in Korea.[19]

Turgenev in Japan and Korea

In Japan, Turgenev's works attracted Japanese writers not because it felt familiar but because of either their literary novelty or their political elements. The earliest reception of Russian writers in Japan, which took place in the late 1870s, was stimulated from the beginning by the political subjects to be found in Russian literature. The early reception of Turgenev clearly shows Japanese interest in the political element of his novels.[20] Turgenev's *Fathers and Sons* was introduced in a newspaper, *Chōya shinbun*, in 1879. The Russian writer Goncharov, the author of *Oblomov*, had been known in Japan since 1853, when he came to Japan as secretary to Count Putiatin, yet Turgenev was the first writer Japanese intellectuals paid attention to. Turgenev was introduced as the writer who had coined the terms "nihilist" and "nihilism" in *Fathers and Sons*, and this work was thought to deal with these concepts in depth.[21]

The first of Turgenev's works that Futabatei Shimei worked on translating was *Fathers and Sons*, despite the fact that Futabatei's "Aibiki"— a translation of one chapter, "The Tryst," from Turgenev's *A Hunter's Sketches*—has become known as the first translation of Turgenev. Futabatei started working on *Fathers and Sons* in 1886, under the title "The Form and Spirit of Popular Nihilism," but it remained unfinished and unpublished.[22] The working title of this unfinished translation shows how strongly nihilism figured in *Fathers and Sons* for Japanese authors. The Freedom and People's Rights Movement was active in Japan at the time, and it was in light of this that many Japanese intellectuals studied the nihilists' activities. Many books on nihilism were published in the years after 1882, and Futabatei's early attempt at translating *Fathers and Sons* was probably related to this phenomenon.[23]

The next significant event in the reception of Turgenev in Japan was Futabatei Shimei's translation of "The Tryst," in 1888. Its influence on Japanese writers has roughly three aspects. First, the new writing style of Futabatei's translation, *genbun'itchi*, is one of the most significant events in the history of Japanese literature.[24] Second, it changed Japanese writers' views about the description of nature.[25] Third, some writers were influenced by Turgenev's story itself and used it for their own fiction.[26] It was mostly the literary aspects of this story and its translation that attracted Japanese writers, unlike the introduction of nihilism in *Fathers and Sons* about a decade earlier. *A Hunter's Sketches* also inspired Japanese intellectuals because of its role in the abolition of serfdom in Russia.

Whereas the first introduction of Turgenev's work to Japan was connected to political issues, Turgenev's prose poems were what made him known to Korean intellectuals in the 1910s. Translations of these prose poems were published in Japan in 1901 and 1902 by Ueda Bin, and became popular in Korea in the late 1910s.[27] Turgenev's work was published for the first time in Korean in the literary journal *Ch'ŏngch'un* (Youth) in October 1914.[28] Kim Ŏk, a Korean poet and critic, translated a few of Turgenev's prose poems in the literary journal *T'aesŏ munye sinbo* (Journal of Western literature), first appearing in October 1918.[29] The prose poems mostly describe the later Turgenev's mature thoughts and ruminations about everyday life and, unlike his novels, do not include overtly political ideas. The form of Turgenev's prose poems inspired Korean writers who were seeking new free-style forms, different from the traditional ones.[30] Turgenev's poems enjoyed such great popularity that the same poems were retranslated and republished in several different journals, and other new poems of Turgenev's were also translated. This tendency continued until the early 1930s.[31] But in the 1920s in Korea, Turgenev's novels became recognized as radical, and *On the Eve, Fathers and Sons*, and *Virgin Soil* in particular were frequently employed by Korean proletarian literature writers in the 1920s.

There are similarities and differences in the reception of Turgenev's literary works between in Japan and Korea. One of the conspicuous differences is that Turgenev's *On the Eve* was the novel that was most often introduced and referred to by Korean intellectuals, whereas it was not as popular in Japan. Turgenev's *Rudin*, which was first translated into Japanese by Futabatei Shimei in 1897, was probably the novel by Turgenev that was most frequently appropriated by Japanese writers. For example, Nobori Shomu, an alumnus of the Orthodox Theological Seminary and a well-known translator and scholar of Russian literature, does not discuss *On the Eve* at all in his survey of the impact of the Russian literature in Japan, whereas he assigns a whole section to *Rudin*.[32]

However, *On the Eve* was one of the most often read and discussed works in colonial Korea. Yi Hyo-sŏk remembers that there was almost no one in his high school dormitory who did not know the story of *On the Eve*, whether from having read it or having heard about it through conversations among friends.[33] Another anecdote comes from Chang Yŏn-hwa, a Korean *kisaeng* (female entertainer), who recalled being enormously moved by the story when she heard about it in class at the age of sixteen.[34]

It cannot be conclusively explained why a specific foreign literary work strongly appeals to a certain group of readers. Yet when we consider the protagonists of *On the Eve*—a revolutionary fighting for national liberation and a heroine giving up her comfortable life in Russia to support her husband's cause—it is easy to see why colonized Korean intellectuals would have been particularly attracted to this story. Turgenev's *On the Eve* appeared in the *Russian Herald* in January 1860. Its heroine,

Elena, falls in love with Insarov, a young Bulgarian revolutionary. She
sees in him a purposefulness and determination that, for her, contemporary Russian young men lack. She eventually marries Insarov against her
parents' wishes and plans to accompany him back to Bulgaria to support
the revolution and liberate his country from the Turks. He dies in Venice from illness, however, and Elena decides to continue the journey by
herself, to follow her husband's path.[35]

In Japan, the first translation of Turgenev's *On the Eve* was serialized
in *Yamato nishiki* (Japanese silk) with several illustrations, starting in June
1889, one year after Futabatei's translation of "The Tryst" was published.[36]
The second and full translation was done by Sōma Gyofū (1883–1950), a
Japanese poet and critic. He first serialized a few chapters of *On the Eve*
in 1907–8, and translated the whole book and published it in 1908.[37] This
translation was published when the popularity of Turgenev's writings was
at its peak. This was before the Russian department opened at Waseda
University, although Shimamura Hōgetsu (1871–1918), a Japanese critic
and theatrical producer who later adapted Tolstoy's *Resurrection* into a tre-
mendously successful play in 1914, offered lectures on Russian literature
at Waseda, and students in the English department wrote theses about
Turgenev. It was in this atmosphere that Sōma Gyofū graduated from
Waseda and translated Turgenev's *On the Eve*.[38] Two other translations
appeared before 1945.[39]

In addition to these translations, one theatrical adaptation of this
novel was produced in 1915, thanks to the remarkable success of the performance of Tolstoy's *Resurrection* in 1914.[40] The adaptive play was written by Kusuyama Masao—who had helped Sōma Gyofū translate the
novel *On the Eve*—and was presented as a part of Tokyo Art Theater's
(Geijutsuza) fifth performance at the Imperial Theater (Teikoku gekijō)
in 1915. But it fell far short of the popular success of *Resurrection*. This
play of *On the Eve*, however, later became the source text for Hyŏn Ch'ŏl's
Korean translation in 1920.

In Korea, three translations of *On the Eve* were produced during the
colonial period, and they include an adaptation and a summary translation. The content of *On the Eve* was first introduced by Hyŏn Ch'ŏl's
adaptation for theater performance in 1920. The second translation was
Cho Myŏng-hŭi's relatively full and faithful translation in 1924. The
third was a summary translation by Yi T'ae-jun in 1929.

In the preface to his translation, Hyŏn briefly explains in general terms the reason he chose *On the Eve*.[41] He emphasizes the relevance of the characters, who include a Bulgarian revolutionary hero and a Russian heroine who chooses to follow the revolutionary path. He shows sympathy toward these two characters and describes the heroine, Elena, as "a pioneer of a new revolutionary and active female type in 1850s Russia." Although his preface is written as though it is Hyŏn's own phrasing, his description of Elena was taken from Kusuyama Masao's preface.[42]

Kusuyama's adaptation shortens the story itself by cutting off the beginning of the novel, where Insarov and Elena have not met each other, and by mingling some scenes. It does not explain why or how Insarov becomes sick. But one of the most prominent changes is that it describes Elena as a more active and politically involved woman. In Turgenev's novel, Elena is deeply moved by Insarov's determinedness, honesty, and patriotic ideas but does not express her will to join the independence movement until Insarov dies. In Kusuyama's adaptation, however, Elena clearly expresses her desire to go to Bulgaria to join the revolution in the early part of the story. In Act One she talks about Insarov with Bersenev, one of Insarov's friends: "I want to try to go to Bulgaria. In that country, all people (*kokumin*) are eager for freedom and seek vengeance [for Turkey's oppression]. I want to try to go to such a country and work there, waving the flag of revolution together with those people."[43] As expected from Hyŏn's awareness of copyright, he makes a literal and faithful translation from Kusuyama's adaptation. This literal translation of a Japanese adaptation meant that the first Korean introduction of *On the Eve* presented a stronger and more determined Elena than the Elena in Turgenev's original novel.

The second Korean translation of *On the Eve* is Cho Myŏng-hŭi's full translation of 1924, examined thoroughly in the later part of this chapter. The third, a summarized translation, produced by Yi T'ae-jun in 1929, is something like a rewritten short story, including parts of the characters' conversations and the narrator's descriptions.[44] In Yi's summarized translation, the whole novel is condensed into eight pages, including a short preface. His preface indicates his goals in the translation. Because he considers *On the Eve* to be a story of "youth's pure love and liberal loyalty and courage," Yi emphasizes that he will "write only of the beautiful friendship and true love in the novel."[45] Yi kept a clear distance from proletarian or socially engaged literature during the colonial period, and he claims to focus on conveying general human issues rather than on the political elements that Turgenev's *On the Eve* contains. But because he focuses on only three characters—Insarov, Elena, and Bersenev, who are the most serious, sincere, and liberal in the story—and excludes Elena's conservative parents and the seemingly apolitical Shubin, his summary ends up emphasizing Insarov's patriotism, passion, and determination to win his country's independence, and Elena's faith and purposefulness.

The hero Insarov and heroine Elena became embodiments of revolutionary struggle and comradely love, and their names and images often appeared in Korean writers' essays and literary works. The first example is by a Korean writer who read *On the Eve* as a moving love story. This is how the Korean female entertainer, mentioned above, and her classmates interpreted it. Hyŏn Chin-gŏn's unfinished story "Chisae nŭn an'gae" (Fog at dawn), serialized in 1923, tells the story of a young man and his modern love. In chapter 2, Ch'ang-sŏp, the protagonist (who has studied in Japan and then returned to Korea, finding a job at a Korean newspaper company), has a conversation with his cousin and her two friends about the performance of Turgenev's *On the Eve* in Korea. When the three young girls ask Ch'ang-sŏp to tell them a story, he summarizes the whole novel in a passionate voice. Ch'ang-sŏp interprets the novel as a sad, melodramatic love story, but because he is young and is himself caught up in the agony of love, he idealizes Elena's liberal choice and sacrifice for her love. He identifies himself with Insarov, searching for his Elena in a dream, although he is not involved in any political resistance in his own life.[46]

Yŏm Sang-sŏp's novel *Sarang kwa choe* (Love and sin), written in 1927, also utilized the characteristics of the hero and heroine in *On the Eve*. In *Love and Sin*, a few different story lines are intertwined, including subplots involving love and conflict among young people, a man's tricks to possess one of the heroines, and secret resistance activities against the colonial regime. It also has elements of a detective story surrounding a murder case. In the middle of the story, the protagonists—a lawyer, Kim Ho-yŏn; an artist, Yi Hae-ch'un; and a nurse, Chi Sun-yŏng—bring up the issue of revolutionary Russia and start comparing themselves with the characters in *On the Eve*:

> Without answering, Sun-yŏng [the nurse] was about to leave with a water glass while shyly reading Hae-ch'un's [the artist's] face.

"Are you on night duty?"

"Yes," Sun-yŏng answered and went out.

"Is it already dark? It's time to go! Talking about these things, we look like the characters in Russian novels!" said Hae-ch'un and laughed, standing up. There was still some sunlight, but an electrical light was already turned on.

"You are associating us with Turgenev's *On the Eve*, aren't you?" said Ho-yŏn [the lawyer], laughing as well.

"Possibly, if we imagine you to be Insarov and Sun-yŏng to be Elena, it might be a story exciting enough to be a novel," said Hae-ch'un while picking up his hat.[47]

Love and Sin has similarities with *On the Eve* in terms of its characters' vocations and some episodes about them. Ho-yŏn is a lawyer, and law is one of the subjects Insarov studies in Russia. The pro-Japanese Korean viscount Hae-ch'un is an artist, like the apolitical aristocrat Shubin. Finally, Sun-yŏng is a nurse, while Elena eventually becomes a nurse working for Bulgarian revolutionaries after Insarov has dies. The lawyer Ho-yŏn is a central figure of a secret resistance organization and so restrains his love for Sun-yŏng; Insarov is also a leader of a resistance group for Bulgarian independence and suppresses his feelings toward Elena because he needs to focus on his duty to his oppressed country. But unlike *On the Eve*, in which Insarov and Elena marry despite all the obstacles, Ho-yŏn makes Sun-yŏng escape secretly with Hae-ch'un when he himself is arrested.

In a final example, the character of Insarov is transformed into a group of Korean heroes, dubbed "Insarovs," in Sin Sŏk-chŏng's poem "Pang" (Room), written in the late colonial period:

One winter night with a lot of snow falling in feather flakes,
The hope that the new era will come,
The hope that the new era will come,
The desolate hope, redder than camellia,
Blooming by the brazier embraced by *Insarovs* (*Insarop'ŭ-dŭl*)
Repressing the burst of pent-up rage.[48] (Emphasis in original)

This poem does not include any detailed explanation about what the new era means and who the people are who dream the "desolate hope." But

the insertion of one word provides the reader with the background knowledge to interpret the situation described in the poem: the word "Insarov" brings to this short poem the experience of the Bulgarian character
Insarov—that is, the loss of his country's sovereignty, the oppression by
imperial power, his parents' agony and death, and his preparation in
exile for his country's revolution and independence. This shows how
this specific hero from a Russian novel had become one of the figures
that crystallized the image of the colonized Korean intellectual in
1930s Korea.

Turgenev and Korean Proletarian Literature

Although the Korean proletarian literary movement came under the sway
of the Communist International (Comintern) in its later stage, it enjoyed
flexibility and tolerance in the 1920s, particularly until the mid- to late-
1920s. When proletarian literature was introduced, it was an intermingled collection of various strands of ideas and movements, including
the French Clarté movement (discussed below), Russian populism (the
Narodnik movement), nihilism, and an ambiguous neo-idealism (used
by Pak Yŏng-hŭi). The term "proletariat" referred to the broad range of
Korean common people and often came to include intellectuals themselves. At its greatest extension it included the whole Korean people, including the bourgeoisie.

Along with the broad meaning of the word "proletariat" in the 1920s,
the range of proletarian literature in Korea was inclusive enough to embrace engaged literature even when it lacked a clear socialist ideology or
conception of workers' solidarity or class identity. Proletarian literature
in Korea covered not only literary works about or written by workers but
also the works about *and* written by intellectuals. This inclusiveness was
one of the conditions for the reception of Russian bourgeois literary works
as a strand of socialist literature. Prerevolutionary Russian literature that
aspired to social change may even have been more appealing to Korean
intellectuals than Bolshevik literature, such as F. Gladkov's historic
1925 novel *Tsement* (Cement), which described the process of postrevolu-
tionary reconstruction.

Proletarian literature first became an intellectual topic in Korea not through the introduction of actual literary works but as a discussion of what this new kind of literature could be in the near future. The first prediction about the possibilities of proletarian literature in Korea appeared in January 1923 in an essay by Pak Chong-hwa that recollects the previous year's Korean literary world:

> There is one more thing to remember when thinking about the previous year. Nothing was discussed on the surface but, at the bottom, the kernel of the confrontation of bourgeois and proletarian literature started germinating in Korea. The class struggle between laborers and capitalists did not stop at being a social movement but spread to the realm of theories of value and the place of literature, and thus it swirled through the literary circles in the world. When we look at the Japanese literary scene, it is in the middle of an intense struggle between bourgeois and proletarian literature. This whirlwind will not bypass our literary world. It is one of the phenomena that will appear in Korea in the near future.[49]

With no mention of particular works, the "kernel" that Pak Chong-hwa had in mind might have been his and other Korean writers' growing interest in the new type of literature that they encountered mostly during their stays in Japan. Pak describes proletarian literature as though it had already reached a place in the Japanese literary world sufficient to rival bourgeois literature. In fact the term "proletarian literature" did not appear in Japan until 1922, so Pak may have been overstating the new trend simply to create interest in it in Korea.[50]

It was Kim Ki-jin (1903–85) who took one of the first steps toward creating a politically committed literature in Korea, in 1923. He had studied in the English department at Rikkyo University in Japan for three years, and returned to Korea in 1923. He later recalled that he had been a supporter of art for art's sake and was immersed in neoromanticism and French symbolism until early 1922. But he became interested in socialist ideas in the autumn of 1922.[51] As Kim Ki-jin admits, the ideas found in the Japanese journal *The Sower* (*Tane maku hito* in Japanese; *Ssi ppurinŭn saram-dŭl* in Korean) had a profound impact on this change of course: "There was a journal, *The Sower*, in Japan. It was a small general magazine. I was fond of its title. So I wanted to become one of the sowers."[52]

Kim was deeply impressed by Henri Barbusse's essays as introduced in *The Sower,* and later introduced Barbusse's ideas to Korea as well.

The Sower was a cornerstone of proletarian literature in Japan. While in France in 1919, Komaki Ōmi, the founder of the magazine, was involved in the Clarté movement organized by the French novelist Henri Barbusse and other intellectuals. The Clarté movement took its name from Barbusse's novel *Clarté,* which indicted the evil practices of war and imperialism. It was an international movement that promoted the abolition of class discrimination and of war, and supported the proletarian revolution in Soviet Russia. Komaki founded *The Sower* in order to build the Clarté movement in Japan. It started as an intellectual magazine and aimed to be an ideological movement rather than a forum for proletarian literature itself. But *The Sower* nevertheless combined with the growing movement toward a literature imbued with class consciousness, and played a central role in the Japanese proletarian literary movement until 1923, when it was shut down under political oppression.[53]

A letter from Kim in 1922, sent from Tokyo to his high school friend and fellow member of the *White Tide* coterie Pak Yŏng-hŭi, demonstrates how his interest had shifted by this time from art itself toward the social role of literature and the writer:

> Human beings, the world, learning, the people (*minjok*), poetry and art are the things that are occupying my thoughts right now. [Human beings] wander about to seek after truth. Human beings wander about throughout their lives in search of the truth. But the thing that most confuses me is "Chosŏn" (Korea). Recently, whenever I mutter this word "Chosŏn" to myself, tears soon well up. I don't know how to understand what is happening to me. But the question "What are we to do?" is something that never leaves us as long as history continues. "Truth" gains an ultimate victory.[54]

What do "human being" and "truth" mean, and why do they appear in Kim's writing? Why does "Chosŏn" confuse Kim most? We may gain some insight by comparing his letter with a "Declaration" in the first issue of *The Sower*:

> Truth is absolute. Thus we speak the truth that others do not speak. Man is a wolf against man. Country and race are not the question. Under the light of truth, union and disunion arise.

Look! We fight for the truth of modern times. We are the masters of life. He who denies life will never be a modern man. We defend the truth of the revolution for life. *The Sower* stands here—together with its comrades of the world![55]

G. T. Shea speculates that this obscure language may have been intended to avoid confrontation with the authorities, though this Declaration's defense of "the truth of the revolution" and promotion of internationalism—seen in the phrase "Country and race are not the question"—parallel those of the Clarté movement. As Kim himself admitted, he was profoundly moved by the ideas expressed in *The Sower*. His thoughts about the truth may well have been about "the truth of revolution," and the "victory" of truth that he refers to may have been the victory of proletarian revolution that the Clarté movement supported. The movement's emphasis on internationalism may also have triggered Kim's confusion and tears when thinking about Korea. The agony that intellectuals in a colony had to embrace in relation to the issues of nationalism and internationalism thus appears at this very early stage, before the movement even started in colonial Korea.

Although Kim Ki-jin seems to be in the midst of struggle and confusion in his 1922 epistle to Pak Yŏng-hŭi, his ideas on the role of the writer had firmed up considerably by the time he wrote the essay "Promenade Sentimental," one year later. Kim's first two essays about proletarian literature—"Promenade Sentimental," considered the manifesto of Korean proletarian literature, and "Broken Pieces"—demonstrate his idea that literature had to engage itself in people's lives, and that if it did not, it was nothing more than a play.[56]

Ten years later, Kim explained that when proletarian literature was becoming more active around 1922 and 1923 in Japan, he was so impressed that he decided to return to Korea and transform the Korean magazine *White Tide* into something that would be equivalent to *The Sower*.[57] Believing that "art for art's sake is ultimately the idle talk of the well-fed," he started moving from poetry to prose and became a disciple of "Turgenev, Dostoevsky, Gorky and Ibsen."[58] Cho Myŏng-hŭi also changed his literary genre from poetry to prose after he turned from religious mysticism to proletarian literature. Prose may have been a more effective way to convey ideas and detailed descriptions of people's lives. For Kim, at least, poetry was connected with French symbolism and art for art's sake, while prose was associated mostly with Russian writers whose works addressed social problems of their age.

According to Kim, the event that made him to return to Korea to take action was a conversation with Asō Hisashi (1891–1940), a Japanese socialist activist and writer:

> After turning from "art for art's sake" to "art for life," I gradually moved to socialism. I was fond of reading the critiques of Japanese socialists such as Sakai Toshihiko, Yamakawa Hitoshi, Ōsugi Sakae, Asō Hisashi, and Sano Manabu.
>
> "What are you doing literature for, Mr. Kim? You said you liked Turgenev, didn't you? Your Korea has lots of similarities with XXX [Russia] fifty years ago. Sow the seeds in 'virgin soil.' Become Solomin. It is much more meaningful to become Insarov or Solomin rather than to be Turgenev."
>
> This I was told by Asō Hisashi at his house one day, and I worried over whether I should give up literature or not. . . . "I will do both." I finally arrived at this conclusion. I want to express. . . . Want to cry out. Want to clamor. These impulses surged up within me.[59]

The comparison of Korea to prerevolutionary Russia often appeared in the early proletarian writers' essays. The expression "sowing the seeds" relates to *The Sower*, while the phrase "virgin soil" alludes to the title of Turgenev's 1877 novel, as well as to Korea as a wasteland. Insarov and Solomin are the heroes of Turgenev's novels *On the Eve* and *Virgin Soil*, respectively, and both are practical and determined men with no hesitation or skepticism. They are the most positively described among Turgenev's generally weak and indecisive male characters. Kim Ki-jin repeatedly refers to this conversation with Asō in other essays.[60] Asō believed Japanese society would accomplish a revolution in ten years, and Kim returned to Korea thinking that Korea should keep pace in order to liberate itself from colonization.[61] The initial emotional and literary alignment of Japanese and Korean proletarian literature writers with progressive and sympathetic Russian writers and their characters, regardless of their social classes, is clear in these memoirs.

The future proletarian literature was predicted and prepared for by the proletarian literature pioneers as though it was an unavoidable development for the Korean literary world. Just as Pak Chong-hwa foresaw the arrival of proletarian literature in Korea in January 1923, so Kim Ki-jin publicized his belief in its future existence a few months later, by insisting that "although the bud of proletarian culture is not visible yet in Korea, I feel the flow of such indications. I thus talk about it even before a substantial movement has been born."[62] Pak Yŏng-hŭi, who was affected by Kim, also prophesied that Korean literature would move from romanticism and naturalism to neo-idealism (which Pak equated with proletarian art). He himself admitted that "it is not a tendency visible in our literary world, but I should say that it is a prophecy."[63] Pak Yŏng-hŭi's essay was published in February 1924, a year after Pak Chong-hwa's. These essays demonstrate that the pioneers of proletarian literature in Korea discussed its presence in Korea for a full year without much substantial evidence of its actual existence. This certainly paved the way for proletarian literature in Korea once it did begin to develop.

Korean proletarian writers used various names to refer to their own literature, such as New Tendency literature (*sin kyŏnghyangp'a munhak*), neo-idealism (*sin isangjuŭi*), the literature of the dispossessed (*musanja munhak*), class literature (*kyegŭp munhak*), the literature of the dominated (*p'i chibae kyegŭp munhak*), KAPF literature (*kap'ŭ munhak*), and, of course, proletarian literature (*p'uro munhak*). According to Kim Ki-jin, a leading proletarian literature pioneer, the term "New Tendency literature" was coined by Pak Yŏng-hŭi to denote the new group of literary works that described the poverty of the dispossessed and their resistance and vengeance.[64] In an article written in December 1925, Pak Yŏng-hŭi declared that proletarian literature had obviously started in Korea. He coined the terms "New Tendency" and "New Tendency literature" to describe the literary works dealing with social problems that had been produced up to that point. This group had used the term "proletarian literature" from the beginning, as seen in Kim Ki-jin's 1923 article "Promenade Sentimental," whereas Pak coined the term "New Tendency" retrospectively to indicate the literary works of the early period, which he regarded not as mature but as transitional proletarian literature.[65] This term has continued to be used by writers and literary historians up to the present.

In February 1927 (slightly more than a year after Pak Yŏng-hŭi's December 1925 essay had declared the beginning of proletarian literature), Kim Ki-jin asserted that the probationary period of proletarian literature was over, which meant the end of "New Tendency literature."[66] This mode of literary criticism is significant in that it drew its trajectory not after events had occurred but while or even before the events took place. The changes in the production of literary works did not exactly correspond to their declarations.

To understand what kind of literature Korean proletarian writers expected from themselves and other Korean writers, it is necessary to examine what they meant by the terms "proletarian" and "proletarian literature." In Korea, "the proletariat" was equivalent to "colonized Korean people." Kim Ki-jin explains in "Promenade Sentimental" that "the dispossessed class is not the only proletariat. All the oppressed people throughout the world are the proletariat, like us. There is no national boundary for the proletariat."[67] In this essay, influenced by the Clarté movement and socialism, Kim emphasizes the international solidarity of the proletariat—but what does the term "proletariat" mean for Kim? He broadens the boundary of the proletariat far beyond its common association with factory workers or peasants, so that it refers to all oppressed people. The expression "the proletariat, like us" indicates that Kim, a member of the middle-class elite, considered himself a part of the proletariat, along with all Korean people regardless of the class they belonged to.[68] This way of thinking demonstrates that, for Kim, nation was obviously prioritized over class from the beginning.

In his essay "Seoul's Paupers, Paupers' Seoul," published in June 1924, about a year later, the distinction between the proletariat and the bourgeoisie within Korea is erased:

> Paupers are everywhere we go. . . . They say that the unemployed are two hundred thousand among two hundred eighty thousand in Seoul. . . . The proposition that Seoul will become a city of paupers within only six or seven years is being realized. . . . If so, the current bourgeoisie (*puyu kyegŭp*) will be the proletariat (*pinmin kyegŭp*) six or seven years from now. Paupers! You do not have to hate the current bourgeoisie who will soon belong to the same class as you. When it comes down to it, Seoul belongs to paupers, and in the same sense, Korea belongs to paupers.[69]

Ironically, it is Kim, the proletarian literature writer, who here seeks to persuade the proletariat not to hate the Korean bourgeoisie. Though not directly stated, this passage implies that colonization is the cause of the Korean proletariat's miserable life. It thus promotes the consolidation of the proletarian and bourgeois classes in Korea while insinuating that the ultimate enemy for the Korean proletariat is Japanese imperialism. Pak coined another term, "proletarianized Korea" (*musan-jŏk chosŏn*), when commenting on New Tendency literary works in December 1925.[70]

For both Kim and Pak, it was prerevolutionary Russian literature that served as a model, rather than Bolshevik literature. They explained that Chekhov's Russia—around the 1880s and 1890s—was the era of disillusionment, and argued that Korea had arrived at the same situation as Chekhov's Russia.[71] They also compared Korea to the period of the 1860s and 1870s populist movements in Russia, which Turgenev's novels describe. They thus referred to prerevolutionary nineteenth-century Russia to explain the situation of Korean society.

Pak believed that prerevolutionary Russian literature showed the path that they should take: "Literature accompanies the circumstances where it is placed—whether it is of personal or social thoughts. It is everything about prerevolutionary Russia that shows us [the connectedness of] circumstantial changes, thought, life, and literature."[72] The logic behind this argument is again explained in Pak's memoir published in 1959:

> When life in Korea was so restless, we could not be satisfied with the literature of beautiful dreams. Our skepticism and anxiety grew more serious day by day. Writing itself seemed meaningless. We needed something that could empower our cramped and tired nerves.
>
> We tried to find this something in *Tsarist Russian literature*. Under the Tsarist regime, there was no people's freedom, only hunger and cruelty. Russian literature represented this reality as it was. It mostly described the revolutionaries' lives, wretched people's miserable lives and cries, numerous thinkers' exile in Siberia, and their appeals and ideals about how to live through [their era]. This is the reason we reapprehended our reality (*hyŏnsil-sŏng*) and ideals (*isang-sŏng*) in Russian literature.[73] (Emphasis added)

While comparing Korean society to Russian, Pak effectively utilizes the theme of sleep and awakening, and goes on to explain the contribution of nineteenth-century Russian writers to the revolution:

> Korean people! Do not fall asleep! Look! . . . Look at Russia! Chekhov was very tired. But Turgenev's *Virgin Soil* shook Russia, saying, "Do not sleep! Do not sleep!" Dostoevsky's hero, Raskolnikov of *Crime and Punishment*,

took up an ax and killed the Russia that was falling asleep. Russia thus came to be revolutionized. Korea might be in the middle of a deep sleep.[74]

Infusing life into the fictional characters of Russian works, Pak is asserting the necessity of politically committed literature in leading Korean society toward revolution and liberation.

Not only Pak but Kim promoted prerevolutionary Russian literature:

> There are many people who write short stories and novels. But why is there no one whom we can call "Our dear writer!"? I mourn the absence of such a writer whom this poor, lonesome, and tired people can sincerely call their writer. There are about five Maupassants or Zolas. But there is not a single Gogol. There are some literary critics. But there is not a single Belinsky.[75]

It is not clear why Kim singled out Gogol and Belinsky, though they were both pioneers of Russian critical realism.[76] It may not be a coincidence that they both also critically affected Futabatei Shimei, in terms of his writing style and thoughts on literature. Both Kim and Pak repeatedly invoked prerevolutionary Russian writers and their characters as role models for themselves and for Korean proletarian literature. While explaining historical materialism, Kim went further, to point out that Turgenev and Dostoevsky are close to Marx and Engels.[77] He did not develop his idea, but it is quite obvious that he considered Turgenev and Dostoevsky to be materialists, in the sense that their literary works have a firm grounding in the Russian people's life and reality.

Among nineteenth-century Russian writings, it was Turgenev and his characters who were most often cited and appropriated by both Pak and Kim. Explaining that Turgenev was one of the pioneers who worked for the liberation of the serfs, Pak eulogized the nihilist Bazarov, Turgenev's hero in *Fathers and Sons*, emphasizing that Bazarov's nihilism did not stop at destruction but paved the way for the construction of new era, which, for Pak, was the process Korean society must now undergo.[78]

For Kim, Turgenev was the most inspiring writer. He asserts that Turgenev described Russia's reality more precisely and supplied deeper insight into its social tendencies than did Tolstoy, whom Lenin considered the mirror of Russia. He then asks, "What kind of life did young educated and conscious Russian intellectuals intend to live when they saw their people starving and exhausted under the outrageous aristocrats in Tsarist Russia?"[79] He seeks an answer to this question—which is also one about the role of intellectuals in Korea—through Turgenev's characters, particularly those in *Virgin Soil* and *On the Eve*. Kim's manifesto vis-à-vis Korean proletarian literature is thus full of Turgenev characters. Although he defines himself as a proletarian and declares his intention to be an activist writer in his other essays, discussed above, he admits the limits that intellectuals face and identifies himself with Nezhdanov, Turgenev's tragic and agonized intellectual figure, rather than with Solomin, a solid and practical factory manager of common stock whom Turgenev hinted embodied the future of Russia.[80] Kim also calls for the emergence of a new type of woman, but rather than describing her characteristics, he cites Turgenev's female characters Elena from *On the Eve* and Marianna from *Virgin Soil*, who are more determined and mentally stronger than most of his male characters.[81]

Turgenev's last novel, *Virgin Soil* (*Nov'* in Russian), published in 1877, was a response to Russia's Narodnik movement. It is the most overtly political of his novels but at base describes the failure of radical intellectuals in the movement, who ended up committing suicide or getting arrested. The Narodnik movement was a Russian populist movement that was led by socially conscious members of the Russian intelligentsia during the 1860s and 1870s. Under the call "V Narod" (Going to the people), hundreds of educated Russians left the cities for the countryside to try to enlighten the peasants and generate a mass movement. Despite their self-sacrifice and passion, the result was tragic. In the majority of cases, the peasants were suspicious of and hostile toward these idealists, and in the cases where revolts did occur, these were brutally crushed by the Russian imperial police. The Narodniks and their supporters were imprisoned and persecuted. After this severe repression, the Narodnik group organized an underground party, "The People's Will," and turned toward terrorism, leading to the assassination of Tsar Alexander II in 1881. In Cho Myŏng-hŭi's story "Naktong River," discussed below, after the failure of their resistance to the severe repression of the Japanese imperial police, the hero Sŏng-un's friend despairs and tells Sŏng-un that he will go abroad because there is nothing they can do in Korea apart from terrorism. Sŏng-un's friend's turn to terrorism in the story reflects the real trajectory of the Russian Narodnik movement. As Richard Freeborn accurately points out, the Narodnik (populist) movement had a quasi-religious belief in the peasantry, and its appeal and ideals were "humanistic," "subjective," "utopian," and "more emotional than rational."[82]

Rather than focusing on the failure of the Narodnik movement, Kim Ki-jin accepts this as a process that will pave the way for future success. As we will see in Cho Myŏng-hŭi's translation and appropriation of Turgenev's *On the Eve* (discussed in the next section), Korean intellectuals tended to dismiss Turgenev's ambivalence toward radical intellectuals and his pessimistic view of life. The reason *Virgin Soil* became one of the most recognized novels in Korea, whereas Russian critics paid less attention to it, was its theme of a populist movement that related to the socialist movement in Russia in a broad sense. In tandem with the Clarté movement, the Russian populist movement provided Korean proletarian writers with a role model. Kim's exclamatory remarks on the Narodnik movement demonstrate his belief in it: "Let's move forward, following those Russian intellectuals of sixty years ago, young people of the aristocratic class who cried out *V Narod* and bravely moved forward, dashing toward the spiritual liberation of all mankind in order to construct a valuable life!"[83]

Kim Ki-jin's poem "Paeksu ŭi t'ansik" (The sigh of the man with white hands), published in June 1924, also addresses the theme of the Narodnik movement in Russia and Korea:

Sitting at Café chairs
Being proud of their white arms
Clamoring V Narod!
Russian young men sixty years ago are in front of us . . .
Café Chair Revolutionist, [English in original]
How white your hands are!

Being proud of their white arms
Their lips speak out *V Narod!*
The vain sigh of young Russian men sixty years ago
Is within us.
Café Chair Revolutionist,
How white your hands are!

You are *the man with white hands*—
The peasants you are approaching
Do not have
Even the slightest bit of ambiguous *taste*.
Café Chair Revolutionist,
How white your hands are!

Ah, the past of sixty years ago,
The sigh of Russian young men with white hands
Was the sigh with which they did their best
By killing their taste.
Ah! Café Chair Revolutionist,
How white your hands are![84] (Emphasis in original)

Here, as in his 1923 essay "Ruins of the Heart—Standing in Winter," Kim compares Korean society with the Russia of sixty years before and Korean intellectuals with Russian Narodniks. Kim expresses the intellectuals' agony and limitations, and at the same time declares his belief in the Narodniks' sincerity and self-sacrifice, onto which he then projects himself and Korean intellectuals.

This poem has a connection not only with Russian intellectuals but also with Japanese intellectuals. And in the essay "Broken Pieces," also written in 1923, before he composed "The Sigh of the Man with White Hands," Kim Ki-jin recollects a part of a Japanese writer's poem that impressed him:

The young people who are tired from a long debate sit together.
They look like Russian youth of fifty years ago.
But there is no one who, clenching his teeth and fist and banging the desk,
Cries V NAROD! with a powerful voice.

A Japanese poet wrote a poem like this one ten years ago. After ten years, is Korea standing in a position where it can cry out "V Narod!"? Ah! It is not. "V Narod," which Russian young people clamored for sixty years ago, might still be early for Korea.[85]

The stanza that Kim cites is a part of Japanese poet Ishikawa Takuboku's (1886–1912) poem "Hateshinaki giron no ato" (After endless debates), written in 1911. Kim does not cite Takuboku's poem from a written text but simply paraphrases a single stanza of it. It is thus slightly different from the original poem, though it preserves the content and similar wording. The whole 1911 poem "After Endless Debates" can be translated as follows:

We continue our debate while reading books,
Thus our shining eyes
Are not inferior at all to those of young Russian men fifty years ago.

We debate about what we should do.
But there is no one who, banging the table with his clenched fist,
Stands up crying out *V NAROD!*

We know what we are seeking.
We know, too, what the people want.
Thus, we know what we should do.
Indeed, we know better than young Russian people fifty years ago.
But there is no one who, banging the table with his clenched fist,
Stands up crying out *V NAROD!*

The people who gather here are all young people,
Young people who always make things new to the world.
We know that the old people will be gone first, so we will win in the end.
Look how our eyes shine, and how intense our debate is.
But there is no one who, banging the table with his clenched fist,
Stands up crying out *V NAROD!*

Ah, the candles were already changed three times.
Small dead insects are floating in the teacups.
Although a young woman's passion has not cooled,
The fatigue after the endless debate is in her eyes.
But, still, there is no one who, banging the table with his clenched fist,
Stands up crying out *V NAROD!*[86] (Emphasis in original)

Ishikawa Takuboku lived a short life and, in his last years, started paying attention to socialist ideas and the relationship between literature and society.[87] "After Endless Debates" was written in 1911, after his development toward socialism, and it is obvious from it that he related socialism to the Narodnik movement. Takuboku's poem acknowledges the Japanese intellectuals' sincerity about their role in society but simultaneously points out their indecisiveness and lack of focus and action. Kim's poem, in turn, ridicules Korean intellectuals to some extent and points to the gap between them and the people, by repeatedly referring to the intellectuals' "white hands."

Kim Ki-jin's 1924 poem "The Sigh of the Man with White Hands" may possibly have appropriated Turgenev's prose poem "The Workman and the Man with White Hands—A Dialogue," written in 1878. This prose poem was introduced to Korean readers with Turgenev's other prose poems, and was translated three times during the colonial period:

WORKMAN. Why do you come crawling up to us? What do ye want? You're none of us. . . . Get along!

[THE] MAN WITH WHITE HANDS. I am one of you, comrades!

THE WORKMAN. One of us, indeed! That's a notion! Look at my hands. D'ye see how dirty they are? And they smell of muck, and of pitch— but yours, see, are white. And what do they smell of?

THE MAN WITH WHITE HANDS (*offering his hands*). Smell them.

THE WORKMAN (*sniffing his hands*). That's a queer start. Seems like a smell of iron.

THE MAN WITH WHITE HANDS. Yes; iron it is. For six long years I wore chains on them.

THE WORKMAN. And what was that for, pray?

THE MAN WITH WHITE HANDS. Why, because I worked for your good; tried to set free the oppressed and the ignorant; stirred folks up against your oppressors; resisted the authorities. . . . So they locked me up.

THE WORKMAN. Locked you up, did they? Serve you right for resisting!

Two Years Later

THE SAME WORKMAN TO ANOTHER. I say, Pete. . . . Do you remember, the year before last, a chap with white hands talking to you?

THE OTHER WORKMAN. Yes; . . . what of it?

THE FIRST WORKMAN. They're going to hang him to-day, I heard say; that's the order.

THE SECOND WORKMAN. Did he keep on resisting the authorities?

THE FIRST WORKMAN. He kept on.

THE SECOND WORKMAN. Ah! . . . Now, I say, mate, couldn't we get hold of a bit of the rope they're going to hang him with? They do say, it brings good luck to a house!

THE FIRST WORKMAN. You're right there. We'll have a try for it, mate.[88]

Although Kim appropriated the image of the intellectuals with white hands, his poem differs fundamentally from Turgenev's in terms of its persona's attitude toward radical intellectuals. Whereas Turgenev's shows ambivalence toward the radical intellectuals' involvement in workers' lives, Kim's self-ridicule is not about the intellectuals' action but about their *lack* of action. Kim ultimately shows his belief in Russian intellectuals' sincerity, and the result of their action, and goes on to urge Korean intellectuals to follow Russian intellectuals' path, just as Takuboku's poem exhorts Japanese intellectuals to action. Although Turgenev looked favorably on radical intellectuals, he was always somewhat skeptical about the results of their agitations.[89] The belief that Turgenev fully supported Russian radical intellectuals is therefore an image that Japanese and Korean intellectuals constructed by projecting their desires and hopes onto his literature. In other words, this image of Turgenev was the product of translation in order to create a foreign "other" who would ground their activities.

Translating for the Newspaper: Serialization and the Production of Meaning

In Korea, most of Turgenev's literary works were translated quite early, but nothing equaled the fervor surrounding *On the Eve*. Cho Myŏng-hŭi recalled that Turgenev's *On the Eve* was one of the Western literary works that impressed him most when he started his career as a poet and prose writer. Others included Victor Hugo's *Les Misérables* and Dostoevsky's *Crime and Punishment*, along with Turgenev's novella *Torrents of Spring*.[90] Cho later translated and serialized *On the Eve* in the *Chosŏn Daily* in 1924. Cho's translation provides an interesting example of the institutional and material factors that affect literary translation. Translation is not an activity that occurs simply between the source text and the translator's linguistic and artistic needs, but is embedded within an institutional and material system.

Cho Myŏng-hŭi was born the son of a poor aristocrat (*yangban*) in Chinch'ŏn, Ch'ungch'ŏng Province, in 1894, the year the Kabo Reforms and Sino-Japanese War took place in Korea. He went to Japan to study in 1919, after serving a few months in prison for his involvement in the March First independence movement. He studied Hindu philosophy at Tōyō University (Tōyō Daigaku) in Tokyo from 1919 to 1923. He returned to Korea in early 1923 due to financial problems. At this time, he was immersed in the work of Rabindranath Tagore (1861–1941). He valued meditation in absolute solitude, and his early poems contain mysticism and romanticism. But as he confessed in his essay "A Sketch of My Life," after witnessing the poverty of his family and the Korean people, he began to feel that his pursuit of the metaphysical was meaningless. He soon realized that "life (*saenghwal*) gave birth to thought (*sasang*)," and decided to make a critical turn from "Tagore's neoromanticism" to "Gorky's realism."[91] With this, he started writing short stories. His first proletarian short story, "Ttang sok ŭro" (Into the earth), was written in 1925.

It is worth pointing out that Cho's 1924 translation of Turgenev's *On the Eve* preceded his own short stories of 1925. This precedence of translation practice was true of many Korean intellectuals at the beginning of their careers as writers. Cho joined the founding of KAPF in 1925 and published his historic short story "Naktonggang" (Naktong River) in the journal *Chosŏn chi kwang* (The light of Korea) in July 1927. He continued producing proletarian literature in Korea until his defection to Soviet Russia in 1928. There he lived in different areas, such as Vladivostok and Khabarovsk, having a profound impact on Soviet Korean writers until he was falsely accused of pro-Japanese espionage and executed in 1938.[92]

Because Cho did not know Russian, it is very likely that he translated Turgenev's *On the Eve* from Japanese. There are four Japanese translations that Cho might have referred to for his own translation, and three of these are full and faithful to Turgenev's text. Two were serialized in journals, whereas the other two were published in book form from the beginning. As discussed above, the first Japanese translation of *On the Eve* was serialized in the journal *Yamato nishiki* in 1889, but only part of it was published because the journal was discontinued. Parts of the novel were translated again by Sōma Gyofū and published in irregular installments in journals in 1907–8, and later compiled in book form in 1908. In both these cases of serial publication, each installment followed Turgenev's original chapter divisions, of which there were thirty-five. The Russian novel was not a serialized publication, but the Japanese serializations retained the original Russian chapter segmentation. In Cho's case, however, the novel had to be restructured to fit the format of newspaper serialization: the length of the installments he had to submit was shorter than the original chapters, so his translation had to reorganize the narrative.

The first Korean newspaper, *Hansŏng sunbo* (Seoul thrice-monthly gazette), was published by the Korean government in 1883, to be followed by several privately run newspapers. The first serialization of a novel in a newspaper was in 1898, in the *Hansŏng sinbo* (Seoul newspaper), a newspaper published by a Japanese company.[93] Other newspapers soon followed suit, but most of their serializations were adaptations of foreign literary works, or stories that are hard to distinguish from newspaper reports. After Japan's annexation of Korea in 1910, there was only one newspaper in Korea: the *Maeil sinbo* (Daily News), published by the Japanese Government-General. Serialization continued during this time, with *Mujŏng* (The heartless), recognized as the first modern Korean novel, published in this newspaper in 1917. In 1920, the Japanese colonial policy relaxed slightly and Korean companies were permitted to start publishing their own newspapers. The two major Korean newspapers at that time were the *Tong'a ilbo* (Tong'a Daily) and the *Chosŏn ilbo* (Chosŏn Daily). The *Chosŏn ilbo* carried Cho's translation of *On the Eve*. Newspaper serialization of novels was standard, with about one hundred novels and short stories appearing in newspapers up until 1945.[94]

Serial publication had a few customary limitations. First, each installment was limited in length, usually to about 1,200 characters per installment (about 600 words in English). Second, each installment was supposed to have a suspenseful ending and some dramatic turn: readers had to feel they had gotten their money's worth each time and be curious to read the next installment. Third, newspaper publications generally emphasized dialogue over descriptions of the characters' psychology. Finally, serial novels had simpler and clearer plots than novels published in book form.[95]

Cho Myŏng-hŭi started serializing his translation of *On the Eve* on August 4, 1924, and continued daily installments for seventy-eight days, until October 26, 1924.[96] Unlike serialization of a novel, serialization of a translation must balance constraints from two sides—the source text on the one hand, and publishing norms on the other.

Cho, in this case, intended to remain faithful to the source text as far as was possible, meaning that, ideally, he would not have altered the story at all, either to create a climax or hook at the end of each installment or to make the story easier for the average reader. Thus his translation of Turgenev's novel, when compared to other serialized translations from this period, is relatively unaffected by the medium. Even so, we can see that, whether or not Cho intended it, his translation was restructured by the institution of newspaper publication. Turgenev's *On the Eve* consists of thirty-five chapters, and between each chapter there is a change of scene. But Cho's translation could not follow the original segmentation, and thus his episodes break off in the middle of scenes and conversations. The newspaper assigned about 1,200 characters per day, but in Cho's case there was some flexibility: his segments varied from 1,200 to 1,500 characters, and later from 1,500 to 1,800. Hence Cho did have some degree of agency in constructing intermediate endings through his process of re-editing the novel.

For instance, the first chapter of *On the Eve* is a conversation between two male characters, Shubin and Bersenev, who talk about nature, love, and art, and who introduce and comment on the main characters for the reader. This conversation is one chapter in Turgenev, but five-and-a-half segments in Cho's serialization. In one case, Cho ends a segment with Shubin's question, "Have you met Stakhov?" This question introduces a new character, the heroine Elena's father, and in Turgenev's chapter it is immediately followed by an explanation. But Cho's translation leaves the reader in suspense, and this increases the drama surrounding the introduction of the new character.

More significant, however, is the fact that Cho's first six segments all end with one of Shubin's questions or comments, so that the next segment starts with Bersenev's answer or response. This has the effect of steering the reader's attention to Bersenev's opinions. It implicitly shows the translator's preference for Bersenev's ideas of altruistic love and unification of the people over Shubin's argument for the importance of personal happiness.

In this way, even though Cho did not change Turgenev's plot, he restructured how the text was read by manipulating pauses in the divulgence of information. The most dramatic example of this may be the ending of the fifty-sixth segment, in which Insarov has to leave for Bulgaria and Elena begs him to come to see her one last time before he departs. Insarov does not show up, and Elena goes out to search for him. When she unexpectedly runs into him in a cathedral, she asks in desperation whether he was really going to leave without seeing her. Cho's segment ends there, leaving the reader wondering whether Insarov really loves Elena. In Turgenev's chapter, however, the reader is immediately provided with Insarov's explanation that he loves her but that his private happiness cannot come before his duty to his country. Cho's translation does not allow readers this immediacy but leaves them, in some sense, together with Elena, in despair and anxiety, waiting for Insarov's answer. He did not alter the plot at all yet created a suspense that the source text does not have, simply by cutting the story in a different place. The publication in daily installments thus changed the sensibility with which readers encountered and understood the text.

Cho faithfully translated the first twenty-seven chapters of Turgenev's thirty-five. But from the end of Turgenev's chapter 28, Cho's work suddenly changes: he begins summarizing and editing the text. This was not Cho's decision but resulted from the newspaper deciding to end the serial earlier than planned. After the final episode, Cho included a short note in which he apologized to readers for the abridged translation, attributing it to "a certain situation at the newspaper company."[97]

We do not know what lay behind the decision, though it may have been prompted by the reorganization of newspaper sections. On October 2, 1924, the serialization of another translated novel, *The Power of Love*, ended abruptly with the translator's apology that he had to finish the serialization because of the reorganization of newspaper sections.[98] Ownership of the *Chosŏn ilbo* changed due to financial problems in 1924, and this led to the renovation of newspaper editorial and sectional organization.[99] Whatever the reason for the decision, it drastically affected Cho's translation. To compensate for the lack of time, he summarized the plot from the end of chapter 28 to chapter 31. In these chapters Elena secretly marries Insarov and prepares to leave for Bulgaria with him. Her parents find out and are furious, but later reluctantly accept their daughter's decision. When the time comes, Insarov leaves with Elena for Bulgaria, to serve in his country's war of independence, but dies on the way, in Venice. Elena, however, decides to continue on to Bulgaria, following her husband's path. Cho skipped the scenes about Elena's parents, friends, and other characters but fully translated chapter 32, which describes Elena's painful farewell to her parents and to her country, Russia, as wells as Insarov's purposefulness despite his illness. Cho then omitted chapters 33 and 34, which deal with Insarov's illness and the couple's stay in Venice.

In the final installment, Cho faced the task of translating Turgenev's entire final chapter in a single installment. In his translation, Cho left out much of what happened to minor characters, and also Turgenev's pessimistic musings on human existence and death. What he concentrated on instead was the letter that Elena sends to her parents, explaining her plans to continue on to Bulgaria and fight in the war against the Turks.

Elena's letter is only one-seventh of Turgenev's last chapter, but it makes up more than half of the final newspaper installment of Cho's translation. The letter tells the reader that Elena plans to serve as a nurse in Bulgaria. Within the letter, Cho translates "war" as "war of independence," alluding to the independence movement in colonial Korea. By excluding the parts about Elena's despair and Turgenev's observations about a human being's fate before death, Cho's editing and selective translation succeed in highlighting Elena's determination and sacrifice as an activist, which color the story with a nationalist and socialist emphasis.

Cho's selection of this text, which tells the story of a Bulgarian revolutionary and his follower Elena, reflects his faith that art could be political. Just as important for the form and content of the translation, however, was Cho's decision to publish it in the *Chosŏn ilbo*. As we see in this example, it was not issues of linguistic equivalence and translatability but institutional and material forces governing the venue of publication that most affected the concrete form of the translation. Triggered both by his political preference and by the material condition of the newspaper medium, Cho deliberately minimized apolitical and selfish characters and erased Turgenev's pessimistic notes, while foregrounding the determined and altruistic characters. In doing so, Cho colored his translation with a more positive and progressive perspective than was found in the source text. This prefigures, I would argue, the way in which he appropriated this novel in creating a revolutionary hero and heroine in his proletarian short story "Naktong River."

On the Eve *and "Naktong River"*

A few years after the Korean proletarian literature movement began, its writers sought to produce more politically conscious works. This "first change of direction" (*panghyang chŏnhwan*) was affected by changes in the Korean socialist movement that started in late 1926 with the purpose of channeling workers' spontaneously generated economic struggles into conscious political acts. In the history of Korean proletarian literature, Cho Myŏng-hŭi's "Naktong River" is credited with being the representative work of this period of change. This is a judgment shared both by

Cho's contemporaries and by literary historians in later periods. When the story appeared in 1927, it was at the center of the debate about proper literary works after the so-called change of direction. Kim Ki-jin argued excitedly that Cho's "Naktong River" was unprecedented in the history of Korean proletarian literature, asking rhetorically, "Before this, were there any impressive literary works that showed everything in front of us? It is not an individual's record of life but a true record of Korean people's lives as they have been since 1920."[100] But Cho Chung-gon, a proletarian literary critic, disagreed with Kim, holding that it might be a successful work for the first period but not the second, where works had to express "objective consciousness" (*mokchŏk ŭisik*).[101] Whether or not it is a work of the second period, "Naktong River" is different from the previous proletarian literature in that it deals with class struggle and collective resistance instead of spontaneous acts of vengeance and individual resistance. This is one of the reasons "Naktong River" has survived in the history of Korean proletarian literature.[102]

"Naktong River" is the story of Pak Sŏng-un, an activist, and Rosa, his female comrade and lover. Sŏng-un leaves his hometown because of political oppression and poverty, and returns to Korea after being involved in the independence movement in the Kando area of Northeast China for five years. After returning, he actively leads social movements in his hometown area before he is arrested. The story begins when he is released from prison due to an illness that developed after severe torture, and introduces the protagonists' pasts through several flashbacks. The final scene is Sŏng-un's funeral, after which Rosa leaves to head for a northern area, presumably either China or Russia, to follow Sŏng-un's path.

The protagonists Insarov in Turgenev's *On the Eve* and Sŏng-un in Cho's "Naktong River" are both passionate and patriotic intellectuals. Despite their enthusiasm and passion, they die at an early age from illness—Insarov succumbs to pneumonia and Sŏng-un to torture—before fulfilling their self-avowed missions. Illness is an effective device for interrupting the heroes' dreams, and may have been more realistic in their real historical situations than their heroic success would have been. But their illnesses are also an opportunity to show the reader their unstoppable will and bravery despite their failure, and add a tragic note to the stories that consecrate the heroes. In addition, because their failure is not due to their mental weakness, their spirit can continue through their female successors.

In both stories, the deaths of the heroes are associated with the flow of water. Sŏng-un crosses the Naktong River with Rosa by boat a few days before he dies. Insarov moves along the Grand Canal with Elena by gondola the day before he dies, and his dead body crosses the sea between Venice and Bulgaria the next day. Their acts symbolize a "crossing" from one world to another, and the sea and river stand for the flow that continues eternally, regardless of their deaths. The flow also generates emotional effect by conveying the sorrow of the heroes' early deaths and unfulfilled lives through the image of waves.

Songs also appear prominently around the deaths of both heroes. Sŏng-un sings about the Naktong River and is then joined by everyone singing along with him. In *On the Eve*, Violetta, the heroine of the opera *La Traviata*, which Insarov and Elena watch together the day before Insarov's death, dies from tuberculosis and sings in a song, "O, God! To die so young." These songs parallel the flowing image of water, further dramatizing the two young men's deaths and elevating the overall sentimentalism.

The protagonists' parents in both stories also share similar characteristics. The two heroes' parents suffer from social oppression, and all of them die before their time. Insarov's parents are murdered by Turks before he comes to Russia. Sŏng-un's mother dies in Korea while he is in prison; his father also dies because of poverty. The two heroines' parents have different social statuses—Elena's parents are aristocrats, whereas Rosa's used to be butchers, one of the lowest classes in premodern Korea—but they are alike in being conservative and philistine. Rosa's parents, despite their low social status, are described as similar to petit bourgeoisie. Both Elena's and Rosa's parents disagree with their daughters and severely criticize them, wanting them to continue a comfortable and socially respected life without concerning themselves with their society and other peoples' lives. Completely different from their parents, Elena and Rosa are progressive, independent, and compassionate. Both young women dislike their parents' conservatism and ignorance of the reality of their society, but at the same time they pity them.

The most significant similarity in these stories is the relationship between the heroes and heroines. Although both Elena and Rosa are independent and determined, their lives change drastically and they become more resolute after meeting Insarov and Sŏng-un, respectively. Both stories end with the heroine's pursuit of her lover's path after his

death. Elena leaves for Bulgaria to join the revolution and independence movement. Rosa heads northward, implying she will go to China
or Russia to continue the Korean independence movement from there.
Upon leaving, they each explain their decision and determination to
other people. Elena writes a letter to her parents, which, apart from a
short epilogue, constitutes the end of the story:

> My Dear Parents.—I am saying goodbye to you forever. You will never see
> me again. Dmitri [Insarov] died yesterday. Everything is over for me. Today
> I am setting off with his body to Zara. I will bury him, and what will become
> of me, I don't know. But now I have no country but Dmitri's country. There,
> they are preparing for revolution, they are getting ready for war. I will join
> the Sisters of Mercy; I will tend the sick and the wounded. I don't know what
> will become of me, but even after Dmitri's death, I will be faithful to his
> memory, to the work of his whole life.[103] (Russian, 8:165; English, 286)

"Naktong River" also ends with Rosa's funeral ode at Sŏng-un's funeral
and her leaving for the north:

> There were too many [banners] to count. There is [sic] also this banner in
> verse:
>
>> You used to tell me
>> 'Be a bombshell, exploding, bursting from the lowest class.'
>> Yes. A bombshell I will be.
>> Even when you were dying, you told me,
>> 'Be a bombshell. Truly, I say.'
>> Yes. A bombshell I will be.
>
> He knows [sic] [People knew] without asking that this is [sic] Rosa's
>   streamer.
>
> It is late one morning, the year's first snow drifts down in fitful flurries,
> and a train bound for the north eases out of Tortoise Eddy Station. A
> woman in the passenger coach stares vacantly out the window until the
> train has passed all the open country. It is Rosa. Perhaps she too means to
> tread the path along which her dead lover has gone. But in the end, before
> too long, there will be a day when she too returns to this unforgettable
> land.[104] (Korean, 30–31; English, 31)

Compared to Rosa, who has no hesitation about her future path, Elena
is indecisive about her future life, although she is determined and

passionate. This is so in part because Cho does not describe Rosa's psychology in detail, whereas Turgenev assigns many pages to describing Elena's inner self, by means not only of the narrator's description but also of her diary and letter. Although Cho's creation of the new type of heterosexual relationship of lover-comrade in "Naktong River" resulted from his incorporating the hero and heroine of Turgenev's *On the Eve*, the comradeship between the hero and heroine is more emphasized in "Naktong River." Just as Yŏm Sang-sŏp's protagonists, discussed above, compared themselves to Insarov and Elena, so Korean intellectuals were inspired by *On the Eve* to create a new type of fictional relationship— and to aspire to its possibility in real life. (And as already mentioned, when Kim Ki-jin and Pak Yŏng-hŭi call out in their essays for a new kind of Korean woman, they cite as examples Elena and other female characters in Turgenev's novels.)

Sŏng-un and Insarov differ from each other in terms of their political activities in their home countries. Whereas Insarov dies right before he arrives back in his country, Sŏng-un successfully returns to Korea and tries to run a night school, founds a tenant farmers' union, and leads a resistance movement against landowners' exploitation. But except for a small success in the first year, the movements fail under the severe oppression of the time, and Sŏng-un is tortured into illness. One of the prominent proletarian literary components in "Naktong River" may be the fact that its heroine is from the lowest class. As mentioned above, whereas Elena is a daughter of aristocrats, Rosa is a butcher's daughter. Rosa had another name given to her by her parents, but Sŏng-un renames her after Rosa Luxemburg (1871–1919), a Polish-born Jewish-German Marxist theorist and activist. This naming functions as a symbolic gesture in the story, presenting Rosa as a serious activist. Another difference, in terms of the narration, is that "Naktong River" does not have much description or explanation about other characters due to its short length. Whereas Bersenev and Shubin, and Insarov and Elena's friends and acquaintances describe and comment on the hero and heroine in *On the Eve*, it is the narrator who introduces and remarks on the hero and heroine in "Naktong River."

"Naktong River" has two different kinds of narratives juxtaposed throughout the story. The narrator generally keeps a certain distance, tries to describe nature and people without stepping forward, and conveys characters' words without intervention. But occasionally the narrator cuts into the story and becomes the author's spokesman. This narrator explains the history of class and oppression and contextualizes the current suffering of the people who live around the Naktong River. Although many events occur, quite a few parts of the story are not described but summarized by the omnipresent narrator. Because the story includes a significant amount of statement and explanation, the role of narrator becomes more important than usual. After opening with a description of the Naktong River and an introduction to the song about it that Sŏng-un sang when he first left Korea, the narrator explains the origin of class and inequality and the emergence of socialism in Korea. Before this digressive but important explanation, the narrator cuts the flow of the story by saying, "Now it had become difficult to coax out even one mouthful of milk. They had no recourse but to depart this earth and roam the land. Let us reflect on this plight a moment" (Korean, 17; English, 24). The strategic mingling of these two narrators makes it possible to integrate a novel-length plot into a short story.

"Naktong River" is only seventeen pages long in Cho Myŏng-hŭi's *Complete Works*, and it takes place over only two days—the day of Sŏng-un's discharge and the day of his funeral. But the events that it handles through flashbacks and narrator's explanation cover both the whole past lives of the hero and heroine and the socio-political context of their struggle. The compositional time and space of "Naktong River" are also equivalent to the scale of a novel. Because Cho creates a novel-scale story within the length of a short story, there are disjunctures and narrative leaps, such as abrupt changes of topic, shifts into narrator's direct address, juxtaposition of lyrical and essay-like analytical passages, and sudden changes in the narrator's distance from the reader. One scholar has noticed this mismatch between the form and content of "Naktong River" and pointed out that it is a shortcoming of Cho's story.[105]

If we do not insist on applying the conventions of the modern short story to this work, however, these disjunctures and leaps need not be viewed as shortcomings. Rather, they may be seen as generating a uniquely experimental narrative style. Although the formal consistency and stability of the story line are broken, "Naktong River" tries to give the reader the sense of totality that realist literature ultimately aims for (and that the short story genre is not generally suited to convey). This may be the result, to some extent, of Cho's experimental attempt to translate the plot structure of the novel *On the Eve* into a short story, rather than to write a story with components that fit the short story genre.

It is the song about the Naktong River that, as a literary device, provides Cho's more or less fragmentary narrative with a certain unity. The song describes a sort of utopian past of the people living around the Naktong River—a past that functions as a metonym for Korean soil. It is placed at the beginning of the story and takes up one page out of seventeen. Half of the song is repeated in the middle of the story. In addition to this, a couple of lines of a different song about the Naktong River, which might also be considered part of the first song, appear a bit later. As the title suggests, the Naktong River functions as a focal point of the story. Its continuous flow, along with the recurrent songs about the river, passes around and embraces the ruptures in the description of characters and events.

In the early stages of proletarian literature, writers chose shorter and more accessible forms such as short stories, poems, and plays. Producing novels required time to pass, to allow writers to reach maturity.[106] In Korea it took approximately ten years after the proletarian literary movement started before the first novel appeared.[107] In this context, Cho Myŏng-hŭi's rewriting of Turgenev's novel into a short story is not surprising. In addition, the popularity and prominence of the short story genre in modern Korean literature might partly explain Cho's choice.[108] In translation practice as well, summarized translation was a popular practice during the colonial period, so transforming a foreign novel into a short story was not an exceptional task for Korean writers, as in the example of Yi T'ae-jun's summarized translation of Turgenev's *On the Eve*, mentioned earlier.

Although the heroes of both stories face tragic early deaths, one of the major differences between "Naktong River" and *On the Eve* is the narrator/author's attitude toward the protagonists' fates. Whereas Cho's ending is more or less triumphant despite the hero's death, Turgenev's wraps up *On the Eve* on a pessimistic note:

> However it [the rumor about Elena after she left for Bulgaria] was, all trace of Elena had disappeared beyond recovery for ever; and no one knows whether she is still living, whether she is hidden away somewhere, or whether the petty drama of life is over—the little ferment of her existence is at an end; and she has found death in her turn. It happens at times that a man wakes up and asks himself with involuntary horror, 'Can I be already thirty . . . forty . . . fifty? How is it life has passed so soon? How is it

death has moved up so close?' Death is like a fisher who catches fish in his
net and leaves them for a while in the water; the fish is still swimming but
the net is round him, and the fisher will draw him up—when he thinks
fit. (Russian, 166; English, 288)

This passage clearly shows Turgenev's pessimistic perspective on human
beings' limits before the law of nature. The simile of death as a fisherman
and human beings as fish doomed to be caught fuses Turgenev's fatalism
with Insarov's tragic early death and Elena's unknown future. Cho clearly
departs from this. Even when Cho translated Turgenev's *On the Eve* quite
faithfully, he rendered Elena's whole letter line by line but excluded Turgenev's musings about his characters' fate and death. Though Insarov's
death is quiet and private, Sŏng-un's death generates a festive and collective commemoration, with a long march of many people holding banners
such as "A brave man has gone. But his hot blood still leaps in our breasts,"
and Rosa's inspirational banner, quoted earlier (Korean, 30; English, 31).

As Cho's short story shows, in the process of appropriating and
rewriting nineteenth-century Russian literature, Korean intellectuals'
political commitment was indubitably at work. The act of revisiting
bourgeois literature and refashioning it as proletarian literature may
have been especially effective and prominent in Korea precisely because
its writers associated their own social reality more with prerevolutionary
Russia than with Soviet Russia, which had already differentiated itself
from its own past.

What might Turgenev and nineteenth-century Russian writers have
meant to Korean proletarian writers? Korean proletarian literature is a literature that came into being with the aspiration for the revolution *to
come,* whereas Soviet proletarian literature was built on/with the revolution that had already arrived.[109] In Russia, the literature that embodied
the aspiration for the revolution to come was that of the last few decades
of the nineteenth century—the time when Turgenev's revolutionary characters were molded. If a study discusses Korean proletarian literature
only in relation to Soviet literature and its theories *after* revolution, it cannot properly capture the direction that early Korean proletarian literature pursued.

Korean proletarian literature aimed at a clear break from the literature of the past, as proletarian literatures in other countries did. But while
emphasizing its discontinuity from its own tradition—especially that of

art for art's sake, which itself had a very short history—it was simultaneously constructing a connection with the tradition of nineteenth-century prerevolutionary Russian literature. It is worth noting that because Korea had a relatively short tradition of modern literature (it had been less than ten years since the first modern Korean novel was produced), proletarian literature was less troubled by the necessity of distinguishing itself from existing bourgeois literature. Instead, it paid more attention to creating a legitimate basis for a literary movement by emphasizing the role of engaged literature in nineteenth-century Russia, and by stressing the similarity between prerevolutionary Russian and 1920s Korea.

Unlike in revolutionary Russia, the principal motivation and aspiration of proletarian literature in Korea was based not on its successful revolution or the growth of the working class, but on hope for the advent of social revolution in the near future. As we have seen in Kim Ki-jin's recollections, for instance, Korean writers' belief that revolution was imminent in Japan and Korea ignited their will to change the Korean literary world, and ultimately to alter Korean society. Nineteenth-century Russian literature had played a self-conscious counter-hegemonic role against tsarist tyranny, deliberately engaging with ordinary people's lives and with needed social change. This was the image of Russian literature that attracted Korean intellectuals throughout the colonial period. If the success of the Russian revolution gave Korean socialist writers a future that they could dream of, then it was nineteenth-century Russian literature that showed a possible path through which revolution might come.

In a 2002 article, Ch'oe Wŏn-sik, a renowned scholar of modern Korean literature, argues that Korean proletarian literature was the result of external transplantation of a worldwide movement of left-wing literature. He enumerates three specific features of Korean proletarian literature in its heyday in the 1920s and early 1930s: external transplantation, international synchronism, and the contemporaneity (*hyŏndaesŏng*) that Korean proletarian literature acquired as a result of intensive, self-conscious development. Emphasizing contemporaneity and transplantation, Ch'oe defines Korean proletarian literature as "a revolutionary literature that started and prospered throughout the world under the leadership of the Comintern in the 1920s and the early 1930s."[110]

Ch'oe's definition gives a solid historical grounding to Korean proletarian literature, and effectively conveys its international character in the early twentieth century. But at the same time, it erases the complexities generated by Korea's sociopolitical and cultural context. Despite the influence of the Comintern on the Korean proletarian literary movement in its later stage, 1920s Korean proletarian writers embraced a diverse array of ideas and social movements, particularly Russian nihilism, the French Clarté movement, Russian populism, and an inclusive and eclectic "neo-idealism." They also consciously aligned their era and themselves with nineteenth-century Russia and its realist writers.

Although there seems to be an obvious theoretical contradiction in this alignment, most writers of proletarian literature in colonial Korea, despite their awareness of and belief in socialist international coalition, prioritized the recovery of their national sovereignty and assumed that the revolution that they were waiting for and working toward would always accompany the independence of Korea. For the proletarian writers in colonial Korea, national sovereignty was not a byproduct of revolution but a *motivation* for it. With this prioritization of national independence and their recognition of its resemblance to Russia's pre-revolution reality, Korean proletarian writers sympathized with Russian realists not simply emotionally but logically, as is shown in their manifestos, essays, and fictional writings. Their attachment to and alignment with nineteenth-century Russia may seem anachronistic, but it was in fact colonial Korean writers' emotional and realistic sense of contemporaneity and internationality that Korean proletarian literature pivoted around in the 1920s.

EPILOGUE

Shared Sensibility in East Asia and Imagining Alternative Literary Histories

Russian Literature in Postcolonial Korea

Koreans' interest in Russian literature continued in postliberation (post-1945) Korea. Surges of interest between 1945 and 1950 and in the late 1980s and early 1990s testify to the way that Russian literature proved important to Korean writers and intellectuals during times of rapid social change, while also highlighting the role of cold war politics in discouraging such engagement in the intervening years.[1] The translation of Russian literature in postcolonial South Korea exposes complex interactions among the South Korean government's longstanding anticommunist policy, the lack of institutionalized education in Russian language and literature, and the continuing Korean practice of translating Russian literature from the Japanese.

Trends in translation of Russian literature in postcolonial Korea responded to the vicissitudes of political change in Korea. The first few years between liberation and the Korean War (1945–50) witnessed a resurgence of leftist literature in Korea. Soviet literature was actively translated and translations of Russian/Soviet literature outnumbered those of American literature.[2] However, after the Korean War and the division of Korea, it became almost impossible to publish any Soviet literature in South Korea until the late 1980s when South Korea's military regime ended. South Korea's anticommunist policy was strictly enforced in the 1960s and 1970s and Soviet literature was completely blocked during this period. For instance, in the 1960s, a ten-volume world literature anthology published by the Singu publishing company did not have a section for Soviet literature, and a five-volume Russian literature anthology published by the Munu publishing company did not include any Soviet writers.[3] The situation was same if not worse in the 1970s, but it is noteworthy that the number of translations of Russian literature increased compared to that of 1960s. The increase was primarily a result of a general boom in publishing anthologies in the 1970s, which was possibly caused by Korean industrial and economic growth at the time.[4]

It was in the late 1980s, when South Korea's long-standing military regime ended, that the ban on dissident books was lifted and cultural regulations relaxed. Previously banned Soviet literature started to be translated, and Soviet and East European culture began to be imported. Previously prohibited Korean books also became accessible, which triggered a boom in publishing and researching proletarian literature from the colonial period. The surge in interest in Russian/Soviet literature was matched by initiatives to create departments of Russian language and literature in universities, a trend accelerated by Korea's establishment of diplomatic relations with Russia after the collapse of Soviet Union. There were only three universities that had Russian Department as of the mid-1980s: the first Russian department was founded at the Hankuk University of Foreign Studies in 1954, the second at Korea University in 1974 and the third at Seoul National University in 1984. In the early 1990s, however, about thirty universities created new Russian departments.

This newly established educational infrastructure for Russian language and literature made direct Korean translation from Russian sources possible in a way it had not been before. Up until the late 1980s, translators still relied heavily on relay translation through Japanese translation, although among them there were translators who received higher education in Russian language and literature. In the 1950s and 1960s many prominent writers such as Kim Tong-ni, Hwang Sun-wŏn, and Chu Yo-sŏp who did not know Russian but had a great interest in Russian literature were involved in translating Russian literature. Even translators from the Russian Department of Hankuk University of Foreign Studies, who were the leading translators and professional scholars of Russian literature since 1960s, have been criticized because their translations still significantly utilized Japanese translations.[5] These scholarly translators' continuing use of relay translation from Japanese may seem odd, but

becomes easier to understand when we consider the fact that this generation of translators was educated during the colonial period and were perfectly bilingual in Japanese and Korean.

These translators of Russian literature belong to the generation that
Han Su-yŏng calls "chŏnhu sedae" (postwar generation): the writers who
were born in the 1920s and 1930s received their elementary, secondary,
and college education during the colonial period, and debuted around
the Korean War. This generation was bilingual, yet while they had
command of Japanese in all aspects, they did not learn advanced reading and writing in Korean until Korea was liberated in 1945. Most of
them evidently felt more comfortable with Japanese and read literature in
Japanese.[6] The translators who produced the greatest number of Korean
translations of Russian literature for a few decades after Korea's liberation
were such Russian specialists as Kim Hak-su, Yi Ch'ŏl, Pak Hyŏng-gyu,
and Tong Wan. They were all born in the 1920s and 1930s and had
received their education in Japanese in the colonial period, as did the
"postwar generation" writers. Thus, although they studied Russian language and literature in college, it would have been much easier and effi-
cient for them to read and translate from Japanese, which was often more
familiar to them than their mother tongue.

Japanese mediation thus had a continuous impact on Korean translation and understanding of Russian literature about for eighty years, from
the late 1900s to the late 1980s. The time period extends if we consider
reprints of earlier relay translations from Japanese, which are still being
published. Koreans' introduction of Russian literature during the colonial period, which was prefigured by the Japanese understanding and
translation of Russian literature, still affects the contemporary Korean
production of knowledge about Russian literature. An exceptionally
enthusiastic reception of Tolstoy's novel *Resurrection* by Japanese and
Korean readers in the early twentieth century continues to shape assumptions one hundred years later, although it is not central to the
Tolstoy canon in Russia and elsewhere. Titles of Korean translations
also continue to reveal the history of Japanese mediation. Futabatei
Shimei translated Turgenev's novella "Asya" (1858)—which is the heroine's
name—into Japanese in 1896 under the title "Katakoi" (Unrequited
love). Since the colonial period, Korean translations of the novella have
likewise used the title "Tchaksarang" (Unrequited love). Even Russian
literature specialists such as Yi Ch'ŏl and Kim Hak-su used the title in

their translations, showing how deeply the Japanese colonial legacy is rooted in contemporary Korean translation practice and its culture.

It is often assumed that postcolonial Korea produced direct translations from source texts without further Japanese mediation because there were no active cultural exchanges between Korea and Japan until the 1990s. Japanese mediation, however, permeated Koreans' understanding of Russian literature and its translation, lasting well beyond the agents who first translated Russian literature. Koreans' understanding of Russian literature that had developed during the colonial period significantly affected not only the process of translation but also the deployment of knowledge about Russian literature until very recently. The complicated tripartite configuration through "the regime of translation" mentioned in the introduction, where Korean and Russian literatures are being conceptually articulated while the Korean language was configured vis-à-vis the Japanese language in the context of actual translating practice, holds true for postcolonial Korea.

"A Literature for Life" and Shared Sensibility in East Asia

Korea's engagement with Russian literature in the early twentieth century was one part of an East Asian intellectual community that utilized Russian literature to develop a new literature. Addressing East Asia through the process of its interaction with Russian literature lets us see common cultural denominators in China, Japan, and Korea that do not necessarily surface when we approach East Asian modern literatures vis-à-vis "the West" as modernization is often represented in Western Europe and America.

The process of East Asian interaction with Russian literature highlights the fact that a foreign literature went through layered mediations of various linguistic cultures when it entered the literary world of East Asia. Russian literature was mostly read and translated in East Asia through other Western languages or Japanese. In Japan, many Russian texts were rendered from their English translations (which were themselves translated from French at first), while in China and Korea,

Japanese and English versions of Russian literature often became the source texts for translations.

The case of Russian literature in East Asia provides an extreme example of how general accessibility and proficiency in a foreign language does *not* determine the volume of translation of and the popularity of that literature. It shows that linguistic distance or unfamiliarity between two cultures does not necessarily discourage enthusiastic reception of one culture in the other. Even though many intellectuals hardly knew enough Russian to read or translate Russian texts, Russian literature was the most frequently translated literature in East Asia for a certain period of time and arguably had the greatest intellectual impact of any western literature on Japan, China, and Korea in the late nineteenth and early twentieth century.[7] It is a unique aspect of East Asian modernity that East Asia created an immense field of cultural interest in Russian literature despite the relatively undeveloped infrastructure of language acquisition and related education.

Relatedly, it is noteworthy that each of the three writers of Japan, Korea, and China (Futabatei Shimei, Yi Kwang-su, Lu Xun), who are credited with writing the first modern novel or short story in each culture, had a strong connection with Russian literature in terms of both their literary creation and the directions of their own lives. Futabatei Shimei explained that Russian writers studied the oppression of people as "a human problem" and singled out the expression "sincerely" (*majime-ni*) as a way to describe the way that Russian writers approached the problem of oppression in their literature. He took Turgenev's *A Hunter's Sketches* as an example of a work that influenced the emancipation of the serfs and explained the sacrifices Russian writers made for their literature.[8] Futabatei's view is close to that of Lu Xun, who considered Russian literature a "guide and friend" where he could see "the kindly soul of the oppressed, their sufferings and struggles."[9] It was not coincidence that Yi Kwang-su's life as a writer and his theory of literature incorporated Tolstoy's in many aspects, as discussed in Chapter 1, that the first modern Japanese novel, Futabatei's *Ukigumo*, shows close connections with Russian writers such as Gogol and Turgenev, and that Lu Xun's first modern Chinese story "A Madman's Diary" resembles the title of Gogol's "A Madman's Notes." What these three writers paid primary attention to was not the aesthetic quality or modern-ness of nineteenth-century Russian literature, but the concern with common people and society that it demonstrated. Thus, Russian literature was not merely an "advanced" civilizational technology for East Asian writers to compete with or emulate, but something through and within which they could envision and communicate a shared directionality in the literatures that they were making and would make.

While their aspiration for literature was closely intertwined with their concern with their society and oppressed people, East Asian intellectuals' engagement with Russian literature is also an example of how literature could mold their lives and lived reality. Chapter 2 looks at how translation in early twentieth-century Korea was not a reproduction of "the original" but a productive appropriation through which the translator not only creatively reconstructed the source text but developed new ways of perceiving and reshaping lived reality. In some specific writers' cases, going beyond the perception of their lived reality, literature spelled out the lives they would live and the lives they would ask other people to join. Some writers lived the lives they described in their literature, as we can see in the homology between the Korean writer Cho Myŏng-hŭi and his own characters in "Naktong River," which Cho created through the translation of Russian literature. Cho Myŏng-hŭi, although he was executed in Russia and could not return to Korea in the end, followed in the footsteps of his hero Sŏng-un, who returned to Korea and led a social movement after being involved in the independence movement in Northeast China for five years, as well as in the footsteps of his heroine Rosa, who left for a northern area (Russia or China) after the hero's death. Cho may already have virtually lived the life he would go on to pursue through his own characters and through Turgenev's Insarov and Elena before following his characters' path by leaving for Russia, where he engaged with writing and cultural/political activities for the rest of his life. Similarly, for Chinese writers, "Russian, and then Soviet, literature in China was identified with real life, its fictional characters with living men and women and its authors with teachers."[10] For Chinese intellectual Qian Gurong, Russian literature went beyond a genre and provided a cognitive frame through which he was able to perceive and understand the world around him.[11] When East Asian intellectuals characterized Russian literature using phrases like "literature for life" and cried out for such a literature in their own languages, it may have meant not only the literature that they would produce but also *the literature that, in reverse, they saw producing their own present and future lives.*

As seen in the cases of Futabatei Shimei, Yi Kwang-su, and Lu Xun, Russian literature was promoted as *the* model of their own literature. East Asia shared a blueprint of their modern literature that found its truest reflection in their image and understanding of Russian literature. It was the phrase "literature for life" that not only crystalized East Asian intellectuals' perception of Russian literature but also epitomized their own desire for a new form of literature for a turbulent era. The specific expression "literature for life" was used not only in Korea but also in China. Chinese intellectuals believed that Russian literature endorsed a "literature of man" and "literature for life," which entailed "portraying the oppressed and struggling to achieve a better future for them."[12] Fundamentally East Asian intellectuals saw Russian literature as something that realized humanism through the writer's own life and writing.

The image of Russian literature and writers that East Asian intellectuals built did not necessarily correspond to reality, a clear example being their understanding of Dostoevky as a representative humanist writer. In reality, Dostoevsky was an imperialist and typical orientalist, as we can see in his essay "Geok-Tepe. What is Asia to us?," in which the conquered Asians (Siberia and Central Asia) constitute for him, "an indispensable element in the overall picture of Russian glory."[13] East Asian intellectuals, however, fashioned their ideals in a careful selection of foreign materials, as well as the occasional outright fabrication. They viewed Dostoevsky, despite the evidence, as a humanist who was sympathetic to people of the lower classes and who embraced the thoughts and lives of the oppressed through his literature—by extension, as sympathetic to them. East Asian writers projected the image of the literature they *desired* onto that of Russian literature, which they constructed to fit their purpose.

As recent studies on the relationship between Russia and East Asia show, it is problematic to consider Russia a seamless part of the West in relation to Asia.[14] First, from the Russian side, a historically and culturally complex identity vis-à-vis Western Europe combined with its geographical and ethnic proximity to Asia complicated Russia's own approach to Asia. Meanwhile, East Asia saw Russia as a Western culture—but a Western culture that was familiar to Asia and had some distance from Western European cultures in its geographical proximity and racial proximity to Asia and in its position as one of the late comers in modernization. East Asian intellectuals perceived Russia as an alternative to Western modernity, as is obvious in the example of Russian-Japanese anarchist community in nineteenth- and early twentieth-century Japan.[15] Lu Xun and Zheng Zhenduo in China also considered Russian litera- ture as "an acceptable alternative to 'the West.' "[16]

Incorporating Russia as a comprehensive explanatory tool for East Asian literature helps us elucidate those shared desires for social justice as well as an awareness of choices and alternatives available even amid the tumult of modernization. This perspective does not emerge as read- ily when we approach the impact of Western European and American literature on East Asian literature, nor even when we consider the con- nections between Russia and one or another single East Asian culture. Although literature in twenty-first-century East Asia seems to exist as only one among many forms of art and mass-mediated culture, the shared hu- manist view of literature in modern East Asia—which was imagined and concretized through dialogue with Russian literature, and was crys- talized in the expression "literature for life"—reminds us that literatures in East Asia in particular were born and constructed as a critique of anti- humanist oppression and as a desire for creating a better society.

Translation and Imagining Alternative Literary Histories

By exploring Korean intellectuals' translation and appropriation of Rus- sian literature in the formative period of modern Korean literature, this book ultimately seeks to restore translation as a critical medium generat- ing new value and change in society and as a methodology that allows us to better understand literature as a process with inherent intercultural aspects, in the sense that questions of translation extend to literary writ- ing in general. Most national literary histories treat translation practice teleologically, so that early translation practices such as summaries and adaptive translations are taken to be unsatisfactory or incomplete. For- mation thus becomes viewed as a transitional phase that is overcome in the development of a more exclusive and homogenous national litera- ture. In a similar way, various hybrid forms of writing—for instance, newspaper reports with fictional elements and fragmented narratives— have often been debased as transitional genres doomed to extinguish themselves when more "sophisticated and original" forms of fiction began to appear. But these seemingly transitional and immature hybrid practices, both in translation and modern literary writing, were fully creative and authentic forms of writing, constructively engaging with each other.

Rethinking this forgotten aspect of Korean history lets us approach convoluted and diverse literary practices within and across linguistic and cultural boundaries. It also allows us to reconsider the cognitive and institutional marginalization of translation as a modern cultural product, which is reconfirmed and fortified by legal and customary regulations, publication practices, and histories of national literatures. Our awareness of this history can help us affirm the creativity and enabling force of translation and the possibilities that translation provides. While revealing the complex junctures of cultural translation, this book hopes to rectify the view that essentializes the derivativeness and inferiority of translated modernity that inevitably and profoundly involves translation practice in its historical trajectory.

Understanding the relationship between translation and the formation of modern literature provides us with a way of going beyond the developmental model of the literatures of nation-states, since it entails acknowledging the interaction between, and flow of, literatures from different cultures. It also shows the profound significance of translation, not only as an act of rendering but as a venue that discloses conflicts, struggles, and shared sensibility among cultural agents, and that in the process reveals sociohistorical contingencies and unexpected cultural forces that go beyond these agents' control and choice. This complexity and relationality are the aspects that we must not miss if we are to imagine a different type of literary history, one that is more open to others, and thus begin to write about a collective connectedness among literatures that is not based on the exclusivity of teleological national literary history or reiterating the inevitable imbalances and blind spots of world literature canons. I hope that *Translation's Forgotten History* is a small step toward imagining and writing these new types of literary history.

Notes

Introduction

1. Anderson, *Imagined Communities*, 42.
2. Ibid., 42–43.
3. Ibid., 44.
4. Karatani, "Nationalism and Écriture," 17–18.
5. For the relationship between translation and the *genbun-itchi* (literally, "unification of spoken and written languages"; *ŏnmun ilch'i* in Korean) movement in Japan, see Levy, *Sirens of the Western Shore*, 38–39.
6. Sakai, *Translation and Subjectivity*, 2.
7. Anderson, *Imagined Communities*, 22–31.
8. Moretti, "Conjectures on World Literature," 54.
9. Ibid., 55–56.
10. Jameson, "Foreword: In the Mirror of Alternate Modernities," xiii.
11. Moretti, "Conjectures on World Literature," 58.
12. Ibid., 60–61. One of the problems with this article, which has been raised by other scholars, is Moretti's argument that the English, French, and Spanish novel experienced "autonomous development," which was an exception in the development history of the novel. Jonathan Arac refutes this in his article "Anglo-Globalism?" and Moretti acknowledges that there is no "autonomous development" in Western Europe in his later article "More Conjectures." Moretti's core-periphery model thus becomes weak, but his idea that the novel form develops through a process of compromise becomes universally true, encompassing all Western European countries. For more details, see Arac, "Anglo-Globalism?" 38; Moretti, "More Conjectures," 78–80. Nevertheless, literary scholars still consider Moretti's diffusionist model problematic because it affirms a Eurocentric perspective and ignores the relations among the "peripheries." For more discussion on Moretti and world literature theories, see Chapter 2.
13. Moretti, "Conjectures on World Literature," 64–65.
14. Liu, *Translingual Practice*, 26.
15. Sakai, *Translation and Subjectivity*, 15.

16. Ibid., 22.

17. The ground-breaking example is Kim Yun-sik and Kim Hyŏn, *Han'guk munhaksa*. Later scholars have been rethinking this dichotomous view on Korean literary history, and Kim Yun-sik himself changed his course in the 1990s. Ch'oe Wŏn-sik, who was also a member of the group of scholars promoting the theory of autonomous development, argued that the surge in nationalist investments in literary history resulted from a "neurotic repulsion toward influence" in a short 1993 article. He suggested that scholars try to liberate themselves from this neurotic repulsion and move "beyond the theory of transplantation" and "the theory of autonomous development" (Ch'oe Wŏn-sik, "Isingnon kwa naejaejŏk palchŏnnon ŭl nŏmŏsŏ," 406–7).

18. Ku Chung-sŏ, "Munhaksa wa kŭndaesŏng, kŭndae kichŏm."

19. Bassnett and Lefevere, *Translation, History and Culture*, 24.

20. Liu, *Translingual Practice*, xix.

21. Ibid.

22. Benjamin, *Illuminations*, 71.

23. Ibid., 79.

24. Qian, *Wanqing xiaoshuo shi*, 1; quoted in Liu, *Translingual Practice*, 26.

25. Venuti, ed., *The Translation Studies Reader*, 14.

26. Robinson, *Translation and Empire*, 52.

27. For more detailed explanation about how the term "literature" (*munhak*) was defined as a translated word, see Chapter 1.

28. Wallerstein, *Historical Capitalism with Capitalist Civilization*, 24.

29. Ibid., 24–25.

30. Venuti demonstrates in detail how translation is stigmatized and discouraged by the concept of authorship and copyright law in particular in America and England. For more details, see Venuti, *The Scandals of Translation* and *The Translator's Invisibility*.

31. Watt, *The Rise of the Novel*, 14.

32. Woodmansee, "The Genius and the Copyright: Economic and Legal Conditions of the Emergence of the 'Author,'" 426.

33. Bassnett, *Translation Studies*, 11.

34. Ibid.

35. Venuti, ed., *The Translation Studies Reader*, 221. Bassnett's book has been consistently reprinted in 1980, 1991, and 2002.

36. The series starts with Bassnett and Lefevere's *Translation, History and Culture*, published in 1990.

37. Bassnett and Lefevere, eds., *Translation, History and Culture*, preface.

38. Ibid.

39. For polysystem theory, see Even-Zohar, "Polysystem Theory," 237–310; and its revised version, Even-Zohar, *Polysystem Studies*.

40. Robinson, *Translation and Empire*, 12.

41. Kim Pyŏng-ch'ŏl, *Han'guk kŭndae pŏnyŏk munhaksa yŏn'gu*.

42. Kokuritsu, *Meiji, Taishō, Shōwa hon'yaku bungaku mokuroku*.

43. It is symptomatic that Kim Pyŏng-chŏl includes non–Western European writers such as the Indian poet Tagore and the Norwegian writer Ibsen but excludes the translation of Chinese and Japanese literature from his consideration.

44. Kim Pyŏng-ch'ŏl, *Han'guk kŭndae pŏnyŏk munhaksa yŏn'gu*, 302.

45. For a detailed example, see Bassnett and Lefevere, "Introduction: Proust's Grandmother and the Thousand and One Nights," in *Translation, History and Culture*, 1–13.

46. Kim Pyŏng-ch'ŏl's study also has minor problems. First, when calculating the number of translations, in some cases he counts both a short story and an anthology of short stories as a single instance. Second, he also includes a performance of a foreign play as a translation, though it is not the translation itself of a foreign play. Third, he often concludes that there is a connection to a particular Japanese translation without giving any persuasive reason. Fourth, when he tries to demonstrate the immaturity and unfaithfulness of a translation from the colonial period, he often uses the more recently published Korean translation of the same foreign text. There is no evidence that the more recent translation is better and thus can be a criterion for judging the previously published translation.

47. Kim Young-hee, "Conditions of Literary Translation in Korea," 239. It is unclear what she means by the "texts [translations] that stand as literary works on their own" and how she would distinguish the literariness of the specific recommendable translations from other translations, but I will not discuss these issues further here.

48. Ibid., 245.

49. Ibid., 245–46.

50. Spivak, "The Politics of Translation," 371.

51. Ibid., 371–72.

52. Berman, *The Experiencing of the Foreign*, 87–91.

53. Venuti, *The Translator's Invisibility*, 16.

54. Cho Hŭi-ung, "Naksŏnjae-bon pŏnyŏk sosŏl yŏn'gu," 258.

55. Min Kwan-dong, "Chungguk kojŏn sosŏl ŭi kungnae pŏnyŏksa yŏn'gu," 516–17.

56. Ibid., 516.

57. Ibid., 537.

58. Yi Hyŏn-hŭi et al., *Kŭndae han'gugŏ sigi ŭi ŏnŏgwan, munchagwan yŏn'gu*, 55.

59. Ibid., 72–73. For more details, see Chapter 1 (Introduction) and Chapter 4 of Yi Hyŏn-hŭi et al., *Kundae han'gugŏ sigi ŭi ŏnŏgwan, munchagwan yŏngu*.

60. Ch'oe T'ae-wŏn, "Iljae Cho Chung-hwan ŭi pŏnan sosŏl yŏn'gu," 12.

61. *Maeil sinbo*, October 29, 1914. For more details on Yi Sang-hyŏp's practice of translation, see Heekyoung Cho, "Imagined, Transcultural, and Colonial Spaces in Print," 153–83.

62. Miller, *Adaptations of Western Literature in Meiji Japan*, 4.

63. Ibid., 12–13. When Miller says "Meiji period," he more precisely refers to the last three decades of the nineteenth century; he compares adaptations by three Meiji writers: comic fiction writer Kanagaki Robun (1829–94), professional storyteller San'yōtei Enchō (1839–1900), and dramaturge Tsubouchi Shōyō (1859–1935).

64. For more details on Korean intellectuals' dilemma after the Japanese annexation of Korea, see Schmid, *Korea between Empires 1895–1919*.

65. *Taehan maeil sinbo*, July 9, 1909.

66. Yi Ik-sang, "Yesulchŏk yangsim i kyŏryŏhan uri mundan," 106.

67. In this essay, Yi Kwang-su criticizes Korean writers' decadent lifestyle and argues this lifestyle came from Japan. Yi Kwang-su, "Munsa wa suyang" (A writer and self-cultivation), in *Yi Kwang-su chŏnjip*, 10:355.

68. Yi Ik-sang, "Yesulchŏk yangsim i kyŏryŏhan uri mundan," 112.

69. Kim Tong-in, "Munhak kwa na" (Literature and I), in *Kim Tong-in chŏnjip*, 8:390–91.

70. Kim Tong-in, "Munhak ch'ulbal" (The start of my literary career), in *Kim Tong-in chŏnjip* 8:394–95.

71. Yi Kwang-su's Japanese short story "Ai ka" (Is it love?) was written in 1909. For Kim Tong-in's case, see Kim Tong-in, "Munhak kwa na," in *Kim Tong-in chŏnjip*, 8:392–93.

72. Pak Yŏng-hŭi, "Chayŏnjuŭi esŏ sin-isangjuŭi e kiurŏjinŭn chosŏn mundan ŭi ch'oesin kyŏnghyang" (A recent tendency in the Korean literary world that moves from naturalism to new-idealism), *Pak Yŏng-hŭi chŏnjip*, 3:19–22. Korean intellectuals never actively acknowledged Japanese literature as their model, although some of them referred to Japanese writers' names and their fictional and nonfictional works in their essays. For example, Yi Kwang-su lists Japanese references on literature that he recommends to future writers in his article "Munhak e ttŭt ŭl tunŭn i ege" (p. 3), but he never promoted Japanese literature as one of the models that Korean literature should follow despite its great impact on his own and other Korean writers' work in many aspects.

73. Koreans' active use of Japanese literature and the close literary connections among Japan, China, Korea, and Taiwan are well demonstrated in Thornber's *Empire of Texts in Motion*.

74. Kim Pyŏng-ch'ŏl, *Han'guk kŭndae pŏnyŏk munhaksa yŏn'gu*, 307, 369. After the 1920s, the number of translations rapidly increased, so Kim does not have statistics.

75. The late Qing practice of translation in China was also roughly defined, encompassing "paraphrasing, rewriting, truncating, translation relays, and restyling" (Wang, "Translating Modernity," 303). The translators conceived of their own translations as distinct from the "original" texts, in order to make them serve their ideological goals, and the unintended mistranslations and intended distortions engendered unpremeditated alternative aspects of modern literature. For specific case studies, see Wang, "Translating Modernity," 303–29.

76. Kim Pyŏng-ch'ŏl, *Han'guk kŭndae pŏnyŏk munhaksa yŏn'gu*, 308.

77. For the distinctions between adaptation and appropriation, see "Introduction" and "Part I" in Sanders, *Adaptation and Appropriation*, 1–41. "Adaptations and appropriations can vary in how explicitly they state their intertextual purpose. Many of the film, television, or theatre adaptations of canonical works of literature that we look at in this volume openly declare themselves as an interpretation or re-reading of a canonical precursor. Sometimes this will involve a director's personal vision, and it may or may not involve cultural relocation or updating of some form; sometimes this reinterpretative act will also involve the movement into a new generic mode or context. In appropriations the intertextual relationship may be less explicit, more embedded, but what is often inescapable is the fact that a political or ethical commitment shapes a writer's, director's, or performer's decision to re-interpret a source text" (ibid., p. 2).

78. For more about the relationship between translation and the formation of modern Japanese literature, see Levy, *Sirens of the Western Shore*, 28–33. She explains that the history of modern Japanese literature started with translation in three aspects. First, *bungaku*, the Japanese term for "literature," gained a new meaning as it took on the nineteenth-century European concept of literature. Second, Niwa Jun'ichirō's translation in *kanbun-kuzushi* style, a Japanese modification of literary Chinese, helped establish an

educated, elite audience for the genre of the novel. Third, Futabatei Shimei's translating predated his novel-writing, and his successful employment of *genbun-itchi* style, practiced through the process of translation first, became the foundation of the modern Japanese novel. For the role of translation in the formation of modern Japanese identities, see Levy, ed., *Translation in Modern Japan.*

79. Pak Chin-yŏng, "Han'guk ŭi kŭndae pŏnyŏk mit pŏnan sosŏlsa yŏn'gu"; Ch'oe T'ae-wŏn, "Iljae Cho Chung-hwan ŭi pŏnan sosŏl yŏn'gu"; and Heekyoung Cho, "Literary Translation and Appropriation." Pak's dissertation was published as a book in 2011. (Pak Chin-yŏng, *Pŏnyŏk kwa pŏnan ŭi sidae*). Chŏn Ŭn-gyŏng's dissertation also deals with adaptive translations published in the 1910s but it is fundamentally a study of the readership of that period. (Chŏn Ŭn-gyŏng, "1910-nyŏndae pŏnan sosŏl yŏn'gu.") A part of Yi Hŭi-jŏng's dissertation on novels published in the colonial government bulletin, *Maeil sinbo,* in the 1910s also discusses translated novels in relation to colonial policies and discourse. (Yi Hŭi-jŏng, "1910-nyŏndae *Maeil sinbo* sojae sosŏl yŏn'gu.")

80. There are also some significant studies in English that pay attention to translation in a broad sense, although their main topic is not the role of translation in the formation of modern literature. For East Asian literary contact and interactions in the Japanese Empire, see Thornber, *Empire of Texts in Motion.* For the relationship of translation to colonial and national discourses, see Suh, *Treacherous Translation.*

81. There were 89 total translations from Western literature during the 1910s, compared with 671 in the 1920s. (Kim Pyŏng-ch'ŏl, *Han'guk kŭndae pŏnyŏk munhaksa yŏn'gu,* 414). In the 1920s, 81 Russian, 78 French, 55 English, 24 American, and 23 German literary works were translated. Of the 81 Russian works, 23 were Chekhov's short stories and plays. For details, see Kim Pyŏng-ch'ŏl, *Han'guk kŭndae sŏyang munhak iipsa yŏn'gu,* 188–712.

82. Yi Hyo-sŏk "Na ŭi suŏp sidae" (My literary experience), in *Yi Hyo-sŏk chŏnjip,* 7:156–57.

83. Russian language education is discussed in detail later in this introduction.

84. Ng, *The Russian Hero in Modern Chinese Fiction,* 7.

85. For the reception of Russian literature in European countries, see May, *The Translator in the Text,* 11–55.

86. Ng, *The Russian Hero in Modern Chinese Fiction,* 4.

87. For Lu Xun's discussion on the Chinese national character, see Liu, *Translingual Practice,* 45–76; and Yi Kwang-su, "Munhak ŭi kach'i" (The value of literature) in *Yi Kwangsu chŏnjip,* 1:545–46.

88. Il So, "Tuong," 39.

89. Ng, *The Russian Hero in Modern Chinese Fiction,* 4–5.

90. Lu Hsun [Lu Xun], "China's Debt to Russian Literature," in *Selected Works of Lu Hsun,* 3:181.

91. Chu Yo-sŏp "Nosŏa ŭi tae munho Ch'eekhopŭ," 88; Kim Ki-jin, *Kim P'al-bong munhak chŏnjip,* 4:341; Pak Yŏng-hŭi, *Pak Yŏng-hŭi chŏnjip,* 3:24; An Hwak, "Segye munhakkwan," 41.

92. Il So, "Tuong," 39.

93. Kim Myŏng-sik, "Nosŏa ŭi san munhak" (A living literature of Russia), *Sinsaenghwal,* no. 1:3 (April 1922): 5–6; quoted in Kim Pyŏng-ch'ŏl, *Han'guk kŭndae sŏyang munhak iipsa yŏn'gu,* 607–8.

94. Mochizuki Tetsuo, "Japanese Perceptions of Russian Literature in the Meiji and Taishō Eras," in Rimer, ed., *A Hidden Fire*, 17.

95. Berton and Langer, "The Russian Impact on Japan: Supplementary Illustrative Data by Peter Berton and Paul F. Langer," in *The Russian Impact on Japan: Literature and Social Thought*, 112.

96. Hŏ Tong-hyŏn, "Kaehwa ilche-gi han'guk-in ŭi rŏsia insik e poinŭn kojŏng kwannyŏm," 31–57.

97. Im Hwa may have taken this position because he was one of the prominent proletarian literary critics/writers who had close interaction with Japanese intellectuals pursuing international cooperation. Im Hwa, "Chosŏn munhak yŏn'gu ŭi il kwaje," 378–79.

98. Pak Kwang-hyŏn, "Kyŏnggye rŭl nŏmŏsŏn hwahae ŭi sidae," 205–6.

99. Kim Pyŏng-ch'ŏl, *Han'guk kŭndae pŏnyŏk munhaksa yŏn'gu*, 537–38.

100. For the statistics, see Ŏm Sun-ch'ŏn, "Han'guk eso ŭi rŏsia munhak pŏnyŏk hyŏnhwang chosa mit punsŏk," 258–60.

101. May, *The Translator in the Text*, 19.

102. Berton, Langer, and Swearington, *Japanese Training and Research in the Russian Field*, 5.

103. Ibid., 4–8.

104. Ibid., 11, 18.

105. Araya Keizaburō, "Nihon ni okeru rosia bungakku" (Russian literature in Japan), in Mitsuharu et al., eds., *Ōbei sakka to nihon kindai bungaku*, 3:12.

106. Ibid., 12.

107. Berton, Langer, and Swearington, *Japanese Training and Research in the Russian Field*, 19.

108. Naganawa Mitsuo, "The Japanese Orthodox Church in the Meiji Era," in Rimer, *A Hidden Fire*, 161–62.

109. For Nobori Shomu's explanation about Father Nikolai and Russian-language education in Orthodox Theological Seminary, see Nobori, "Nikorai dai-shukyō no shōgai to gyōseki," 103–26.

110. Nihon Rosia Bungakkukai, ed., *Nihonjin to rosiago: rosiago kyōiku no rekishi*, 39–40.

111. Berton, Langer, and Swearington, *Japanese Training and Research in the Russian Field*, 13–15; Nihon Rosia Bungakkukai, ed., *Nihonjin to rosiago*, 42–44.

112. The reason the school was suddenly closed is not known. It might have been due to financial considerations or Mori's doubt about the school's usefulness. Berton, Langer, and Swearington, *Japanese Training and Research in the Russian Field*, 15.

113. Nihon Rosia Bungakkukai, ed., *Nihonjin to rosiago*, 73.

114. Berton, Langer, and Swearington, *Japanese Training and Research in the Russian Field*, 27. For more about Futabatei Shimei and the Russian Department of the Tokyo School of Foreign Languages, see Chapter 1 in *Japan's First Modern Novel: Ukigumo of Futabatei Shimei*, translation and critical commentary by Marleigh Grayer Ryan.

115. Berton, Langer, and Swearington, *Japanese Training and Research in the Russian Field*, 40.

116. Nihon Rosia Bungakkukai, ed., *Nihonjin to rosiago*, 107.

117. Ibid., 106. For a detailed history and curriculum of the Russian Department of Waseda University, see Chapter 3 in Waseda Daigaku Daigaku-shi Henshūjo, ed., *Waseda daigaku hyaku-nen shi bekkan 1*.

118. Yi Kwang-rin, *Han'guk kaehwasa yŏn'gu*, 163–76. For N. N. Biriukov and the Russian-language school, see Pak Chong-hyo, "Kwallip aŏ hakkyo sŏllip kwa piryukop'ŭ ŭi hwaltong (1896–1916)," 7–26.

119. Kim Pyŏng-ch'ŏl, *Han'guk kŭndae pŏnyŏk munhaksa yŏn'gu*, 494.

120. Chin Hak-mun translated Chekhov's "Album" (Sajin ch'ŏp) (*Ch'ŏngch'un*, no. 2, 1916), Gorky's "Chelkash" (Ch'erŭkatsyu) (*Tong'a Daily*, August 2–September 16, 1922), Turgenev's prose poem "A Laborer and a Person with White Hands" (Nodongja wa son hŭin saram) (*Kongje*, no. 1:1, Sept. 1920), and so forth.

121. Yasuda Yasuo, "Tsurugenefu" (Turgenev), in Fukuda, Kenmochi, and Kodama, eds., *Ōbei sakka to nihon kindai bungaku*, 3:75.

122. Quoted in Yanagi Tomiko, "Chehofu: meiji taishō no shōkai, hon'yaku o tsūshin ni," in Hukuda et al., eds., *Ōbei sakka to nihon kindai bungaku*, 100.

123. For more about the reception of Turgenev in Japan and Korea, see Chapter 3.

124. For a detailed explanation, see Chapter 1.

125. For more about the reception of Tolstoy as humanist in Japan and Korea, see Chapter 1. For Dostoevsky in Korea, see Yi Sang-hwa, "Tokhuingsang"; and I. K. P., "Ttŏsŭt'ŏep'ŭsŭk'i," 55, 57.

126. May, *The Translator in the Text*, 22–23.

127. For a detailed explanation of the introduction of Turgenev in Japan and Korea, see Chapter 3.

128. May, *The Translator in the Text*, 15, 29.

129. Lefevere, *Translation, Rewriting, and the Manipulation of Literary Fame*, 5. Lefevere's "rewriting" means "the translation, editing, and anthologization of texts, the compilation of literary histories and reference works, and the production of criticism . . . mostly in the guise of biographies and book reviews" (ibid., 4).

130. For a detailed explanation, see Chapter 3.

131. Tolstoy, Chekhov, and Turgenev were the three most often translated Russian writers in Meiji and Taishō Japan, and in colonial Korea. Between 1868 and 1926 in Japan, Tolstoy was translated 783 times, Chekhov 232 times, and Turgenev 167 times (not counting his poems), Gorky 160 times, and Dostoevsky 114 times. Kokuritsu Kokkai Toshokan, ed., *Meiji, Taishō, Shōwa hon'yaku bungaku mokuroku*. Between 1909 and 1929 in Korea, Tolstoy was translated 52 times (including eight essays), Chekhov 32 times, Turgenev's prose 20 times, Gorky 16 times (including five essays), and Dostoevsky 4 times. This is based on data I compiled by expanding and editing the information in Kim Pyŏng-ch'ŏl, *Han'guk kŭndae pŏnyŏk munhaksa yŏn'gu*.

1. Manipulation of Fame and Anxiety

1. Yi Kwang-su, "Munhak iran hao" (What is literature?), *Maeil sinbo* (November 10–23, 1916), reprinted in *Yi Kwang-su chŏnjip*, 1:547. All text translations are by author unless otherwise specified.

2. The Korean idea of *munhak* up until that time was significantly affected by that of *wenxue* (literature) in Chinese. *Wenxue* meant both writing and erudition until the

Zhou and Qin dynasties; *wen* (*mun*; writing) and *xue* (*hak*; study) were not differentiated from each other. *Wen* and *xue* were separated only during the Han Dynasty, and *wenxue* and *wenzhang* (*munjang* in Korean) were used to refer to scholarship and aesthetic writing, respectively. In the Song Dynasty, *wenxue* was articulated under the strong influence of Confucian ideas and it denoted writing that would convey the Way. Chosŏn Korea shared this idea of literature, so this concept of *munhak* continued to be dominant throughout the Chosŏn Dynasty. In the meantime, despite the spread of novels, starting in the seventeenth century, novels were considered merely entertainment until the end of nineteenth century when ideas and perceptions of *munhak* in Korea changed dramatically. It was against this backdrop that Yi Kwang-su tried to enunciate his concept of *munhak* as a translation. For further explanation of how the concept of literature developed and functioned in Korea, see Kim Tong-sik, *Han'guk ŭi kŭndae chŏk munhak kaenyŏm hyŏngsŏng kwajŏng*, 54–60; and Hwang Chong-yŏn, "Munhak iranŭn yŏgŏ," 458–59. For more about the concept and use of *mun* (writing) in the 1900s, see Kwŏn Podŭrae, *Han'guk kŭndae sosŏl ŭi kiwŏn*, 79–101.

3. For more details, see Kim Pyŏng-ch'ŏl, *Han'guk kŭndae sŏyang munhak iipsa yŏn'gu*; and Kim Pyŏng-ch'ŏl, *Han'guk kŭndae pŏnyŏk munhaksa yŏn'gu*.

4. For more about the reception of Turgenev in Japan and Korea, see Chapter 3.

5. Hong Il-sik, "Yukdang ŭi saeng'ae wa munhak," II-17. The *chung'in* class is discussed in more detail later in this chapter.

6. Ibid., II-18.

7. Ibid., II-20.

8. Kim Yun-sik, *Yi Kwang-su wa kŭ ŭi sidae*, 1:151.

9. Shirakawa, "Kan, nichi, chū sangoku bunjin no ryūgaku taiken-kō," 138–39.

10. Hong Il-sik, "Yuktang ŭi saeng'ae wa munhak," II-21.

11. Ibid., II-22–23.

12. Shirakawa, "Kan, nichi, chū sangoku bunjin no ryūgaku taiken-kō," 142–43.

13. Yanagi, *Torusutoi to nihon*, 10–11; Nobori Shomu, "Russian Literature and Japanese Literature," in Nobori and Akamatsu, *The Russian Impact on Japan: Literature and Social Thought*, 22–23, 34–35.

14. This was part of the series "Twelve Great Writers of the World" (*Senkai jūni bungō*), published by *Min'yūsha* in 1897. Nobori Shomu, "Russian Literature and Japanese Literature," 35.

15. Its Russian title is *"Odumaites!"* Because of its antiwar content, the article could not be published in Russia. It was published in 1906 and 1911, but both of these runs were seized. David Wells, "The Russo-Japanese War in Russian Literature," in Wells and Wilson, eds., *The Russo-Japanese War in Cultural Perspective, 1904–05*, 123, 132.

16. Sandra Wilson, "The Russo-Japanese War and Japan: Politics, Nationalism and Historical Memory," in Wells and Wilson, eds., *The Russo-Japanese War in Cultural Perspective, 1904–05*, 174.

17. For detailed examples of Japanese intellectuals' ambivalence toward Tolstoy's antiwar stance, see Yanagi, *Torusutoi to nihon*, 24–26.

18. Wells and Wilson, "The Russo-Japanese War in Russian Literature," 124.

19. Ibid.

20. Tolstoy, "Bethink Yourselves!," *The Times* (London), June 27, 1904.

21. Kōtoko, "Torusutoi ō no hisenron o hyōsu," 36.

22. Wilson, "The Russo-Japanese War and Japan: Politics, Nationalism and Historical Memory," 174.

23. Yanagi, *Torusutoi to nihon*, 28–29.

24. Tolstoy's reply, written in October 1904, arrived after *Heimin shinbun* had been discontinued; it was eventually published in both English and Japanese in the socialist journal *Chokugen*. "Torusutoi ou no henji" (Mr. Tolstoy's reply), *Chokugen* 2, no. 30 (August 1905): 1, 3.

25. Nobori and Akamatsu, *The Russian Impact on Japan: Literature and Social Thought*, 38–39.

26. It was not until the 1920s that anarchism was combined with Tolstoysm in Korea. Tolstoyan anarchism was called "humanistic anarchism" or "pacifist anarchism," and aimed at achieving social revolution by peaceful means, in opposition to destruction for destruction's sake. Yi Ho-ryong, *Han'guk ŭi anak'ijŭm*, 254–55; O Chang-hwan, *Han'guk anak'ijŭm undongsa yŏn'gu*, 46.

27. Yi Kwang-su, "T'olsŭt'oi ŭi insaenggwan—kŭ chonggyo wa yesul" (Tolstoy's ideas on life—his religion and art), *Chogwang*, no. 1 (November 1935), 10:489.

28. Yi Kwang-su, "Tuong kwa hyŏndae" (Tolstoy and the contemporary era), *Chosŏn ilbo* (November 26–27, 1935), 9:464–65.

29. Anderson, *Imagined Communities*, 119.

30. Kwŏn Podŭrae, *Han'guk kŭndae sosŏl ŭi kiwŏn*, 179.

31. Sin Yong-ha, "Sinminhoe ŭi ch'anggŏn kwa kŭ kukkwŏn hoebok undong (sang)," 31–33.

32. Ibid., 33.

33. Sin Yong-ha, "Sinminhoe ŭi ch'anggŏn kwa kŭ kukkwŏn hoebok undong (ha)," 133–34.

34. Ibid., 134–37.

35. Ch'oe Nam-sŏn, "Ch'ŏngnyŏn haguhoe ch'wijisŏ" and "Ch'ŏngnyŏn haguhoe sollip wiwŏnhoe chŏnggŏn."

36. Twelve Sinminhoe members were involved in founding *Ch'ŏngnyŏn haguhoe*. Ch'oe Nam-son, Ch'oe Kwang-ok, and An Ch'ang-ho were core members. Ch'oe Ki-yŏng, "Hanmal Ch'oe Kwang-ok ŭi kyoyuk hwaltong kwa kukkwŏn hoebok undong," 58.

37. Ch'oe Nam-sŏn, "Chinsil chŏngsin" (True mind), *Saebyŏk* (September 1954), reprinted in *Yuktang Ch'oe Nam-sŏn chŏnjip*, 247.

38. Sin Yong-ha, "Sinminhoe ŭi ch'anggŏn kwa kŭ kukkwŏn hoebok undong (ha)," 147–48.

39. Ch'oe Nam-sŏn, *Sonyŏn* 1, no. 1 (November 1908), front page.

40. Ch'oe Nam-sŏn, "Han'guk mundan ŭi ch'och'anggi rŭl mallham," 38.

41. Kuksa Pyŏnch'an Wiwŏnhoe, ed., *Ilche ch'imnyak ha han'guk samsimyungnyŏn sa*, vol. 1, 222; Sin Yong-ha, "Sinminhoe ŭi ch'anggŏn kwa kŭ kukkwŏn hoebok undong (ha)," 137–38.

42. Ch'oe Nam-sŏn, *Sonyŏn* 1, no. 1 (November 1908): 56.

43. Ch'oe Nam-sŏn, "Han'guk mundan ŭi ch'och'anggi rŭl mallham," 37–38.

44. See Nihon Kindai Bungakukan, ed., *Nihon kindai bungaku daijiten*, 4:323–24 for the reception of Ibsen, and 4:387–88 for that of Hugo.

45. The articles on Tolstoy that Ch'oe Nam-sŏn wrote are "Tolssŭtoi sŏnsaeng ŭi kyosi" (Tolstoy's teaching), "Uridŭl ŭi ŭimu" (Our duty), "Sŏnsaeng ŭi soon silhaeng"

(Tolstoy's practice), "Tolssŭtoi sŏnsaeng ŭi ilgwa" (Tolstoy's daily plan), and "Tolssŭtoi sŏnsaeng ŭi ŏryŏtsŭl ttae ŭi sŏrŭm" (Tolstoy's sorrow in his childhood), all in *Sonyŏn*, no. 2:6 (July 1909); "Tolssŭtoi sŏnsaeng ŭi ilsang saenghwal sipgye" (Tolstoy's ten principles for everyday life), *Sonyŏn*, no. 3:3 (March 1910); and "Tolssŭtoi sŏnsaeng ŭl kokham" (Lamentation on Tolstoy's death), "Sojŏn" (A short biography of Tolstoy), "Sangmo" (Tolstoy's countenance), "Yŏnbo" (A chronology on Tolstoy), "Ŏrok" (Tolstoy's sayings), all in *Sonyŏn*, no. 3:9 (December 1910).

46. The six Tolstoy stories that Ch'oe translated are "Sarang ŭi sŭngjŏn" (The victory of love; the English translation of the original Russian title is "Evil Allures, but Good Endures," 1885), *Sonyŏn*, no. 2:6 (July 1909); "Choson samdae" (Three generations; "A Grain as Big as a Hen's Egg," 1886), *Sonyŏn*, no. 2:7 (August 1909); "Ŏrun kwa ahae" (A child and adult; "Little Girls Wiser than Men," 1885), *Sonyŏn*, no. 2:10 (November 1909); and "Han saram i ŏlmana ttang i issŏya hana" (How much land does a man need?, 1886), "Nŏ ŭi niut" (Your neighborhood; "A Spark Neglected Burns the House," 1885), and "Tagwan" (Teahouse; "The Coffee-House of Surat," 1893), all in *Sonyŏn*, no. 3:9 (December 1910).

47. Ch'oe Nam-sŏn, "T'olssŭt'oi sŏnsaeng ŭi kyosi" (Tolstoy's teaching), *Sonyŏn*, no. 2:6 (July 1909): 10.

48. Nakazato, *Torusutoi genkōroku*.

49. Yanagi, *Torusutoi to nihon*, 252.

50. Ibid., 29.

51. Lefevere, "Translation and Canon Formation: Nine Decades of Drama in the United States," in Álvarez and Vidal, eds., *Translation, Power, Subversion*, 138–54.

52. Ch'oe Nam-sŏn, "T'olssŭt'oi sŏnsaeng ŭi kyosi" (Tolstoy's teaching), 5.

53. Nakazato, *Torusutoi genkōroku*, preface, 1; preface for 2nd edition, 1.

54. Ch'oe Nam-sŏn, "T'olssŭt'oi sŏnsaeng ŭi kyosi" (Tolstoy's teaching), 12–13.

55. Ibid., 9.

56. Ibid.

57. Ibid., 10–13.

58. Ibid., 8.

59. Leo Tolstoy, *My Confession*, in *The Complete Works of Count Tolstoy*, vol. 13, 59–60. The term that Tolstoy used is *trud* (labor, work, toil), or *trudit'sia* (to work hard).

60. Leo Tolstoy, *My Confession*, 1–90; for a Russian text, see *Polnoe sobranie sochinenii Lva Nikolaevicha Tolstogo*, vol. 15.

61. Ch'oe Nam-sŏn, "Uridŭl ŭi ŭimu" (Our duty), *Sonyŏn*, no. 2:6 (July 1909), 13. This is Ch'oe's translation of Kaizan's "Oshifuru wa gimu ni arazu" (Teaching is not a duty), in *Torusutoi genkōroku*, 211–12.

62. Ch'oe Nam-sŏn, "Sŏnsaeng ŭi soŏn silhaeng" (Tolstoy's practice), *Sonyŏn*, no. 2:6 (July 1909), 13. This is Ch'oe's translation of Kaizan's "Ō no jikko" (Tolstoy's practice), in *Torusutoi genkōroku*, 152.

63. Ch'oe Nam-son, "T'olsŭt'oi sŏnsaeng ŭi ilgwa" (Tolstoy's daily plan), *Sonyŏn*, no. 2:6 (July 1909): 17. This is Ch'oe's translation of Kaizan's "Ō no nikka" (Tolstoy's daily plan), in *Torusutoi genkōroku*, 208–9.

64. Ch'oe Nam-sŏn, "Ch'ŏngnyŏn haguhoe ch'wijisŏ" and "Ch'ŏngnyŏn haguhoe sollip wiwŏnhoe chŏnggŏn," 14–15.

65. Ch'oe Nam-sŏn, *Yuktang Ch'oe Nam-sŏn chŏnjip*, 116.

66. Ch'oe Nam-sŏn, "Ch'ŏngnyŏn haguhoe ŭi chuji" (The aims of the Youth Association), *Yuktang Ch'oe Nam-sŏn chŏnjip*, 10:424.

67. Kim Kyo-sik, *Ch'oe Nam-sŏn*, 25.

68. Kwŏn Chŏng-hwa, "Ch'oe Nam-sŏn ŭi ch'ogi sŏsul e nat'ananŭn chiri chŏk kwansim," 3–5.

69. Simmons, *Leo Tolstoy*, 584–86.

70. Ch'oe Nam-sŏn, "T'olsŭt'oi sŏnsaeng ŭi kyosi" (Tolstoy's teaching), 10.

71. Nakazato, *Torusutoi genkōroku*, 241.

72. Ibid., 245.

73. Ch'oe Nam-sŏn, "T'olsŭt'oi sŏnsaeng ŭi kyosi" (Tolstoy's teaching), 11–12.

74. Chŏng Kŭn-sik, "Singminji Kŏmyŏl ŭi yŏksa chŏk kiwŏn," 36.

75. Ibid., 37. For recent discussions of censorship in colonial Korea, see two edited volumes published in Korea: Kŏmyŏl yŏn'guhoe, ed., *Singminji kŏmyŏl: chedo, t'eksŭt'ŭ, silch'ŏn*; Tongguk taehakkyo munhwa haksurwŏn han'guk munhak yŏn'guso, ed., *Singminji sigi kŏmyŏl kwa han'guk munhwa*; Kyeong-Hee Choi, *Beneath the Vermilion Ink*. For the relationship between translation and censorship, see Thornber, "Early Twentieth-Century Intra–East Asian Literary Contact Nebulae," and Heekyoung Cho, "Translation and Censorship."

76. Nakazato, *Torusutoi genkōroku*, 241.

77. Ch'oe Nam-sŏn, "T'olsŭt'oi sŏnsaeng hase kinyŏm" (Remembering Tolstoy), *Sonyŏn*, no. 3:9 (December 1910): 1.

78. Under colonization, this kind of metonymic displacement was also used by authors such as Ch'ae Man-sik, whose satirical fictional narratives attacked the corruption of Korean elites collaborating with the Japanese instead of directly criticizing Japanese authority.

79. Ch'oe Myŏng-ik, "Lepŭ T'olsŭt'oi sŏnsaeng e taehan tansang," 156.

80. Ch'oe Nam-sŏn, "T'olsŭt'oi sŏnsaeng ŭl kokham" (Lamentation on Tolstoy's death), *Sonyŏn*, no. 3:9 (December 1910): 1–5.

81. Ibid., 5.

82. Ibid.

83. Yi Kwang-su, "Tuong kwa na" (Tolstoy and I), *Chosŏn ilbo* (November 20, 1935), 10:594–95.

84. Kim Yun-sik, *Yi Kwang-su wa kŭ ŭi sidae*, 1:224.

85. Yi Kwang-su, "Uri munye ŭi panghyang" (The direction of our art), *Chosŏn mundan* no. 13 (November 1925), 10:430.

86. Yi Kwang-su, "Munhak e taehan sogyŏn" (My opinions on literature), *Chosŏn mundan* no. 13 (November 1925), 10:456.

87. Honda, *Shirakabaha no bungaku*, 137.

88. Ibid., 138.

89. Ibid., 142.

90. Keene, *Dawn to the West*, 447.

91. Nobori Shomu, in Nobori and Akamatsu, *The Russian Impact on Japan: Literature and Social Thought*, 40.

92. Keene, *Dawn to the West*, 441–42.

93. Nobori and Akamatsu, *The Russian Impact on Japan: Literature and Social Thought*, 40.

94. Honda, *Shirakabaha no bungaku*, 139.

95. Yanagi, *Torusutoi to nihon*, 87.

96. *Torusutoi kenkyū* (Tolstoy studies), no. 1 (September 1916), 71.

97. Ibid., no. 2 (October 1916), 70.

98. Ibid., no. 4 (December 1916), 71.

99. Tolstoy's *What Is Art?* gives the clearest exposition of his theory of art from his later period.

100. Yi Kwang-su, "Tuong kwa na," 10:595.

101. Yi Kwang-su, "Tolstoy ŭi insaeng kwan—kŭ chonggyo wa yesul," *Chogwang*, no. 1 (1935), 10:487.

102. Kim Yun-sik, *Yi Kwang-su wa kŭ ŭi sidae*, 335–38.

103. Simmons, *Leo Tolstoy*, 330.

104. Yanagi, *Torusutoi to nihon*, 44.

105. Ibid.

106. Tolstoy, *Geijutsuron* (The theory of art).

107. Yanagi, *Torusutoi to nihon*, 49.

108. Shimamura, "Torawaretaru bungei" (Shackled art), 40–41.

109. Yi Kwang-su, "Tuong kwa na," 10:595.

110. Yi Kwang-su, "Munhak kanghwa" (A lecture on literature), *Chosŏn mundan*, no. 5 (October 1924–February 1925), 10:378.

111. Tolstoy, *What Is Art?*, 48. Tolstoy, *Polnoe sobranie sochinenii*, 30:64. Page numbers for all further quotations from these books are given directly in the text: English and Russian, in that order.

112. Hwang Chong-yŏn, "Munhak iranŭn yŏgŏ," 475–76.

113. Tolstoy's emphasis on man's capacity to be infected with others' feelings by means of art echoes David Hume's explanation of sympathy, which was part of the eighteenth-century European discourse about feeling that affected Romanticism, although Tolstoy does not discuss Hume. Hume explains that no other qualities of human nature are more significant "than that propensity we have to sympathize with others, and to receive by communication their inclinations and sentiments." (Hume, *A Treatise of Human Nature*, 316; quoted in Wertz, "Human Nature and Art," 76.) Both Hume and Tolstoy were interested in explaining "socially constituted feelings—not private inner feelings of an individualistic nature, but ones that come about through intersubjectivity (love, friendship, respect, esteem, and so on)." (Wertz, "Human Nature and Art," 77.)

Hume's thoughts on feeling/emotions were within the changing understanding of emotion in eighteen-century European philosophy. In her book on epistemologies of emotion, Adela Pinch describes this aspect of eighteenth-century European philosophy as follows: "Feelings often seem to have lives of their own in eighteen-century writing. Not always lodged within the private, inner lives of individual persons, they rather circulate among persons as somewhat autonomous substances. They frequently seem as impersonal, and contagious, as viruses, visiting the breasts of men and women the way diseases visit the body" (Pinch, *Strange Fits of Passion*, 1). She explains that the eighteenth century's revolution in epistemology had an interesting influence on the way philosophers represented the relationships between people and their feelings. Their representations of them are often conflicting, showing that on the one hand feelings are personal and private and on the other one's feeling may be someone else's, impersonal, and transsubjective. These two different views coexist and are inseparable in Hume's writing. (For a detailed discussion of Hume's ideas on feelings, see Pinch, *Strange Fits of Passion*, 17–50.) As Pinch's chapters on Romantic literature show, this discourse on feeling that appeared in eighteen-century philosophical writings was the context with which Western Romantic literature engaged.

114. The literal translation of *tongp'o* is "compatriots." The issue of "people," which distinguishes Yi's theory from Tolstoy's, is discussed later.

115. Yi Kwang-su, "Munhak kwa munsa wa munjang" (Literature, writer and writing), *Han'gŭl* (June–October 1935), 10:472.

116. Yi Kwang-su, "Munhak e taehan sogyŏn," 10:454.

117. Yi Kwang-su, "Munsa wa suyang" (A writer and self-cultivation), 10:355.

118. The stark difference between Yi and Tolstoy in terms of their approaches to the concept of "nation" is also mentioned in Michael Shin, "Interior Landscapes," in *Colonial Modernity in Korea*, 258.

119. Yi Kwang-su, "Munhak e taehan sogyŏn," 10:456; Yi Kwang-su, "Chilliin" (A man of truth), 9:464.

120. Yi Kwang-su, "Uri munye ŭi panghyang," 10:430.

121. Yi Kwang-su, "Chŏnjaenggi ŭi chakka chŏk t'aedo" (A writer's proper attitude in wartime), *Chosŏn ilbo* (January 6, 1936), 10:490.

122. Tolstoy's idea that all mankind can be united in Christendom might be itself unrealistic and self-contradictory because "Christian" cannot be equated with "universal." But he includes all human beings, regardless of nationality and religion, at least on the theoretical level, which differentiates him from Yi.

123. Yi Kwang-su, "Munhak e taehan sogyŏn," 10:456.

124. Yi Kwang-su, "Chilliin," 9:464.

125. Yi Kwang-su, "Uri munye ŭi panghyang," 10:430.

126. Yi Kwang-su, "Chŏnjaenggi ŭi chakka chŏk t'aedo," 10:492.

127. Yi Kwang-su, "Munhak iran hao," 1:549.

128. Ibid., 1:548.

129. Ibid., 1:546.

130. Yi Kwang-su, "Yesul kwa insaeng" (Art and life), *Kaebyŏk*, no. 19 (January 1922), 10:360.

131. Gregory Jusdanis, *Belated Modernity and Aesthetic Culture*, 102–3.

132. Yi Kwang-su, "Munhak ŭi kach'i" (The value of literature), 1:545–46.

133. Yi Kwang-su, "Munhak iran hao," 1:547.

134. Ibid., 1:547–48.

135. Chu Si-kyŏng, "Kugŏ wa kungmun ŭi p'iryo," 39.

136. Ibid.

137. Yi Kwang-su, "Uri munye ŭi panghyang," 10:428.

138. Yi Kwang-su, "Munhak iran hao," 1:552–53.

139. Yi Kwang-su, "Chosŏn sosŏlsa" (The history of Korean literature), *Sahae kongron* (May 1935), 10:469.

140. Ibid.

141. Yi Kwang-su, "Munhak iran hao," 1:555.

142. Kim T'ae-jun, a prominent Korean literary historian in the colonial period, also included Korean translations of Chinese works in his discussion of Korean literature,

although, unlike Yi, he did not make a clear statement that Korean translations were "Korean literature." Kim T'ae-jun, *Kyoju Chŭngbo Chosŏn sosŏlsa*.

143. How the notion of *shōsetsu* in the Meiji period incorporated the concept of emotion, or human feelings, is well explained in Tomi Suzuki, *Narrating the Self*, 19–26.

144. The other two are Mori Ōgai and Natsume Sōseki. Yi Kwang-su, "Munsa wa suyang," 10:355.

145. Tsubouchi Shōyō, *Shōsetsu shinzui* (The essence of the novel), 16.

146. Tomi Suzuki, *Narrating the Self*, 21.

147. Ibid.

148. Tsubouchi Shōyō, *Shōsetsu shinzui*, 4.

149. Ibid., 8–16.

150. Yi Kwang-su, "Munhak iran hao," 1:549. For the connection that Korean writers, specifically Yi Kwang-su and Kim Tong-in, have with Shōyō's *Shōsetsu shinzui*, see Hwang Chong-yŏn, "Nobŭl, ch'ŏngnyŏn, cheguk," 268–73.

151. Ch'oe Tu-sŏn, "Munhak ŭi ŭiŭi e kwanhaya," 29.

152. An Hwak, "Chosŏn ŭi munhak," 64.

153. Yi Kwang-su, "Munhak iran hao," 1:548.

154. Yi Kwang-su, "Kŭmil ahan ch'ŏngnyŏn kwa chŏng'yuk" (Korean youth and the fostering of their emotion), *Taehan hŭnghakpo*, no. 10 (February 1910), 1:526.

155. Yi Kwang-su, "Munhak iran hao," 1:548.

156. Takashima Heizaburō, *Shinri hakuwa*, 9; Chŏng Byŏng-ho, "Hanil kŭndae munyeron e issŏsŏ 'chŏng' ŭi wich'i," 282.

157. Natsume Sōseki, *Theory of Literature and Other Critical Writings*, 206–7.

158. Chŏng Byŏng-ho, "Hanil kŭndae munyeron e issŏsŏ 'chŏng' ŭi wich'i," 284–85. For more detailed discussions of rhetoric in Japan, see Ueda, "*Bungakuron* and 'Literature' in the Making," 25–46, and Tomasi, "Studies of Western Rhetoric in Modern Japan," 161–90.

159. Yi Kwang-su, "Munhak iran hao," 1:550.

160. Ibid., 1:550–51.

161. An Hwak, "Chosŏn ŭi munhak," 73.

162. Yi Kwang-su, "Munhak iran hao," 1:550.

163. Yi expands upon his idea about the function of literature in his descriptions of the writing process and of the benefits of literature. According to Yi, "when a person experiences something and tries to *transmit* it to other people, when a person tries to *move people's emotions* by a certain expression . . . literature comes into being" (emphasis added; Yi Kwang-su, "Munhak kwanghwa," 10:388.) This function of literature is described in more detail in Yi's explanation of the benefits of literature: "Literature allows people to obtain knowledge of the spiritual aspects of life: A humble man can know a noble man's thought and emotion, a wealthy man can know a poor man's life, a villain can know a virtuous man's emotion, and a person can truly understand even a foreigner and an ancestor through literature" (Yi Kwang-su, "Munhak iran hao," 1:550).

164. Yi Kwang-su, "Munhak iran hao," 1:547–48.

165. Ibid., 551.

166. Ibid., 554.

167. Ibid.

168. Brownstein, "From *Kokugaku* to *Kokubungaku*," 436–38.

169. Mikami and Takasu, *Nihon bungakushi*, 29.

170. Ibid., 11–12.

171. Haga, *Kokubungakushi jikkō*, 7.

172. Ibid., 265–66.

173. The wording in Yi's definition of Korean national literature is as follows: "Korean literature (*Chosŏn munhak*) is the literature that Korean people (*Chosŏnin*) written in the Korean language (*Chosŏnmun*)" (Yi Kwang-su, "Munhak iran hao," 1:554).

174. Ibid., 554–55.

175. Ibid.

176. Suzuki Sadami, *Nihon no "bungaku" gainen*, 221.

177. Brownstein, "From *Kokugaku* to *Kokubungaku*," 457.

178. For more detailed explanation of "art for life's sake" and Korean intellectuals' description of Russian literature, see the introduction to this book.

179. Yi Kwang-su, "Munsa wa suyang," 10:353.

180. Ibid., 10:355.

181. *Tong'a ilbo* (Tong'a Daily), August 14, 1922, quoted in Pak Hŏn-ho, "'Munhwa chŏngch'i-gi sinmun ŭi wisang kwa pan-gŏmyŏl ŭi naechŏk nolli," 216.

182. For a detailed explanation of the role of newspapers in colonial Korea, see Pak Hŏn-ho, "'Munhwa chŏngch'i-gi sinmun ŭi wisang kwa pan-gŏmyŏl ŭi naechŏk nolli," 217.

183. For a detailed explanation of the complicated relationships and fluid boundaries among literature, journalistic writings, social discourse, and translation in colonial Korea, see Chapter 2.

184. Ueda, *Concealment of Politics, Politics of Concealment*, 5.

185. Ibid., 6.

186. This irony is, of course, not uncommon at all in the process of the formation of modern nation-states. The emphasis on particularity is truly an international phenomenon, in the sense that every nation-states promotes its uniqueness in the process of nation-building.

187. Ch'oe and Yi's anxiety may also have originated from their personal history and experience. Neither man was from the aristocratic class—Ch'oe was from the middle class and Yi was an orphan—and they were still in their teens when they started writing their important essays and works of fiction. Their social status, therefore, was not naturally established at the beginning of their careers.

2. Rewriting Literature and Reality

1. Anonymous, "Injae sullye (1)," 30.

2. The term "productive" is used here as defined by Paul Ricoeur. Ricoeur defines fiction as a "productive reference" in terms of the relationship between representation and referent: "Fiction does not refer in a 'reproductive way' to reality as already given," but rather "may refer in a 'productive' way to reality as intimated by the fiction." For Ricoeur, fiction changes reality in the sense that it "invents" and "discovers" it. Paul Ricoeur, "The Function of Fiction in Shaping Reality," in Valdés, ed., *A Ricoeur Reader*, 121. Taking this cue, the term "productive appropriation" used here refers to translation as an activity that does not reproduce an "original" text but produces a new one with a

productive relationship to its own present. Translation is an activity through which the translator may develop new ways of perceiving and reshaping his or her reality.

3. For instance, Hyŏn praised the short story "Pakdol ŭi chugŭm" (The death of Pakdol) by Ch'oe Sŏ-hae, a representative proletarian writer. He noted that its content and artistic composition differed from the "flat description" of other (proletarian) literary works. Hyŏn Chin-gŏn et al., "Chosŏn mundan happ'yŏnghoe che-4-hoe" (A joint review of *Chosŏn mundan* [The Korean literary world]), *Chosŏn mundan*, in Yi Kang-ŏn, Yi Chu-hyŏng, Cho Chin-gi, and Yi Chae-ch'un, eds., *Hyŏn Chin-gŏn munhak chŏnjip*, 6:111. For further comments on proletarian literature, see Hyŏn Chin-gŏn, "Mulkkot tonnŭn taero" (As things go), *Hyŏn Chin-gŏn munhak chŏnjip*, 6:141–44. For Hyŏn's criticism of art for art's sake, see Hyŏn Chin-gŏn, "Irŏk'ung chŏrŏk'ung" (This and that), *Hyŏn Chin-gŏn munhak chŏnjip*, 6:27–33.

4. Hyŏn acknowledged his use of Chekhov at the end of "Blindman's Bluff." Hyŏn Chin-gŏn, "Kkamakchapki" (Blindman's Bluff), 222. In the case of "A Lucky Day" and "Fire," we can infer the relationship from significant similarities in plot and character.

5. Mirsky, *A History of Russian Literature*, 369–70.

6. For a detailed description of the types of Chekhovian characters, see Kenneth A. Lantz, "Chekhov's Case of Characters," in Clyman, ed., *A Chekhov Companion*, 71–75.

7. This figure includes repetitive publication of the same stories. For the list of translations, see Kokuritsu Kokkai Toshokan, ed., *Meiji, Taishō, Shōwa hon'yaku bungaku mokuroku*, 252–75. The first Japanese translations of Chekhov's short stories were "Tsuki to hito" (Moon and people, 1903; Russian title "Dachniki" [Holiday visitors in the country]), and "Shashinchō" (Album, 1903; Russian title "Al'bom" [Album]). These stories were translated jointly by Senuma Kayō and Ozaki Kōyō. Senuma Kayō (1875–1915) was a graduate of Nikolai Orthodox Women's School and a disciple of Ozaki Kōyō. She studied Russian with Father Nikolai (Ivan Dmitrievich Kasatkin, 1836–1912), the founder of the school, and started translating Russian authors' stories and novels. In addition to translations of individual literary works, anthologies of Chekhov's short stories played a significant part in establishing him as a literary figure in Japan. Senuma Kayō's *Chehofu kessaku shū* (Chekhov's masterpieces, 1908), Maeda Akira's *Tanpen jisshu Chehofu shū* (Chekhov's ten short stories, 1913), and Hirotsu Kazuo's *Seppun hoka hachihen* ("The Kiss" and eight other stories, 1916) are the most important of these published in the 1910s. Chekhov's complete translated works began to be prepared by Akita Toshihiko and others at the Shinchōsha publishing company in 1919, and the full ten volumes had been published by 1928. In Korea, Chekhov's "Album" was the first work to be translated, in 1916, by Chin Hak-mun (pen name Sunsŏng), under the title "Sajinchŏp" (Album), in *Hakchigwang*, no. 10 (September 1916). The first Korean anthology of Chekhov stories was published in June 1924 as Anton Chekhov, *Chehop tanp'yŏnjip* (Chekhov's short stories), trans. Kwŏn Po-sang (Seoul: Chosŏn tosŏ chusik hoesa, 1924).

8. Kropotkin, *Russian Literature*, 314.

9. Yanagi Tomiko, "Chehofu—Meiji Taishō no shōkai hon'yaku wo chūshin ni" (The introduction and translation of Chekhov in Meiji and Taishō Japan), in Fukuda Mitsuharu, Kenmochi Takehiko, and Kodama Kōichi, eds., *Ōbei sakka to nihon kindai bungaku*, 3:84–136.

10. Sōma Gyofū's "Chehofu ron" (A study of Chekhov) was serialized in the *Tokyo niroku shinbun* from September 23 to October 1, 1909. Nakajima, *Nihon ni okeru Chehofu shoshi: 1902–2004*, 87.

11. Maeda, "Chehofu shōden." A less detailed version of Maeda's article had been published anonymously in 1908. Following the 1913 reprint, it was again reprinted in Maeda and Shimamura's *Ōshū kindai shōsetsuka kenkyū* in 1915.

12. In addition to Chu Yo-sŏp and Pak Yŏng-hŭi's pieces, there were two other introductions to Chekhov in Korean between 1916 and 1924, but these were very short pieces: Sunsŏng, "Sajinch'ŏp sŏ: Che-hopŭ ŭi sogae," 50; and the introduction to the first Korean anthology of Chekhov stories—Chekhov, *Chehop tanp'yŏnjip*.

13. Chu Yo-sŏp, "Nosŏa ŭi tae munho Ch'eekhopŭ," 88.

14. Ibid., 90–91.

15. Ibid., 94.

16. Maeda, "Che-hofu shōden."

17. Kropotkin, *Russian Literature*, 308–17.

18. Ibid., 314.

19. Ibid., 308.

20. Pak Yŏng-hŭi, "Ch'ehopu hŭigok e nat'anan nosŏa hwanmyŏlgi ŭi kot'ong," 56.

21. Shestov's essay on Chekhov was translated first in 1920 and four more times in the 1930s. Shestov, "Anton Tchekhov (Creation from the Void)," 1–60.

22. Ibid., 4–5.

23. In the late 1920s and 1930s, Ham Tae-hun and Kim On, who were members of the Haeoe Munhak-p'a (School of Foreign Literature), played an important role in the continuing importation and introduction of Chekhov. They started focusing more on aesthetic analysis of literary works and showed an increasing preference for the plays. For the group's reception of Chekhov, see An Suk-hyŏn, *Han'guk yŏn'gŭk kwa Anton Ch'ehop*, 92–165.

24. Kwŏn Yŏng-min, *Han'guk hyŏndae munhaksa*, 1:218.

25. Ku In-hwan, "Hyŏn Chin-gŏn ŭi saeng'ae wa munhak," II-13; Sŏ Hyŏn-ju, "Hyŏn Chin-gŏn sosŏl yŏn'gu: sahoe hyŏnsil kwa yŏsŏngsang ŭl chungsim ŭro," 45–48.

26. Yun Pyŏng-ro, "Pinghŏ Hyŏn Chin-gŏn ŭi saeng'ae wa pip'yŏng," 109.

27. Ch'oe Wŏn-sik, "Hyŏn Chin-gŏn sosŏl e nat'anan chisigin kwa minjung," 200.

28. For an analysis of the female characters in Kim Tong-in's stories and Korean literature of the 1920s, see Yu Nam-ok, "1920-nyŏndae tanpyŏn sosŏl e nat'anan peminijŭm yŏn'gu."

29. Hyŏn Chin-gŏn, "Munhak chonghoengdam" (Miscellaneous conversations on literature), in *Hyŏn Chin-gŏn munhak chŏnjip*, 6:307–8.

30. Ibid., 306.

31. Hyŏn Chin-gŏn, "Chosŏn mundan happ'yŏnghoe che-1-hoe" (A joint review of *Chosŏn mundan* [The Korean literary world]) in *Hyŏn Chin-gŏn munhak chŏnjip*, 6:68.

32. Kim Pyŏng-ch'ŏl, *Han'guk kŭndae pŏnyŏk munhaksa yŏn'gu*, 441.

33. Chekhov, "Let Me Sleep," in *Chekhov: The Early Stories 1883–88*, 191–96, and in Chekhov, *Polnoe sobranie sochinenii i pisem*, 7:12–17.

34. Hyŏn Chin-gŏn, "Pul" (Fire), in *Hyŏn Chin-gŏn munhak chŏnjip*, 1:145–52. All translations are author's unless otherwise specified.

35. Hyŏn Chin-gŏn, "Nae sosŏl kwa model" (My stories and their model), in *Hyŏn Chin-gŏn munhak chŏnjip*, 6:213.

36. Of course, these discussions are a part of the modernizing project of Korean society and its politics of gender. For more on this subject, see Yoo, *The Politics of Gender in Colonial Korea*; Hyaeweol Choi, *Gender and Mission Encounters in Korea*; Jeong, *Crisis of Gender and Nation in Korean Literature and Cinema*; and Lee, *Women Pre-scripted*.

37. Kim Tu-hŏn, "Chosŏn ŭi chohon kwa mit kŭ kiwŏn e taehan il koch'al," 46–86.

38. "Honinron" (About marriage), *Tongnip sinmun* (The Independent), January 20, 1899; ibid., July 20, 1899.

39. *Cheguk sinmun* (Imperial Newspaper), May 11, 1900; ibid., March 25, 1901; "Saram maemae" (Human trafficking), *Taehan maeil sinbo* (Korean Daily News), December 11, 1907.

40. "Honinjyoch'ik" (A royal edict on marriage), *Taehan maeil sinbo*, August 17, 1907.

41. "Ronsyŏl" (Editorial), *Taehan maeil sinbo* (Korean Daily News), December 11, 1907; "Hanjungmanp'yŏng" (Rambling criticism), *Hwangsŏng sinmun* (Capitol Daily), August 23, 1907; "Chohon ŭi p'yehae rŭl t'ongnon" (A sincere opinion on the harmful effects of early marriage), ibid., September 3–4, 1909.

42. "Chohon ŭi p'yehae rŭl t'ongnon" (A sincere opinion on the harmful effects of early marriage), *Hwangsŏng sinmun*, September 3–4, 1909.

43. Chŏn Mi-gyŏng, "Kaehwagi chohon tamnon ŭi kajok yulli ŭisik ŭi hamŭi," 195–202.

44. Hyŏn Sang-yun, "Ingu chŭngsik p'iryoron"; C. Y. Saeng, "Kwabu haebangnon"; Kang In-t'aek, "Na ŭi pon chosŏn sŭpsok i sam"; Kim Tong-ik, "Chohon ŭro manhi saengginŭn saengsikgŭi sŏngsin'gyŏng soeyakchŭng" (Sexual neurasthenia frequently caused by early marriage), *Tong'a ilbo*, February 27–28, 1932; "Chohon kwa pumo ŭi ŭimu" (Early marriage and parents' duties), ibid., October 19, 1938.

45. *Chosŏn ch'ongdokbu kwanbo* (Government-General Gazette), August 7, 1915; *Maeil sinbo* (Daily News), August 15, 1915.

46. Han'guk Yŏsŏngsa P'yŏnch'an Wiwŏnhoe, *Han'guk yŏsŏngsa*, 152.

47. The percentage of females marrying before the age of fifteen increased slightly after 1932, as people's lives grew less secure following the Manchurian Incident in 1931, though it remained under 10 percent. For the records between 1912 and 1936, see Ryu, "Ku-hanmal, Ilcheha yŏsŏng chohon ŭi silt'ae wa chohon p'yeji undong," 18–20.

48. "Chohon yŏp'ye ŭi hwaljünggŏ" (A real evidence of early marriage's harmful effect), *Tong'a ilbo*, December 27, 1921.

49. Ibid., October 12, 1922.

50. Ibid., April 6, 1927; ibid., May 31, 1928; *Chung'oe ilbo* (Chung'oe Daily), June 7, 1928; *Tong'a ilbo*, July 24, 1928; ibid., August 18, 1928; ibid., April 11, 1929; ibid., May 14, 1929.

51. *Tong'a ilbo*, April 11, 1929.

52. Ibid., July 24, 1928.

53. Ibid., May 31, 1928.

54. Ibid., December 22, 1930; ibid., January 16, 1931; ibid., August 29, 1931; *Chung'ang ilbo*, March 15, 1932; *Tong'a ilbo*, May 15, 1932; ibid., December 22, 1932; *Chosŏn chung'ang ilbo* (Chosŏn Chung'ang Daily), August 25, 1933; *Tong'a ilbo*, March 30, 1934; ibid.,

August 31, 1934; ibid., September 9, 1935; ibid., November 14, 1935; ibid., November 28, 1935; *Chosŏn ilbo* (Chosŏn Daily), December 21, 1935.

55. *Chosŏn chung'ang ilbo*, August 25, 1933.

56. *Chung'oe ilbo*, January 23, 1930.

57. *Tong'a ilbo*, February 11, 1938.

58. Chŏng Chin-sŏk, *Inmul han'guk ŏllonsa*, 211–12.

59. Pak Yong-gyu, "Singminji sigi munin kijadŭl ŭi kŭlssŭgi wa kŏmyŏl," 83–86.

60. Hyŏn Chin-gŏn, *Hyŏn Chin-gŏn munhak chŏnjip*, 1:317–20.

61. *Tong'a ilbo*, July 24, 1928.

62. Ibid., May 31, 1928.

63. Ibid., August 18, 1928.

64. Ibid., May 22, 1929.

65. For a detailed explanation of this process, see Kim Yŏng-min, *Han'guk kŭndae sosŏlsa*.

66. Hyŏn's story "Hae ttŭnŭn chip'yŏngsŏn" (A horizon above which the sun rises), published in 1927, shows an interesting interaction between newspaper reports and a piece of fiction writing. Hyŏn's protagonist writes a story based on newspaper reports, to reveal "the truth existing behind the 'objective' reports." In this story, the usual hierarchy of journalism being considered more truthful than fiction is overturned. See Hyŏn Chin-gŏn, "Hae ttŭnŭn chip'yŏngsŏn," *Chosŏn mundan*, no. 18–20 (January–March 1927), in *Hyŏn Chin-gŏn munhak chŏnjip*, 1:191–214.

67. Masamune, "Tamatsukiya" (A billiard room), in *Masamune Hakuchō zenshū*, 1:278–81; Mansfield, "The Child-Who-Was-Tired," in, *In a German Pension*, 163–83.

68. For a brief historical explanation of child labor in Japan, see Kakinami, "History of Child Labor in Japan," 881–87, and Grabowski and Self, "Education and Child Labor in Japan," 888–90.

69. Hill, "Nana in the World," 75–103.

70. Moretti, "Conjectures on World Literature," 54–68; Casanova, *The World Republic of Letters*. The criticisms of Moretti include Kristal, " 'Considering Coldly . . .': A Response to Franco Moretti," 61–74; Arac, "Anglo-Globalism?" 35–45; Shi, "Global Literature and the Technologies of Recognition," 16–30. The criticisms of Casanova are Sapir, "The Literary Field between the State and the Market," 441–64; Prendergast, "The World Republic of Letters," 7; Hill, "Nana in the World."

71. For more detail discussion on Moretti's argument, see the introduction.

72. Damrosch, *What Is World Literature?*, 4.

73. "Happ'yŏnghoe" (A panel discussion), *Chosŏn mundan* (March 1925), in *Hyŏn Chin-gŏn munhak chŏnjip*, 6:68; G. H., " 'Tamatsukiya' to 'surīpi heddo,' " 565–67; New, *Reading Mansfield and Metaphors of Form*, 33.

3. Aspirations for a New Literature

1. Due to Japanese surveillance, the Communist Party in Korea had to remain clandestine. For a history of the communist movement in 1920s Korea, see Suh, *The Korean Communist Movement 1918–1948*, 53–114; Nam, *The North Korean Communist Leadership*, 1–12, 116–25.

2. For more about literary movements after 1919 in Korea, see Im Hwa, *Sinmunhaksa*, 343–70; Paek Ch'ŏl, *Chosŏn sinmunhak sajosa*, 115–84; and Kwŏn Yŏng-min, *Han'guk kyegŭp munhak undongsa*, 13–20.

3. For a detailed explanation of Yŏmgunsa and PASKYUL and the process of the formation of KAPF, see Kwŏn Yŏng-min, *Han'guk kyegŭp munhak undongsa*, 21–84.

4. There are a number of recently published studies in English that take different approaches to Korean proletarian literature. For the relations among literature, film, and art in proletarian movement, see Hughes, *Literature and Film in Cold War South Korea*. For a new perspective on Korea in the Japanese proletarian movement, see Perry, *Recasting Red Culture in Proletarian Japan*. For an explanation that situates Korean realism within the context of colonial leftist culture, see Park, *The Proletarian Wave*.

5. For more about the journal *Kongje*, see Kwŏn Hŭi-yŏng, "Chosŏn nodong konjehoe wa *Kongje*," 139–57. For a history of the Korean Labor Mutual Aid Association, see Yi Kyŏng-yŏng, "1920-nyŏndae ch'oban nodong undong ŭi punhwa kwajŏng," 103–14; and Pak Ae-rim, "Chosŏn nodong kongje-hoe ŭi hwaltong kwa inyŏm."

6. All translations are author's unless otherwise specified. Chŏng Se-yun, "Ch'anggan ŭl ch'ukham," 22.

7. Ibid., 22–23.

8. Tongwŏn, "Nodong ŭl chŏju hanŭn kungmin ege," 108.

9. Ibid., 109.

10. Yu Chin-hŭi, "Nodong undong ŭi sahoejuŭi-jok koch'al," 11.

11. Ibid., 13.

12. Ibid., 15.

13. Ibid., 19.

14. Yi Kwang-su, "Munhak iran hao," *Maeil sinbo*, November 10–23, 1916, reprinted in *Yi Kwang-su chŏnjip*, 1:549.

15. Kim Yu-bang, "Tolsŭtoi ŭi yesulgwan," 123.

16. Ibid., 131.

17. Pak Yŏng-hŭi, "Ch'oegŭn munye sogam" (My recent opinions on literature), in *Pak Yŏng-hŭi chŏnjip*, 3:316.

18. Ibid., 3:317.

19. For comprehensive studies of Turgenev's life and literary works, see Freeborn, *Turgenev: The Novelist's Novelist*; Seeley, *Turgenev: A Reading of His Fiction*; and Moser, *Ivan Turgenev*.

20. Another big surge in Japanese writers' interest in Russian literature was triggered by Tolstoy's antiwar sentiments during the Russo-Japanese War, as examined in Chapter 1.

21. Nobori, "Russian Literature and Japanese Literature," in Nobori and Akamatsu, *The Russian Impact on Japan: Literature and Social Thought*, 21, 34–42; Yasuda Yasuo, "Tsurugenefu" (Turgenev), in Fukuda Mitsuharu et al., eds., *Ōbei sakka to nihon kindai bungaku*, 3:47.

22. Nobori, "Russian Literature and Japanese Literature," in Nobori and Akamatsu, *The Russian Impact on Japan Literature and Social Thought*, 22.

23. Yasuda Yasuo, "Tsurugenefu," in Fukuda Mitsuharu et al., eds., *Ōbei sakka to nihon kindai bungaku*, 47–48.

24. Futabatei used the written style he developed in translating Russian works in writing his own novel, *Ukigumo*, in Japanese. Hiroko Cockerill investigates Futabatei's

translations of Turgenev and Gogol in order to show how his appropriation of new verb endings and other elements in the narrative style from Russian appear in *Ukigumo*. Cockerill makes a detailed and effective argument, but her assumptions about translation and receiving cultures need to be examined. She assumes that a literary work that maintains a consistent narrational stance is superior, endorsing a teleological perspective that makes Russian literature into an ideal model that Futabatei should have followed. She argues the work was the site of "a struggle between the conflicting influences of Gogol's [third-person narrative] and Turgenev's [first-person] narrative style," and thinks that Futabatei might have left it unfinished because he was not able to resolve this conflict. She goes on to claim that "the shift from one narrator to the other resulted in an inconsistent narrative point of view, leaving a flawed novel. Had he instead maintained the narrator's synchronous point of view, as in *Shōzōga* [Gogol's *"Portret"* (The Portrait)], Japan's first modern novel would have maintained a single narrative point of view." By claiming that Futabatei's work is "flawed" compared to Gogol's, she is adopting a West-centered perspective, which a scholar in comparative studies particularly should be careful not to take. Cockerill, "Futabatei Shimei's Translations from Russian," 237.

"The Tryst" was also translated into Korean by Kim Ŏk in *T'aesŏ munye sinbo*. Kim Ŏk, "Milhoe" (The tryst), 1–2. Kim Pyŏng-ch'ŏl argues that Kim Ŏk probably translated Turgenev's *"Svidanie"* (The tryst) from Futabatei Shimei's first translation of it, and takes several examples from the two translations to prove their similarity. (Kim Pyŏng-ch'ŏl, *Han'guk kŭndae pŏnyŏk munhaksa yŏn'gu*, 390–91.) If this is the case, Kim Ŏk's Korean translation (1918) of "The Rendezvous" demonstrates an interesting use of verbal endings in relation to Futabatei's. According to Cockerill, Futabatei used " '-ta' form verbs . . . only in dialogue to indicate the past tense in a surrounding narrative, while the past tense of the surrounding narrative was normally expressed using the classical auxiliary verbs '-keri' and '-ki' " (Hiroko Cockerill, "Futabatei Shimei's Translations from Russian," 231). In his translation, Kim Ŏk adopted the verbal ending "-haptida" for the past tense of the surrounding narrative, which is usually used only in dialogue, while using verb ending forms "-handa," and "-haetta" in his other writings and translations in the same newspaper. In the case of the Korean language, however, Kim Ŏk's "-haptida" for the translation of Futabatei's "-ta", which corresponds to the Russian past perfect/imperfect forms, is more prominent in revealing the existence of a mediator who conveys the story. This example demonstrates the fact that a relay translation from a translation can sometimes bring about quite a different narrative style from that of the source text.

25. The impact of Futabatei's translation of Turgenev's "The Tryst" was tremendous, not only for its new writing style, but also in the impact it exerted on Japanese writers' way of seeing nature. For more details, see Futabatei, *Japan's First Modern Novel: "Ukigumo" of Futabatei Shimei*, 118.

26. Yasuda Yasuo, "Tsurugenefu," in Fukuda Mitsuharu et al., eds., *Ōbei sakka to nihon kindai bungaku*, 53–54.

27. In *Mi wo tsukushi* (The destruction of life), (Tokyo: Bun'yūkan, 1901), Ueda Bin translated 10 prose poems of Turgenev's: "The Country," "A Conversation," "Prayer," "The Old Woman," "The Dog," "My Adversary," "The Beggar," "A Contented Man," "A Rule of Life," and "We will still fight on." The next year, he translated and published another three prose poems in *Myōjō* (Venus), no. 2 (August 1902): "The Monk,"

"To-morrow! To-morrow!," and "The Russian Tongue." These titles formed the repertoire of Korean translations of Turgenev's prose poems.

28. The translator of the poem "Munŏgu" (Threshold) is unknown but is probably Ch'oe Nam-sŏn because he published the journal *Ch'ŏngch'un* and was a main writer for it. "Munŏgu" (Threshold), *Ch'ŏngch'un*, no. 1, (October 1914): 120–21.

29. Kim Ŏk, "Myŏng'il? Myŏng'il?" (Tomorrow? Tomorrow?) and "Muŏt ŭl naega saenggak hagenna?" (What do I think?), *T'aesŏ munye sinbo*, no. 4 (October 26, 1918): 4; "Kae" (Dog) and "Pŏrŏngbaeng'i" (The beggar), *T'aesŏ munye sinbo*, no. 5 (November 2, 1918): 9; "Nŭlgŭni" (The old woman) and "N. N." *T'aesŏ munye sinbo*, no. 7 (November 16, 1918): 6.

30. For the connection between Turgenev's prose poems and Korean poets, in particular Kim Ŏk, see Mun Sŏk-u, "Han'guk kŭndae munhak e kkich'in tturŭgenep'ŭ ŭi yŏnghyang," 115–38; Cho Yong-hun, "T'urŭgenep'ŭ ŭi iip kwa yŏnghyang," 291–338.

31. Adaptations as well as translations of Turgenev's prose poems appeared continuously through 1939. Yun Tong-ju, a well-known Korean poet who was actively involved in the independence movement and who died in prison, composed a poem, "Turgenev's Hill," which rewrote Turgenev's prose poem "The Beggar." Yun Tong-ju, "Turŭgenepŭ ŭi ŏndŏk" (Turgenev's hill), in idem, *Yun Tong-ju chŏnjip*, 100.

32. For the impact of *Rudin* on Oguri Fūyō (1875–1926), see Nobori Shomu, "Russian Literature and Japanese Literature," in Nobori and Akamatsu, *The Russian Impact on Japan Literature and Social Thought*, 29–30, and Levy, *Sirens of the Western Shore*, 9. For the relationship between Futabatei's translation of *Rudin* and Kunikida Doppo, see Yasuda Yasuo, "Tsurugenefu," in Fukuda Mitsuharu et al., eds., *Ōbei sakka to nihon kindai bungaku*, 62–66.

33. Yi Hyo-sŏk, "Na ŭi suŏp sidae" (My literary experience), in *Yi Hyo-sŏk chŏnjip*, 7:157.

34. Chang Yŏn-hwa, "Munhak kisaeng ŭi kobaek," 140–42.

35. There were real-world archetypes for the characters Elena and Insarov. In 1854, V. V. Karateev, a neighboring landowner of Turgenev, gave Turgenev a notebook in which he had written down a short story about a girl he loved. She instead fell in love with a Bulgarian student and left with him for Bulgaria, where he soon died. Seeley, *Turgenev: A Reading of His Fiction*, 200.

36. Tsurugenefu (Ivan Turgenev), *Tsurugenefu shū 2*, eds. Kawato and Sakakibara, 358.

37. Tsurugenefu (Ivan Turgenev), *So no zenya* (On the eve), trans. Sōma Gyofū (Tokyo: Naigai Shuppan Kyōkai, 1908). For a list of translations of the sections and their publication information, see Tsurugenefu, *Tsurugenefu shū 2*, 351–52.

38. Yasuda Yasuo, "Tsurugenefu," in Fukuda Mitsuharu et al., eds., *Ōbei sakka to nihon kindai bungaku*, 75.

39. Tsurugenefu [Turgenev], *So no zenya* (On the eve), trans. Tanaka Jun, in Tsurugenefu, *Tsurugenefu zenshū* (Complete works), vol. 4 (Tokyo: Shinchōsha, 1918); Tsurugenefu, *So no zenya*, trans. Ono Hiroshi (Tokyo: Tōkasha, 1921).

40. Yasuda Yasuo, "Tsurugenefu," in Fukuda Mitsuharu et al., eds., *Ōbei sakka to nihon kindai bungaku*, 77.

41. Hyŏn Ch'ŏl, "Kakpon kyŏgya omak," 152.

42. Kusuyama Masao, *Kyakuhon so no zenya*, preface, 1.

43. Ibid., 40.

44. Yi T'ae-jun, "Kŭ chŏnnal pam," 78–85.

45. Ibid., 78.

46. Hyŏn Chin-gŏn, "Chisae nŭn an'gae" (Fog at dawn), in *Hyŏn Chin-gŏn munhak chŏnjip*, 52–55.

47. Yŏm Sang-sŏp, *Sarang kwa choe* (Love and sin), in *Yŏm Sang-sŏp chŏnjip*, 2:60.

48. Sin Sŏk-jŏng, "Pang" (Room), in *Sŭlp'ŭn mokka*, 28–29.

49. Pak Chong-hwa, "Mundan ŭi il-nyŏn ŭl ch'uŏkhaya," 5.

50. Shea, *Leftwing Literature in Japan*, preface, i.

51. Kim Ki-jin, "Na ŭi hoegorok" (My memoirs), in *Kim P'al-bong munhak chŏnjip*, 2:189.

52. Kim Ki-jin, "Han'guk mundan ch'ŭkmyŏnsa" (Bypaths in the history of Korean literary world), in *Kim P'al-bong munhak chŏnjip*, 2:99.

53. For more about *The Sower*, see Yamada Seizaburō, *Proretaria bungakushi*, vol. 1, 265–77, and Shea, *Leftwing Literature in Japan*, 69–87.

54. Pak Yŏng-hŭi, "Hwayŏm sok e innŭn sŏganch'e" (Epistles in flames), in *Pak Yŏng-hŭi chŏnjip*, 67.

55. *Tane maku hito* (The sower) 1, no. 1 (October 1921): 2, quoted in Shea, *Leftwing Literature in Japan*, 74.

56. Kim Ki-jin, "Ttŏrŏjinŭn chogakjogak" (Broken pieces), in *Kim P'al-bong munhak chŏnjip*, 4:338–44; Kim Ki-jin, "P'ŭromŭnadŭ sangt'imant'al" (Promenade sentimental), in *Kim P'al-bong munhak chŏnjip*, 1:409–26.

57. Kim Ki-jin, "Na ŭi munhak ch'ŏngnyŏn sidae—Turŭgenepŭ-nya soromin-inya" (The period of my literary youth—Turgenev or Solomin), in *Kim P'al-bong munhak chŏnjip*, 2:423.

58. Ibid., 2:421.

59. Ibid., 2:422.

60. Kim Ki-jin, "Na ŭi hoegorok," in *Kim P'al-bong munhak chŏnjip*, 2:189; Kim Ki-jin, "Sosŏlga ŭi kil" (A writer's path), in *Kim P'al-bong munhak chŏnjip*, 5:136.

61. Kim Ki-jin, "Na ŭi hoegorok," in *Kim P'al-bong munhak chŏnjip*, 2:204–5; Kim Ki-jin, "P'yŏnp'yŏn yahwa" (Fragmentary stories), in *Kim P'al-bong chŏnjip*, 2:344.

62. Kim Ki-jin, "K'ŭlrarŭte undong ŭi segyehwa" (The globalization of the Clarté movement), in *Kim P'al-bong munhak chŏnjip*, 1:429.

63. Pak Yŏng-hŭi, "Chayŏnjuŭi esŏ sin-isangjuŭi e kiurŏjinŭn chosŏn mundan ŭi ch'oesin kyŏnghyang" (A recent tendency in the Korean literary world that moves from naturalism to neo-idealism), in *Pak Yŏng-hŭi chŏnjip*, 3:20–21.

64. Kim Ki-jin, "Na ŭi hoegorok," in *Kim P'al-bong munhak chŏnjip*, 2:196–97.

65. Pak Yŏng-hŭi, "Singyŏnghyangp'a ŭi munhak kwa kŭ mundan-jŏk chiwi," in *Pak Yŏng-hŭi munhak chŏnjip*, 3:122.

66. Kim Ki-jin, "Musan munye chakp'um kwa musan munye pip'yŏng—tongmu hoewŏl ege" (Proletarian literature and criticism—My dear friend, Pak Yŏng-hŭi), in *Kim P'al-bong munhak chŏnjip*, 1:99.

67. Kim Ki-jin, "P'ŭromŭnadŭ sangt'imant'al," in *Kim P'al-bong munhak chŏnjip*, 1:428.

68. Kim's father was a magistrate of a county in Hamgyŏng Province (and later in other provinces), and his uncle was a large landowner. Kim Ki-jin, *Kim P'al-bong munhak chŏnjip*, 1:499.

69. Kim Ki-jin, "Kyŏngsŏng ŭi pinmin, pinmin ŭi kyŏngsŏng" (Seoul's paupers, paupers' Seoul), in *Kim P'al-bong munhak chŏnjip*, 4:274–75.

70. Pak Yŏng-hŭi, "Singyŏnghyangp'a ŭi munhak kwa kŭ mundan-jŏk chiwi," in *Pak Yŏng-hŭi chŏnjip*, 3:119.

71. Pak Yŏng-hŭi, "Ch'ehopŭ hŭigok e natanan nosŏa hwanmyŏlgi ŭi kot'ong" (The agony of the disillusioned period of Russia described in Chekhov's dramas), in *Pak Yŏng-hŭi chŏnjip*, 3:24; Pak Yŏng-hŭi, "Chayŏnjuŭi esŏ sin-isangjuŭi e kiurŏjinŭn chosŏn mundan ŭi ch'oesin kyŏnghyang, in *Pak Yŏng-hŭi chŏnjip*, 3:21; Kim Ki-jin, "Maŭm ŭi p'yehŏ—kyŏul e sŏsŏ" (Ruins of the heart—standing in winter), in *Kim P'al-bong munhak chŏnjip*, 4:251.

72. Pak Yŏng-hŭi, "Ch'ehopŭ hŭigok e natanan nosŏa hwanmyŏlgi ŭi kot'ong," in *Pak Yŏng-hŭi chŏnjip*, 3:23–24.

73. Pak Yŏng-hŭi, "Ch'och'anggi ŭi mundan ch'ŭkmyŏnsa" (Byways in the history of early modern Korean literature), in *Pak Yŏng-hŭi chŏnjip*, 2:325–26.

74. Pak Yŏng-hŭi, "Chosŏn ŭl chinae kanŭn penŏsŭ" (Venus passing by Korea), in *Pak Yŏng-hŭi chŏnjip*, 3: 66.

75. Kim Ki-jin, "I-wŏl ch'angjakgye ch'ongp'yŏng" (A critique of literary production in January), in *Kim P'al-bong munhak chŏnjip*, 1:215.

76. Nikolai Gogol (1809–52) is credited as a father of Russian realism. Vissarion Belinsky (1811–48) was a Russian literary critic who was associated with populist Alexandr Gertsen (Alexander Herzen) and anarchist Mikhail Bakunin as well as with other critical intellectuals.

77. Kim Ki-jin, "P'ŭromŭnadŭ sangt'imant'al," in *Kim P'al-bong munhak chŏnjip*, 1:413–14.

78. Pak Yŏng-hŭi, "Chosŏn ŭl chinae kanŭn penŏsŭ" (Venus passing by Korea), in *Pak Yŏng-hŭi chŏnjip*, 3:72; Pak Yŏng-hŭi, "Chunbi sidae e innŭn ppasaroppu ŭi chŏngsin—T'urugenepu chak *Abŏji wa adŭl* eso" (Bazarov's nihilism in the period of preparation—from Turgenev's *Fathers and Sons*), in Pakyŏng-hŭi, 3:123, 129–30.

79. Kim Ki-jin, "Turŭgenepŭ wa Barŭbwisŭ" (Turgenev and Barbusse), in *Kim P'al-bong munhak chŏnjip*, 2:436.

80. Kim Ki-jin, "P'ŭromŭnadŭ sangt'imant'al, in *Kim P'al-bong munhak chŏnjip*, 1:422–23.

81. Ibid., 1:425.

82. For a brief description of Russian populism, see Freeborn, *Turgenev: The Novelist's Novelist*, 166–67.

83. Kim Ki-jin, "Chibae kyegŭp kyohwa, p'i-jibae kyegŭp kyohwa" (The education of the ruling class, the education of the dominated class), in *Kim P'al-bong munhak chŏnjip*, 1:489.

84. Kim Ki-jin, "Paeksu ŭi t'ansik," 136–37.

85. Kim Ki-jin, "Ttŏrŏjinŭn chogakjogak" (Broken pieces), in *Kim P'al-bong munhak chŏnjip*, 4:343.

86. Ishikawa Takuboku, *Ishikawa Takuboku zenshū*, 2: 416.

87. Ishikawa Takuboku recalled the change in his life as follows: "The conspiracy case of Kōtoku Shūsui and others was made known and my thoughts much changed. Afterwards, bit by bit, I read books and magazines concerned with socialism. . . . It was an important year [1910] in my thinking. In this year I found a chain to unify my character, tastes, and inclinations. It is the problem of socialism" ("Meiji Shijūsannen no Jūyō Kiji" [Important Events of 1910], quoted in Shea, *Leftwing Literature in Japan*, 28). For

Takuboku's critical realism and inclination toward socialism, see Shea, *Leftwing Literature in Japan*, 23–30. For his influence on Japanese proletarian poets, see Yukihito Hijima, *Ishikawa Takuboku*, 177–87. For Takuboku's experience reading Russian literature, see Yasumoto Takako, *Ishikawa Takuboku to Roshia*.

88. Turgenev, *Polnoe sobranie sochinenii i pisem*, 13:164–65; Turgenev, *Novels of Ivan Turgenev*, 10:271–73.

89. Garnett, *Turgenev: A Study*, 158–59.

90. Cho Myŏng-hŭi, "Nŭkkyŏbon il myŏt kaji" (A few things I thought about), in *Cho Myŏng-hŭi chŏnjip*, 398–99.

91. Cho Myŏng-hŭi, "Saenghwal kirok ŭi tanp'yŏn—munye e ttŭt ŭl tudŏn ttaebut'ŏ" (A sketch of my life—from the beginning of my first interest in literature), in *Cho Myŏng-hŭi chŏnjip*, 412.

92. For Cho Myŏng-hŭi's biography and discussion of his works, see Chŏng Tŏk-jun, "P'osŏk Cho Myŏng-hŭi ŭi saeng'ae wa munhak," in *Cho Myŏng-hŭi*, 9–67; Kim Sŏng-su, "Soryŏn eso ŭi Cho Myŏng-hŭi," 100–112; and Yi Sŏn-ok, "Cho Myŏng-hŭi chakp'um yŏn'gu." For an English reference, see King, "Cho Myonghui," 18–23.

93. For a brief history of newspaper serialization, see Han Wŏn-yŏng, *Han'guk kŭndae sinmun yŏnjae sosŏl yŏn'gu*, 9–14; Min Pyŏng-dŏk, "Han'guk kŭndae sinmun yŏnjae sosŏl yŏn'gu," 28–33.

94. Min Pyŏng-dŏk, "Han'guk kŭndae sinmun yŏnjae sosŏl yŏn'gu," 30.

95. Ibid., 34–39.

96. Cho Myŏng-hŭi, *Kŭjŏnnalpam* (On the eve), *Chosŏn ilbo*, August 4, 1924–October 26, 1924.

97. Cho Myŏng-hŭi, *Kŭjŏnnalpam* (On the eve), *Chosŏn ilbo*, October 26, 1924.

98. Yi Min-han, "Ae ŭi ryŏk" (The power of love), *Chosŏn ilbo* (Chosŏn Daily), October 2, 1924. This translation of a novel does not include the original author's name but records the translator's name next to the translated title. The practice of prioritizing the translator's name over the author's name was still prevalent in the mid-1920s.

99. Han Wŏn-yŏng, *Han'guk sinmun han segi*, 344–48.

100. Kim Ki-jin, "Sigam i-p'yŏn" (Two appreciative criticisms), *Chosŏn chi kwang* (The light of Korea), no. 70 (August 1927): 8–11, in *Kim P'al-bong munhak chŏnjip*, 1:293–96.

101. Cho Chung-gon, "Naktonggang kwa che-2-gi chakp'um," 9–13.

102. "Naktong River" is credited with being both one of Cho's representative works and a prime example of proletarian literature in Korean literary history. See, among others, Paek, *Chosŏn sinmunhak sajosa*; Kwŏn Yŏng-min, *Han'guk hyŏndae munhaksa*; and Chŏng Ho-ung and Kim Yun-sik, *Han'guk sosŏlsa*.

103. Turgenev, *Polnoe sobranie sochinenii i pisem*, 8:7–167; Turgenev, *On the Eve*.

104. Cho Myŏng-hŭi, "Naktong kang," in *Cho Myŏng-hŭi chŏnjip*, 15–31; Cho Myŏng-hŭi, "Naktong River," 24–31.

105. Yi Sŏn-ok, "Cho Myŏng-hŭi chakp'um yŏn'gu," 62–63.

106. Denning, *Culture in the Age of Three Worlds*, 54.

107. The first proletarian novel, Yi Ki-yŏng's *Kohyang* (Hometown), was written in 1933–34.

108. For an explanation of the popularity of the short story genre in Korea, see Pak Hŏn-ho, *Singminji kŭndaesŏng kwa sosŏl ŭi yangsik*, 67–101.

109. As Michael Denning correctly points out, Russia was exceptional rather than typical because "in Russia, the literary movement developed largely after the revolution, in alliance (in varying degrees) with the new regime, rather than as an oppositional avant-garde. As a result, proletarian novels were more about reconstructing the nation and building socialism than about struggling against capitalism or colonialism." Denning, *Culture in the Age of Three Worlds*, 61. Samuel Perry's argument that the proletarian literary movement in the Japanese empire was a part of "social formation" and "counter-hegemonic oppositional movement" aligns with Denning's observation about proletarian literature as an oppositional avant-garde in most countries. Perry, "Aesthetics for Justice," 1–12.

110. Ch'oe Wŏn-sik, "P'ŭro munhak kwa p'ŭro munhak ihu," 20.

Epilogue

1. This epilogue discusses only South Korean literature. It goes without saying that North Korean literature in the postcolonial era has developed within a close relationship with Russian/Soviet literature.

2. Of book-length translations published between 1945 and 1950, thirty-five were volumes of Russian literature while twenty-seven were volumes of American literature. Kim Pyŏng-ch'ŏl, *Han'guk hyŏndae pŏnyŏk munhaksa yŏn'gu*, 1:106.

3. Ibid., 1:301.

4. For the list of Korean translations of Russian and Soviet literature from the 1950s to the 1980s, see ibid. For a more statistical analysis of the translations of Russian literature in Korea, see Ŏm Sun-ch'ŏn, "Han'guk eso ŭi rŏsia munhak pŏnyŏk hyŏnhwang chosa mit punsŏk," 241–72.

5. Ŏm, "Han'guk eso ŭi rŏsia munhak pŏnyŏk hyŏnhwang chosa mit punsŏk, 259, 266.

6. Han Su-yŏng, "Chŏnhu sedae ŭi munhak kwa ŏnŏŏk chŏngch'esŏng," 259, 273.

7. According to Mochizuki Tetsuo, "other literatures, French, German, and English in particular, also played an important role in the shaping of modern Japanese literature, but of those introduced during the [the nineteenth and early twentieth centuries], Russian literature is rightly regarded as the most influential." Mochizuki Tetsuo, "Japanese Perceptions of Russian Literature in the Meiji and Taishō Eras" in Rimer, *A Hidden Fire*, 17. In the case of China, Gamsa argues that "by common consent, the literature of no other country had as important and as many-sided an impact on modern China as did the literature of Russia and the Soviet Union." Gamsa, *The Reading of Russian Literature in China*, 4). For the number of Chinese translations of Russian literature in different periods, see Gamsa, *The Chinese Translation of Russian Literature*, 20–25. In his study of Japanese-Russian nonstate intellectual relations from the mid-nineteenth to the early twentieth century, Sho Konishi argues that "in macro historical perspective, the Russian cultural presence in Japan from the mid-nineteenth to the early twentieth century was, for interpretive purposes, comparable to that of the Chinese cultural presence in the intellectual life of Tokugawa Japan before 1860 and the American cultural presence in the intellectual life of Japan after the Asia-Pacific War." Konishi, *Anarchist Modernity*, 5.

8. Futabatei Shimei, "Rokoku bungaku no Nihon bungaku ni oyoboshitaru eikyo," in *Futabatei Shimei zenshū*, 5:283–84.

9. Lu Hsun [Lu Xun], "China's Debt to Russian Literature," in *Selected Works of Lu Hsun*, 3:181.

10. Gamsa, *The Reading of Russian Literature in China*, 12.

11. "The influence of Russian literature on me is far from being limited to the literary aspect, for it has entered my blood and marrow: the way I see and make sense of everything in the world, even my very soul, are inseparable from the moral instruction and upbringing (*taoye xunyu*) of Russian literature." Qian Gurong, "Xu" (Introduction), in Chen Jianhua, *20 shiji Zhong-E wenxue guanxi* (Shanghai: Xuelin chubanshe, 1998), 1; quoted in Gamsa, *The Reading of Russian Literature in China*, 16.

12. Gamsa, *The Reading of Russian Literature in China*, 29–33.

13. Lim, *China and Japan in the Russian Imagination, 1685–1922*, 9.

14. Schimmelpenninck van der Oye, *Russian Orientalism*; Konishi, *Anarchist Modernity*; Lim, *China and Japan in the Russian Imagination, 1685–1922*; Schimmelpenninck van der Oye, *Toward the Rising Sun*.

15. "Anarchism" here means "a cultural, intellectual, and social movement" rather than violent confrontations with the state. For more details, see Konishi, *Anarchist Modernity*, 6–10.

16. Gamsa, *The Reading of Russian Literature in China*, 15.

Bibliography

Newspapers

Cheguk sinmun
Chosŏn ch'ongdokbu kwanbo
Chosŏn chung'ang ilbo
Chosŏn ilbo
Chung'ang ilbo
Chung'oe ilbo
Hwangsŏng sinmun
Maeil sinbo
Sidae ilbo
Taehan maeil sinbo
Tong'a ilbo
Tongnip sinmun

Álvarez, Román, and M. Carmen-África Vidal, eds. *Translation, Power, Subversion.* Clevedon, NZ: Multilingual Matters, 1996.

An Hwak. "Chosŏn ŭi munhak" (Literature of Korea). *Hakchigwang*, no. 6 (July 1915): 64–73.

——. "Segye munhakkwan" (A survey of world literature). *Asŏng* 1, no. 2 (May 1921): 28–54.

An Suk-hyŏn. *Han'guk yŏn'gŭk kwa Anton Ch'ehop* (Korean dramas and Anton Chekhov). Seoul: T'aehaksa, 2003.

Anderson, Benedict. *Imagined Communities.* New York: Verso, 1991.

Anonymous. "Injae sullye (1)" (A pilgrimage for men of talent). *Samch'ŏlli*, no. 4 (January 1930): 28–32.

Arac, Jonathan. "Anglo-Globalism?" *New Left Review*, no. 16 (July–August 2002): 35–45.

Bassnett, Susan. *Translation Studies.* London: Routledge, 2002.

Bassnett, Susan, and André Lefevere, eds. *Translation, History and Culture.* London: Pinter, 1990.

Benjamin, Walter. *Illuminations.* Translated by Harry Zohn. New York: Schocken Books, 1968.

Berman, Antoine. *The Experiencing of the Foreign: Culture and Translation in Romantic Germany.* Translated by S. Heyvaert. Albany: State University of New York Press, 1985.

Berton, Peter, Paul Fritz Langer, and Rodger Swearingen. *Japanese Training and Research in the Russian Field.* Los Angeles: University of Southern California Press, 1956.

Brownstein, Michael C. "From *Kokugaku* to *Kokubungaku*: Canon-Formation in the Meiji Period." *Harvard Journal of Asiatic Studies* 47, no. 2 (December 1987): 435–60.

Casanova, Pascale. *The World Republic of Letters.* Translated by M. B. DeBevoise. Cambridge, MA: Harvard University Press, 2004.

Chang Yŏn-hwa. "Munhak kisaeng ŭi kobaek" (A female entertainer's confession). *Samch'ŏlli* (The whole land of Korea), 6, no. 5 (May 1934): 140–42.

Chekhov, Anton. *Chehop tanp'yŏnjip.* Translated by Kwŏn Po-sang. Seoul: Chosŏn tosŏ chusik hoesa, 1924.

———. *Chekhov: The Early Stories 1883–88.* Translated and edited by Patrick Miles and Harvey Pitcher. London: John Murray, 1982.

———. *Polnoe sobranie sochinenii i pisem* (Complete works and letters). 20 vols. Moscow: Gos. izdat. khudozhestvennoi literatury, 1944–51.

Cho Chung-gon. "Naktonggang kwa che-2-gi chakp'um" ("Naktong River" and the literary works of the second period). *Chosŏn chi kwang* (The light of Korea), no. 72 (October 1927): 9–13.

Cho, Heekyoung. "Imagined, Transcultural, and Colonial Spaces in Print: Newspaper serialization of Translated Novels in Colonial Korea." *East Asian Publishing and Society,* 3, no. 2 (2013): 153–83.

———. "Literary Translation and Appropriation: Korean Intellectuals' Reception of Nineteenth-Century Russian Prose via Japan in 1909–1927." PhD diss., University of Chicago, 2010.

———. "Translation and Censorship: Colonial Writing and Anti-imperial Imagination of Asia in 1910s Korea." In *Spaces of Possibility Korea and Japan: In, Between, and Beyond the Nation.* Edited by Clark W. Sorensen and Andrea Gevurtz Arai. Seattle: University of Washington Press, 2016.

Cho Hŭi-ung. "Naksŏnjae-bon pŏnyŏk sosŏl yŏn'gu" (A study of translations in Naksŏnjae library). *Kugŏ kungmunhak* (Korean language and literature), no. 62–63 (December 1973): 257–73.

Cho Myŏng-hŭi. *Cho Myŏng-hŭi chŏnjip* (Complete works). Edited by Yi Myŏng-jae. Seoul: Pŏmusa, 2004.

———. *Kŭjŏnnalpam* (On the eve). *Chosŏn ilbo,* August 4, 1924–October 26, 1924.

———. "Naktong River." Translated by Ross King. *Korean Culture* 22, no. 3 (Autumn 2001), 24–31.

Cho Yong-hun. "T'urŭgenep'ŭ ŭi iip kwa yŏnghyang: 'sanmunsi' rŭl chungsim ŭro" (The importation and influence of Turgenev: The case of prose poems). *Sŏgang ŏmun,* no. 7 (July 1990): 291–338.

Ch'oe Ki-yŏng. "Hanmal Ch'oe Kwang-ok ŭi kyoyuk hwaltong kwa kukkwŏn hoebok undong" (Ch'oe Kwang-ok's educational activity and the movement to restore national sovereignty). *Han'guk kŭn-hyŏndaesa yon'gu*, no. 34 (Autumn 2005): 37–62.

Ch'oe Myŏng-ik. "Lepŭ T'olsŭt'oi sŏnsaeng e taehan tansang" (Fragmentary thoughts on Tolstoy). *Chosŏn munhak*, no. 9 (1958), 156–60.

Ch'oe Nam-sŏn. "Ch'ŏngnyŏn haguhoe ch'wijisŏ" (The manifesto of the Youth Association) and "Chŏngnyŏn haguhoe sollip wiwŏnhoe chŏnggŏn" (The summary of its establishment committee meeting). *Sonyŏn* 2, no. 8 (September 1909): 14–16.

———. "Han'guk mundan ŭi ch'och'anggi rŭl mallham" (Memories of the beginning of modern Korean literary circles). *Hyŏndae munhak*, no. 1 (January 1955): 37–38.

———. "Sŏnsaeng ŭi soŏn silhaeng" (Tolstoy's practice). *Sonyŏn* 2, no. 6 (July 1909), 13.

———. "T'olsŭt'oi sŏnsaeng hase kinyŏm" (Remembering Tolstoy). *Sonyŏn* 3, no. 9 (December 1910): 1.

———. "T'olsŭt'oi sŏnsaeng ŭi ilgwa" (Tolstoy's daily plan). *Sonyŏn* 2, no. 6 (July 1909): 17.

———. "T'olssŭt'oi sŏnsaeng ŭi kyosi" (Tolstoy's teaching). *Sonyŏn* 2, no. 6 (July 1909): 5–13.

———. "T'olsŭt'oi sŏnsaeng ŭl kokham" (Lamentation on Tolstoy's death). *Sonyŏn* 3, no. 9 (December 1910): 1–5.

———. "Uridŭl ŭi ŭimu" (Our duty). *Sonyŏn* 2, no. 2 (July 1909): 13.

———. *Yukdang Ch'oe Nam-sŏn chŏnjip* (Complete works). Seoul: Hyŏnamsa, 1974.

Ch'oe T'ae-wŏn. "Iljae Cho Chung-hwan ŭi pŏnan sosŏl yŏn'gu" (A study on Cho Chung-hwan's adaptations). PhD diss., Seoul National University, 2010.

Ch'oe Tu-sŏn. "Munhak ŭi ŭiŭi e kwanhaya" (On the meaning of literature). *Hakchigwang*, no. 3 (December 1914): 26–28.

Ch'oe Wŏn-sik. "Hyŏn Chin-gŏn sosŏl e nat'anan chisigin kwa minjung" (Intellectuals and the people represented in Hyŏn Chin-gŏn's stories). In *Han'guk hyŏndae sosŏlsa yŏn'gu* (A study on contemporary Korean literary history). Edited by Kim Kwang-yong. Seoul: Minŭmsa, 1984.

———. "Isingnon kwa naejaeŏk palchŏnnon ŭl nŏmŏsŏ" (Beyond the theory of transplantation and the theory of autonomous development). In Im Hwa, *Sin munhaksa* (The history of new literature). Edited by Im Kyu-ch'an and Han Chin-il. Seoul: Hangilsa, 1993.

———. "P'ŭro munhak kwa p'ŭro munhak ihu" (Proletarian literature and afterwords). *Minjok munhaksa yŏn'gu* (A study of national literary history), no. 21 (December 2002): 10–33.

Choi, Hyaeweol. *Gender and Mission Encounters in Korea: New Women, Old Ways*. Berkeley: University of California Press, 2009.

Choi, Kyeong-Hee. *Beneath the Vermilion Ink: Japanese Colonial Censorship and the Making of Modern Korean Literature*. Ithaca, NY: Cornell University Press, forthcoming.

Chŏn Mi-gyŏng. "Kaehwagi chohon tamnon ŭi kajok yulli ŭisik ŭi hamŭi" (The meaning of family ethics and the discourse on early marriage in the Enlightenment period). *Taehan kajŏng hakhoeji* 39, no. 9 (September 2001): 189–207.

Chŏn Ŭn-kyŏng. "1910-nyŏndae pŏnan sosŏl yŏn'gu: tokcha wa ŭi sangho sot'ongsŏng ŭl chungsim ŭro" (A study on adaptations in the 1910s: communication with the reader). PhD diss., Kyŏngbuk University, 2006.

Chŏng Byŏng-ho. "Hanil kŭndae munyeron e issŏsŏ 'chŏng' ŭi wich'i" (The place of emotion in modern Korean and Japanese literary theories). *Asia munhwa yŏn'gu*, no. 8 (February 2004): 271–98.

Chŏng Chin-sŏk. *Inmul han'guk ŏllonsa* (The history of the Korean press). Seoul: Nanam, 1995.

Chŏng Ho-ung and Kim Yun-sik. *Han'guk sosŏlsa* (History of Korean literature). Seoul: Munhak tongne, 2000.

Chŏng Kŭn-sik. "Singminji kŏmyŏl ŭi yŏksaŏk kiwŏn" (The historical origin of colonial censorship). *Sahoe wa yŏksa*, no. 64 (November 2003): 5–46.

Chŏng Se-yun. "Ch'anggan ŭl ch'ukham" (Congratulations on the first edition). *Kongje* (Mutual aid), no. 1 (September 1920): 22–23.

Chŏng Tŏk-jun. "P'osŏk Cho Myŏng-hŭi ŭi saeng'ae wa munhak" (Cho Myŏng-hŭi's life and literature). In *Cho Myŏng-hŭi*. Edited by Chŏng Tŏk-jun. Seoul: Saemi, 1999.

Chu Si-kyŏng. "Kugŏ wa kungmun ŭi p'iryo" (The necessity of Korean language and Korean writing) (1907). In *Han'guk ŭi munhak pip'yŏng 1 (1896–1945)*. Edited by Kwŏn Yŏng-min. Seoul: Minŭmsa 1995.

Chu Yo-sŏp. "Nosŏa ŭi tae munho Ch'eekhopŭ" (The great Russian writer Chekhov). *Sŏgwang*, no. 6 (July 1920): 88–94.

Clyman, Toby W., ed. *A Chekhov Companion*. Westport, CT: Greenwood, 1985.

Cockerill, Hiroko. "Futabatei Shimei's Translations from Russian: Verbal Aspect and Narrative Perspective." *Japanese Studies* 23, no. 3 (December 2003): 229–38.

C. Y. Saeng. "Kwabu haebangnon" (Liberation of widows). *Hakchigwang*, no. 20 (July 1920): 15–20.

Damrosch, David. *What Is World Literature?* Princeton, NJ: Princeton University Press, 2003.

Denning, Michael. *Culture in the Age of Three Worlds*. New York: Verso, 2004.

Even-Zohar, Itamar. "Polysystem Theory." *Poetics Today* 1, no. 2 (Autumn 1979): 237–310.

———. *Polysystem Studies*. Special issue of *Poetics Today* 11, no. 1. Tel Aviv: The Porter Institute for Poetics and Semiotics, 1990.

Freeborn, Richard. *Turgenev: The Novelist's Novelist*. London: Oxford University Press, 1963.

Fukuda Mitsuharu, Kenmochi Takehiko, and Kodama Kōichi, eds. *Ōbei sakka to nihon kindai bungaku* (Western writers and modern Japanese literature). 3 vols. Tokyo: Kyōiku shuppan senta, 1976.

Futabatei Shimei. *Japan's First Modern Novel: "Ukigumo" of Futabatei Shimei*. Translated and with critical commentary by Marleigh Grayer Ryan. New York: Columbia University Press, 1967.

———. "Rokoku bungaku no Nihon bungaku ni oyoboshitaru eikyo" (The influence Russian literature exerted on Japanese literature). In *Futabatei Shimei zenshū* 5:283–84. Tokyo: Iwanami shoten, 1965.

G. H. "'Tamatsukiya' to 'surīpi heddo'" ("A Billiard Room" and "Sleepy Head"). *Bunko* (A library) (April 1908): 565–67.

Gamsa, Mark. *The Chinese Translation of Russian Literature: Three Studies*. Sinica Leidensia. Leiden, Netherlands: Brill, 2008.

———. *The Reading of Russian Literature in China: A Moral Example and Manual of Practice*. New York: Palgrave Macmillan, 2010.

Garnett, Edward. *Turgenev: A Study*. New York: Haskell House, 1975.

Grabowski, Richard, and Sharmistha Self, "Education and Child Labor in Japan." In *The World of Child Labor: An Historical and Regional Survey*. Edited by Hugh D. Hindman. Armonk, NY: M. E. Sharpe, 2009.

Gromkovskaia, L. L., ed. *Russkaia klassika v stranakh vostoka* (Russian classics in Eastern countries). Moscow: Nauka, 1982.

Haga Yaichi. *Kokubungakushi jikkō* (Ten lectures on the history of national literature). Tokyo: Toyamabō, 1899.

Han Su-yŏng. "Chŏnhu sedae ŭi munhak kwa ŏnŏŏk chŏngch'esŏng" (Post-war generation literature and its linguistic identity). *Taedong munhwa yŏn'gu* (A study of Korean culture) 58 (2007): 257–301.

Han Wŏn-yŏng. *Han'guk kŭndae sinmun yŏnjae sosŏl yŏn'gu* (A study of newspaper serialization of fiction in modern Korea). Seoul: Ihoe munhwasa, 1996.

———. *Han'guk sinmun han segi* (One hundred years of Korean newspapers). Seoul: P'urŭn sasangsa, 2004.

Han'guk Yŏsŏngsa P'yŏnch'an Wiwŏnhoe. *Han'guk yŏsŏngsa* (The history of Korean women). 3 vols. Seoul: Ehwa Women's University, 1972.

Hill, Christopher L. "Nana in the World: Novel, Gender, and Transnational Form." *Modern Language Quarterly* 72, no. 1 (March 2011): 75–103.

Hŏ Tong-hyŏn. "Kaehwa ilche-gi han'guk-in ŭi rŏsia insik e poinŭn kojŏng kwannyŏm" (Stereotypes about Russia in Korea during the Enlightenment period and colonial period). *Han'guk minjok undongsa yŏn'gu* (A study of the Korean nationalist movement), no. 42 (March 2005): 29–77.

Honda Shūgo. *Shirakabaha no bungaku* (The literature of Shirakaba-ha). Tokyo: Dainihon yubenkai kōdansya, 1954.

Hong Il-sik. "Yuktang ŭi saeng'ae wa munhak" (Ch'oe Nam-sŏn's life and literature). In *Ch'oe Nam-sŏn kwa Yi Kwang-su ŭi munhak* (Ch'oe Nam-sŏn and Yi Kwang-su's literature). Edited by Sin Tong-uk. Seoul: Saemunsa, 1981.

Hughes, Theodore. *Literature and Film in Cold War South Korea: Freedom's Frontier*. New York: Columbia University Press, 2012.

Hume, David. *A Treatise of Human Nature*. Edited by L .A. Selby-Bigge. 2nd ed. Oxford: Clarendon Press, 1978.

Hwang Chong-yŏn. "Munhak iranŭn yŏgŏ" (*Munhak* as a translated term). *Tong'ak ŏmun hakhoe*, no. 32 (December 1997): 457–80.

———. "Nobŭl, ch'ŏngnyŏn, cheguk: han'guk kŭndae sosŏl ŭi t'ong-kukka-gan sijak" (The novel, the youth, and empire: The transnational beginnings of the modern Korean novel). *Sang'hŏ hakbo*, no. 14 (February 2005): 263–97.

Hyŏn Chin-gŏn. *Hyŏn Chin-gŏn munhak chŏnjip* (The complete works of Hyŏn Chin-gŏn). Edited by Yi Kang-ŏn, Yi Chu-hyŏng, Cho Chin-gi, and Yi Chae-ch'un. 6 vols. Seoul: Kukhak charyowŏn, 2004.

———. "Kkamakchapki" (Blindman's Bluff). *Kaebyŏk*, no. 43 (January 1924): 211–22.

Hyŏn Ch'ŏl. "Kakpon kyŏgya omak: mudan hŭnghaeng ŭl kŭmham" (A five-act play On the Eve—unauthorized performances are forbidden). *Kaebyŏk* (The creation), no. 1 (June 1920): 151–58.

Hyŏn Sang-yun. "Ingu chŭngsik p'iryoron" (The need for population increase). *Hakchigwang*, no. 13 (July 1917): 57–62.

I. K. P. "Ttŏsŭt'ŏep'ŭsŭk'i" (Dostoevsky). *Chosŏn mundan* (The Korean literary world) 3, no. 4 (June 1926): 55–56.

Il So. "Tuong" (Tolstoy). *Asŏng* 1, no. 4 (October 1921): 38–43.

Im Hwa. "Chosŏn munhak yŏn'gu ŭi il kwaje" (A task of the study of Korean literature). *Tong'a ilbo* (Tong'a daily) January 16, 1940. Reprinted in Im Hwa, *Sinmunhaksa* (The history of new literature). Seoul: Hangilsa, 1993.

———. *Sinmunhaksa* (The history of new literature). Seoul: Hangilsa, 1993.

Ishikawa Takuboku. *Ishikawa Takuboku zenshū* (Complete works). Tokyo: Chikuma shobō, 1978–79.

Jameson, Fredric. "Foreword: In the Mirror of Alternate Modernities." In Karatani Kojin, *Origins of Modern Japanese Literature*. Edited by Brett de Bary. Post-Contemporary Interventions, edited by Stanley Fish and Fredric Jameson. Durham, NC: Duke University Press, 1993.

Jeong, Kelly. *Crisis of Gender and Nation in Korean Literature and Cinema*. Lanham, MD: Lexington Books, 2011.

Jusdanis, Gregory. *Belated Modernity and Aesthetic Culture: Inventing National Literature*. Minneapolis: University of Minnesota Press, 1991.

Kakinami, Atsuko Fujino. "History of Child Labor in Japan." In *The World of Child Labor: An Historical and Regional Survey*. Edited by Hugh D. Hindman. Armonk, NY: M. E. Sharpe, 2009.

Kang In-taek. "Na ŭi pon chosŏn sŭpsok i sam" (My view on a couple of Korean customs). *Kaebyŏk*, no. 5 (November 1920): 81–86.

Karatani, Kojin. "Nationalism and Écriture." *Surfaces* 1.0A (January 11, 1995): 5–25.

Kawato Michiaki and Sakakibara Takanori, eds. *Tsurugenefu shū 2*. Vol. 41, Meiji hon'yaku bungaku zenshu: shinbunzasshi-hen. Tokyo: Ōzorasha, 1997.

Keene, Donald, *Dawn to the West*. New York: Columbia University Press, 1998.

Kim Ki-jin. *Kim P'al-bong munhak chŏnjip* (Complete works). 6 vols. Seoul: Munhak kwa chisŏng, 1988.

———. "Paeksu ŭi t'ansik" (The sigh of the man with white hands). *Kaepyŏk*, no. 48 (June 1924): 136–37.

Kim Kyo-sik. *Ch'oe Nam-sŏn*. Seoul: Kyesŏng ch'ulp'ansa, 1984.

Kim Myŏng-sik. "Nosŏa ŭi san munhak" (A living literature of Russia). *Sinsaenghwal* 1, no. 3 (April 1922): 5–6.

Kim Ŏk. "Milhoe" (The tryst). *T'aesŏ munye sinbo* (News about Western literature), no. 15 (February 1, 1919) and no. 16 (February 17, 1919).

Kim Pyŏng-ch'ŏl. *Han'guk hyŏndae pŏnyŏk munhaksa yŏn'gu* (A history of literary translation in contemporary Korea). 2 vols. Seoul: Ŭryu munhwasa, 1998.

————. *Han'guk kŭndae pŏnyŏk munhaksa yŏn'gu* (A history of literary translation in modern Korea). Seoul: Ŭryu munhwasa, 1998.

————. *Han'guk kŭndae sŏyang munhak iipsa yŏn'gu* (A history of the importation of Western literature to modern Korea). Seoul: Ŭryu munhwasa, 1998.

Kim, Rekho, ed. *Lev Tostoi i literatury vostoka* (Tolstoy and the literature of the East). Moscow: Imli ran, 2000.

Kim Sŏng-su. "Soryŏn eso ŭi Cho Myŏng-hŭi" (Cho Myŏng-hŭi in Soviet Russia). *Ch'angjak kwa pip'yŏng* (Creation and criticism), no. 64 (Summer 1989): 100–20.

Kim T'ae-jun. *Kyoju Chŭngbo Chosŏn sosŏlsa* (A history of Korean literature: a revised and expanded edition). Annotated by Pak Hŭi-byŏng. Seoul: Hangilsa, 1990.

Kim Tong-in. *Kim Tong-in chŏnjip* (Complete works). Seoul: Hongja ch'ulp'ansa, 1964.

Kim Tong-sik. *Han'guk ŭi kŭndaeŏk munhak kaenyŏm hyŏngsŏng kwajŏng* (The formation of literature as a modern concept in Korea). PhD diss., Seoul National University, 1999.

Kim Tu-hŏn. "Chosŏn ŭi chohon kwa mit kŭ kiwŏn e taehan il koch'al" (A study of early marriage in Korea and its origins). *Chindan hakbo* 2 (April 1935): 46–86.

Kim Yŏng-min. *Han'guk kŭndae sosŏlsa* (The history of the Korean novel). Seoul: Sol, 2003.

Kim, Young-hee. "Conditions of Literary Translation in Korea." *Korea Journal* 44, no. 1 (Spring 2004): 235–47.

Kim Yu-bang. "Tolsŭtoi ŭi yesulgwan" (Tolstoy's thoughts on art). *Kaebyŏk* (The creation), no. 9 (March 1921): 123–31.

Kim Yun-sik. *Yi Kwang-su wa kŭ ŭi sidae* (The life and times of Yi Kwang-su). 2 vols. Seoul: Sol, 1999.

Kim Yun-sik and Kim Hyŏn. *Han'guk munhaksa* (A history of Korean literature). Seoul: Minŭmsa, 1973.

King, Ross. "Cho Myonghui: Pioneer of Korean Proletarian Fiction, Father of Soviet Korean Literature" and "Cho Myonghui's 'Naktong River.'" *Korean Culture* (Fall 2001): 18–31.

Kokuritsu Kokkai Toshokan, ed. *Meiji, Taishō, Shōwa hon'yaku bungaku mokuroku* (Index of translated literature in Meiji, Taishō, and Shōwa Japan). Tōkyō: Kazama shobō, 1959.

Kŏmyŏl yŏn'guhoe, ed. *Singminji kŏmyŏl: chedo, t'eksŭt'ŭ, silch'ŏn* (Colonial censorship: regulations, texts, and practice). Seoul: Somyŏng, 2011.

Konishi, Sho. *Anarchist Modernity: Cooperatism and Japanese-Russian Intellectual Relations in Modern Japan.* Cambridge, MA: Harvard University Asia Center, 2013.

Kōtoko Shūsui. "Torusutoi ō no hisenron o hyōsu" (Comments on Tolstoy's anti-war opinion). *Heimin shinbun*, August 14, 1904. Reprinted in Hayashi Shigeru and Nishida Taketoshi, eds., *Hemin shinbun ronsetsushū.* Tokyo: Iwanami shoten, 1961.

Kristal, Efraín. "'Considering Coldly . . .': A Response to Franco Moretti." *New Left Review*, no. 15 (May–June 2002): 61–74.

Kropotkin, Pëtr A. *Russian Literature.* London: Duckworth, 1905.

Ku Chung-sŏ. "Munhaksa wa kŭndaesŏng, kŭndae kichŏm" (A literature history and modernity: The starting point of modern Korean literature). In *Han'guk kŭndae munhak yŏn'gu* (A study of modern Korean literature). Edited by Ch'oe Wŏn-sik and Ku Chung-sŏ. Seoul: T'aehaksa, 1997.

Ku In-hwan. "Hyŏn Chin-gŏn ŭi saeng'ae wa munhak" (Hyŏn Chin-gŏn's life and literature). In Sin Tong-uk, ed., *Hyŏn Chin-gŏn ŭi sosŏl kwa kŭ ŭi sidae insik* (Hyŏn Chin-gŏn's literature and his understanding of his times). Seoul: Saemunsa, 1981.

Kuksa Pyŏnch'an Wiwŏnhoe, ed. *Ilche ch'imnyak ha han'guk samsimyungnyŏn sa* (The history of colonial Korea). Vol. 1, Ilche ch'imnyak ha han'guk samsimyungnyŏn sa. Seoul: Kuksa pyŏnch'an wiwŏnhoe, 1966.

Kusuyama Masao. *Kyakuhon so no zenya* (A play: On the eve). Tokyo: Shinchōsha, 1915.

Kwŏn Chŏng-hwa. "Ch'oe Nam-sŏn ŭi ch'ogi sŏsul e nat'ananŭn chiriŏk kwansim" (Ch'oe Nam-sŏn's interest in geography in his early writings). *Ŭng'yong chiri*, no. 13 (December, 1990): 1–34.

Kwŏn Hŭi-yŏng. "Chosŏn nodong kongje-hoe wa *Kongje*" (Korean Labor Mutual Aid Association and *Mutual Aid*). *Chŏngsin munhwa yŏn'gu* 16, no. 2 (June 1993): 139–57.

Kwŏn Podŭrae. *Han'guk kŭndae sosŏl ŭi kiwŏn* (The origin of modern Korean literature). Seoul: Somyŏng ch'ulp'ansa, 2000.

Kwŏn Yŏng-min. *Han'guk hyŏndae munhaksa* (History of modern Korean literature). Seoul: Minŭmsa, 2002.

———. *Han'guk kyegŭp munhak undongsa* (A history of Korean proletarian literature). Seoul: Munye ch'ulp'ansa, 1998.

Lee, Ji-Eun. *Women Pre-scripted: Reading Women's Issues in Pre-colonial and Colonial Korea*. Honolulu: University of Hawai'i Press, 2015.

Lefevere, André. *Translation, Rewriting, and the Manipulation of Literary Fame*. London; New York: Routledge, 1992.

Levy, Indra. *Sirens of the Western Shore: The Westernesque Femme Fatale, Translation, and Vernacular Style in Modern Japanese Literature*. New York: Columbia University Press, 2006.

———, ed. *Translation in Modern Japan*. Routledge Contemporary Japan Series. Milton Park, UK: Routledge, 2011.

Lim, Susanna. *China and Japan in the Russian Imagination, 1685–1922: To the Ends of the Orient*. New York: Routledge, 2013.

Liu, Lydia H. *Translingual Practice: Literature, National Culture, and Translated Modernity—China, 1900–1937*. Stanford, CA: Stanford University Press, 1995.

Lu Hsun [Lu Xun]. "China's Debt to Russian Literature." In *Selected Works of Lu Hsun*. 4 vols. Translated by Yang Hsien-yi and Gladys Yang. Peking: Foreign Languages Press, 1956–60.

Maeda Akira. "Che-hofu shōden" (A short biography of Chekhov). In Anton Chekhov. *Tanpen jisshu Che-hofu shū* (Chekhov's ten short stories). Translated by Maeda Akira. Tokyo: Hakubunkan, 1913.

Maeda Akira and Shimamura Tamizō. *Ōshū kindai shōsetsuka kenkyū* (A study of modern European writers). Tokyo: Bungaku fukyūkai, 1915.

Mansfield, Katherine. "The Child-Who-Was-Tired" In *In a German Pension*. London: Stephen Swift, 1911.

Masamune Hakuchō. "Tamatsukiya" (A billiard room). In *Masamune Hakuchō zenshū* (Masamune Hakuchō: The complete works). 30 vols. Tokyo: Fukutake shoten, 1983.

May, Rachel. *The Translator in the Text: On Reading Russian Literature in English.* Evanston, IL: Northwestern University Press, 1994.

Mikami Sanji and Takasu Kuwasaburō. *Nihon bungakushi* (History of Japanese literature). Tokyo: Kinkōdō, 1890.

Miller, J. Scott. *Adaptations of Western Literature in Meiji Japan.* New York: Palgrave, 2001.

Min Kwan-dong. "Chungguk kojŏn sosŏl ŭi kungnae pŏnyŏksa yŏn'gu" (A history of Korean translations of Chinese novels). *Chung'ŏ chungmunhak* (Chinese language and literature), no. 21 (December 1997): 511–42.

Min Pyŏng-dŏk. "Han'guk kŭndae sinmun yŏnjae sosŏl yŏn'gu" (A study of modern Korean novels serialized in newspapers). PhD diss., Sŏnggyungwan University, 1989.

Mirsky, D. S. *A History of Russian Literature: From Its Beginning to 1900.* Evanston, IL: Northwestern University Press, 1999.

Moretti, Franco. "Conjectures on World Literature." *New Left Review,* no. 1 (January–February 2000): 54–68.

———. "More Conjectures." *New Left Review,* no. 20 (March–April 2003): 73–81.

Moser, Charles A. *Ivan Turgenev.* New York: Columbia University Press, 1972.

Mun Sŏk-u. "Han'guk kŭndae munhak e kkich'in tturŭgenep'ŭ ŭi yŏnghyang: siin Kim Ŏk ŭl chungsim ŭro" (The influence of Turgenev in modern Korean literature: The case of Kim Ŏk). *Oeguk munhak yŏn'gu* 17, no. 1 (1994): 115–38.

Nakajima Michimasa. *Nihon ni okeru Che-hofu shoshi: 1902–2004* (A bibliography of Chekhov in Japan: 1902–2004). Tokyo: Nakajima Michimasa, 2004.

Nakazato Kaizan. *Torusutoi genkōroku* (Tolstoy's sayings and doings). 2nd ed. Tokyo: Naigai shuppan kyōkai, November 1906.

Nam, Kwon Woo. *The North Korean Communist Leadership.* Tuscaloosa: University of Alabama Press, 1974.

Natsume Sōseki. *Theory of Literature and Other Critical Writings.* Edited by Michael K. Bourdaghs, Atsuko Ueda, and Joseph A. Murphy. New York: Columbia University, 2009.

New, W. H. *Reading Mansfield and Metaphors of Form.* Montreal: McGill-Queen's University Press, 1999.

Ng, Mau-sang. *The Russian Hero in Modern Chinese Fiction.* Hong Kong: Chinese University Press, 1988.

Nihon Kindai Bungakukan, ed. *Nihon kindai bungaku daijiten* (An unbridged dictionary of modern Japanese literature). 6 vols. Tokyo: Kōdansha, 1977–78.

Nihon Rosia Bungakkukai, ed. *Nihonjin to rosiago: rosiago kyōiku no rekishi* (Japanese people and Russian language: The history of Russian-language education). Tokyo: Nauka, 2000.

Nobori Shomu. "Nikorai dai-shukyō no shōgai to gyōseki" (Archbishop Nikolai's life and achievements). *Eui: Rosiya bungaku, sisō* (Eui: Russian literature and thought), no. 17 (April 1989): 103–26.

Nobori Shomu, and Akamatsu Katsumaro. *The Russian Impact on Japan: Literature and Social Thought.* Translated and edited with introductions and illustrative data by Peter Berton, Paul F. Langer, and George O. Totten. Los Angeles: University of Southern California Press, 1981.

O Chang-hwan. *Han'guk anak'ijŭm undongsa yŏn'gu* (A study of the Korean anarchist movement). Seoul: Kukhak charyowŏn, 1998.

Ŏm Sun-ch'ŏn. "Han'guk eso ŭi rŏsia munhak pŏnyŏk hyŏnhwang chosa mit punsŏk" (A survey and analysis of Korean translations of Russian literature). *Noŏ nomunhak* (Russian language and literature) 17, no. 3 (2005): 241–72.

Paek Ch'ŏl. *Chosŏn sinmunhak sajosa* (History of intellectual movements in new literature). Seoul: Susŏnsa, 1948.

Pak Ae-rim. "Chosŏn nodong kongje-hoe ŭi hwaltong kwa inyŏm" (The activities and ideologies of the Korea Labor Mutual Aid Association). Master's thesis, Yonsei University, 1992.

Pak Chin-yŏng. "Han'guk ŭi kŭndae pŏnyŏk mit pŏnan sosŏlsa yŏn'gu" (A study on translation and adaptation in modern Korea). PhD diss., Yonsei University, 2010.

———. *Pŏnyŏk kwa pŏnan ŭi sidae* (The age of translation and adaptation). Seoul: Somyŏng, 2011.

Pak Chong-hwa. "Mundan ŭi il-nyŏn ŭl ch'uŏkhaya" (Recalling a year in the literary world). *Kaebyŏk*, no. 31 (January 1923): 1–14.

Pak Chong-hyo. "Kwallip aŏ hakkyo sŏllip kwa piryukop'ŭ ŭi hwaltong (1896–1916)" (The foundation of the Russian school and Biryukov's activities, 1896–1916). *Han'guk kŭndaesa yŏn'gu* (A study of modern Korean history), no. 46 (Fall 2008): 7–26.

Pak Hŏn-ho. "'Munhwa chŏngch'i-i-gi sinmun ŭi wisang kwa pan-gŏmyŏl ŭi naechŏk nolli" (The status of newspapers and internal logic of anti-censorship under the cultural regime). *Taedong munhwa yŏn'gu*, no. 50 (June 2005): 199–259.

———. *Singminji kŭndaesŏng kwa sosŏl ŭi yangsik* (Colonial modernity and prose genres). Seoul: Somyŏng, 2004.

Pak Kwang-hyŏn. "Kyŏnggye rŭl nŏmŏsŏn hwahae ŭi sidae" (An era of reconciliation beyond borders). *Munhak sasang* (Literary thought), no. 390 (April 2005): 205–10.

Pak Yong-gyu. "Singminji sigi munin kijadŭl ŭi kŭlssŭgi wa kŏmyŏl" (Korean writer-journalists' writing and censorship in the colonial period). *Han'guk munhak yŏn'gu* 29 (December 2005): 79–120.

Pak Yŏng-hŭi. "Ch'ehopŭ hŭigok e nat'anan nosŏa hwanmyŏlgi ŭi kot'ong" (The agony of the disillusioned period of Russia described in Chekhov's dramas). *Kaebyŏk* (The creation), no. 44 (February 1924): 55–72.

———. "Munhak e ttŭt ŭl tunŭn i ege" (To people who aspire to do literature). *Kyaebyŏk* (Creation), no. 21 (March 1922): 1–15.

———. *Pak Yŏng-hŭi chŏnjip* (Complete works). 4 vols. Taegu, South Korea: Yŏngnam taehakkyo, 1997.

Park, Sunyoung. *The Proletarian Wave: Literature and Leftist Culture in Colonial Korea, 1910–1945*. Cambridge, MA: Harvard University Asia Center, 2015.

Perry, Samuel. "Aesthetics for Justice: Proletarian Literature in Japan and Colonial Korea." PhD diss., University of Chicago, 2007.

———. *Recasting Red Culture in Proletarian Japan: Childhood, Korea, and the Historical Avant-Garde*. Honolulu: University of Hawai'i Press, 2014.

Pinch, Adela. *Strange Fits of Passion: Epistemologies of Emotion, Hume to Austen*. Stanford, CA: Stanford University Press, 1996.

Prendergast, Christopher. "The World Republic of Letters." In *Debating World Literature*. Edited by Christopher Prendergast. London: Verso, 2004.

Qian Xingcun. *Wanqing xiaoshuo shi* (A history of late Qing fiction). Taipei, Taiwan: Renren wenku, 1968.

Ricoeur, Paul. "The Function of Fiction in Shaping Reality." In *A Ricoeur Reader: Reflection and Imagination*. Edited by Mario J. Valdés. Toronto: University of Toronto Press, 1991.

Rimer, J. Thomas, ed. *A Hidden Fire: Russian and Japanese Cultural Encounters, 1868–1926*. Stanford, CA: Stanford University Press, 1995.

Robinson, Douglas. *Translation and Empire*. Manchester, UK: St. Jerome, 1997.

Ryu Sŭng-hyŏn. "Ku-hanmal, Ilcheha yŏsŏng chohon ŭi silt'ae wa chohon p'yeji undong" (The state of early marriage and the movements for its abolition in the Enlightenment and colonial periods). Master's thesis, Sŏngsin Women's University, 1999.

Sakai, Naoki. *Translation and Subjectivity: On Japan and Cultural Nationalism*. Minneapolis: University of Minnesota Press, 1997.

Sanders, Julie. *Adaptation and Appropriation*. London: Routledge, 2006.

Sapir, Gisèle. "The Literary Field between the State and the Market." *Poetics* 31 (October–December 2003): 441–64.

Schimmelpenninck van der Oye, David. *Russian Orientalism: Asia in the Russian Mind from Peter the Great to the Emigration*. New Haven, CT: Yale University Press, 2010.

———. *Toward the Rising Sun: Russian Ideologies of Empire and the Path to War with Japan*. DeKalb: Northern Illinois University Press, 2001.

Schmid, Andre. *Korea Between Empires 1895–1919*. New York: Columbia University Press, 2002.

Seeley, Frank Friedeberg. *Turgenev: A Reading of His Fiction*. Cambridge: Cambridge University Press, 1991.

Shea, G. T. *Leftwing Literature in Japan*. Tokyo: Hosei University Press, 1964.

Shestov, Leon. "Anton Tchekhov (Creation from the Void)." In *Anton Tchekhov and Other Essays*. Dublin: Maunsel, 1916.

Shi, Shu-mei. "Global Literature and the Technologies of Recognition." *PMLA* 119, no. 1 (January 2004): 16–30.

Shifman, A. I., ed. *Lev Tolstoii i vostok* (Tolstoy and the East). Moscow: Nauka, 1971.

Shimamura Hōgetsu. "Torawaretaru bungei" (Shackled art). *Waseda bungaku II* (January 1906): 1–45.

Shin, Gi-Wook, and Michael Robinson, ed. *Colonial Modernity in Korea*. Cambridge, MA: Harvard University Asia Center, 1999.

Shirakawa Yutaka. "Kan, nichi, chū sangoku bunjin no ryūgaku taiken-kō" (The experience of studying abroad of Korean, Japanese, Chinese writers). *Irŏilmunhak yŏn'gu*, no. 3 (November 1982).

Simmons, Ernest J. *Leo Tolstoy*. Boston: Little, Brown, 1946.

Sin Sŏk-jŏng. "Pang" (Room). In *Sŭlp'ŭn mokka* (Sad pastoral songs). Puan: Nangju munhwasa, 1947.

Sin Yong-ha. "Sinminhoe ŭi ch'anggŏn kwa kŭ kukkwŏn hoebok undong (sang)" (The formation of Sinminhoe and its restoration of the national rights movement, 1). *Han'guk hakpo* 3, no. 3 (1977): 31–75.

———. "Sinminhoe ŭi ch'anggŏn kwa kŭ kukkwŏn hoebok undong (ha)" (The formation of Sinminhoe and its restoration of the national rights movement, 2). *Han'guk hakpo* 3, no. 4 (1977): 125–188.

Sŏ Hyŏn-ju. "Hyŏn Chin-gŏn sosŏl yŏn'gu: sahoe hyŏnsil kwa yŏsŏngsang ŭl chungsim ŭro" (A study of Hyŏn Chin-gŏn's literary works: centering on social reality and the female figure). Master's thesis, Kyŏnghŭi University, 2003.

Sonyŏn (The young). (November 1908–May 1911). Reprint. Seoul: Yŏngnak, 2001.

Spivak, Gayatri Chakravorty. "The Politics of Translation." In *The Translation Studies Reader.* 2nd ed. Edited by Venuti, Lawrence. New York: Routledge, 2004.

Suh, Dae-Sook. *The Korean Communist Movement 1918–1948.* Princeton, NJ: Princeton University Press, 1967.

Suh, Serk-Bae. *Treacherous Translation: Culture, Nationalism, and Colonialism in Korea and Japan from the 1910s to the 1960s.* Berkeley: University of California Press, 2013.

Sunsŏng [Chin-Hak-mun]. "Sajinch'ŏp sŏ: Che-hopŭ ŭi sogae" (A preface to "Album"— an introduction of Chekhov). *Hakchigwang,* no. 10 (September 1916): 50–52.

Suzuki Sadami. *Nihon no "bungaku" gainen* (The concept of literature in Japan). Tokyo: Sakuhinsha, 1998.

Suzuki, Tomi. *Narrating the Self: Fictions of Japanese Modernity.* Stanford, CA: Stanford University Press, 1996.

Takashima Heizaburō. *Shinri hakuwa* (A story of psychology). Tokyo: Rakuyōdō, 1912.

Thornber, Karen. "Early Twentieth-Century Intra–East Asian Literary Contact Nebulae: Censored Japanese Literature in Chinese and Korean." *The Journal of Asian Studies* 68, no. 3 (August 2009): 749–75.

———. *Empire of Texts in Motion: Chinese, Korean, and Taiwanese Transculturations of Japanese Literature.* Cambridge, MA: Harvard University Asia Center, 2009.

Tolstoy, Leo. *The Complete Works of Count Tolstoy.* Vol. 13, *My Confession.* Translated and edited by Leo Wiener. New York: Colonial, 1904–12.

———. *What Is Art?* Translated by A. Maude. New York: Thomas Y. Crowell, 1979.

Tolstoy, Lev. "Bethink Yourselves!" *The Times* (London), June 27, 1904.

———. *Geijyutsuron* (The theory of art). Translated by Arima Sukemasa. Tokyo: Hakubunkan, 1906.

———. *Polnoe sobranie sochinenii Lva Nikolaevicha Tolstogo* (Complete works of Lev Tolstoy). Edited by P. I. Biriukova. Moscow: Tip. T-va I.D. Sytina, 1913–14.

———. "Torusutoi ou no henji" (Mr. Tolstoy's reply). *Chokugen* 2, no. 30 (August 1905): 1, 3.

Tomasi, Massimiliano. "Studies of Western Rhetoric in Modern Japan: The Years between Shimamura Hōgetsu's *Shin bijigaku* (1902) and the End of the Taishō Era." *Japan Review,* no. 16 (2004): 161–90.

Tongguk taehakkyo munhwa haksurwŏn han'guk munhak yŏn'guso, ed. *Singminji sigi kŏmyŏl kwa han'guk munhwa* (Censorship and Korean culture in the colonial period). Seoul: Tongguk taehakkyo ch'ulp'anbu, 2010.

Tongwŏn. "Nodong ŭl chŏju hanŭn kungmin ege" (To the people who curse labor). *Kongje*, no. 1 (September 1920): 108–110.

Torusutoi kenkyū (Tolstoy studies). Tokyo: Shinchōsha, September 1916–January 1919. Reprint, *Torusutoi Kenkyū*. Tokyo: Ōzorasha, 1985.

Tsubouchi Shōyō. *Shōsetsu shinzui* (The essence of the novel). In Vol. 16, *Tsubouchi Shōyō shū* (Collection of Tsubouchi Shōyō's writings). Meiji bungaku zenshū (Complete works of Meiji literature). Tokyo: Chikuma shobō, 1969.

Turgenev, Ivan. *Novels of Ivan Turgenev*. Translated by Constance Garnett. 15 vols. New York: Macmillan, 1906.

———. *On the Eve*. Translated by Constance Garnett. London: William Heinemann, 1906.

———. *Polnoe sobranie sochinenii i pisem* (Complete works and letters). 28 vols. Moscow: Nauka, 1960–68.

———. *So no zenya*. Translated by Ono Hiroshi. Tokyo: Tōkasha, 1921.

———. *So no zenya* (On the eve). Translated by Sōma Gyofū. Tokyo: Naigai Shuppan Kyōkai, 1908.

———. *So no zenya* (On the eve). Vol. 4, *Tsurugenefu zenshū*. Tokyo: Shinchōsha, 1918.

Ueda, Atsuko. "*Bungakuron* and 'literature' in the making." *Japan Forum* 20, no. 1 (February 2008): 25–46.

———. *Concealment of Politics, Politics of Concealment: The Production of "Literature" in Meiji Japan*. Stanford, CA: Stanford University Press, 2007.

Venuti, Lawrence. *The Scandals of Translation*. London: Routledge, 1998.

———. *The Translator's Invisibility: A History of Translation*. London: Routledge, 1995.

Venuti, Lawrence, ed. *The Translation Studies Reader*. 2nd ed. New York: Routledge, 2004.

Wallerstein, Immanuel. *Historical Capitalism with Capitalist Civilization*. London: Verso, 2003.

Wang, David. "Translating Modernity." In *Translation and Creation: Readings of Western Literature in Early Modern China, 1840–1918*. Edited by David Pollard. Philadelphia: John Benjamins, 1998.

Waseda Daigaku Daigaku-shi Henshūjo, ed. *Waseda daigaku hyaku-nen shi bekkan* (A one-hundred year history of Waseda University: Appendix). Vol. 1. Tokyo: Waseda University Press, 1990.

Watt, Ian. *The Rise of the Novel: Studies in Defoe, Richardson and Fielding*. Berkeley: University of California Press, 1962.

Wells, David, and Sandra Wilson, eds. *Russo-Japanese War in Cultural Perspective, 1904–05*. New York: St. Martin's, 1999.

Wertz, S. K. "Human Nature and Art: From Descartes and Hume to Tolstoy." *Journal of Aesthetic Education*, 32, no. 3 (Autumn, 1998): 75–81.

Woodmansee, Martha. "The Genius and the Copyright: Economic and Legal Conditions of the Emergence of the 'Author.'" Special Issue: The Printed Word in the Eighteenth Century, *Eighteenth-Century Studies* 17, no. 4 (Summer 1984): 425–48.

Yamada Seizaburō. *Proretaria bungakushi* (A history of proletarian literature). 2 vols. Tokyo: Rironsha, 1954.

Yanagi Tomiko. *Torusutoi to nihon* (Tolstoy and Japan). Tokyo: Waseda University Press, 1998.

Yasumoto Takako. *Ishikawa Takuboku to Roshia* (Ishikawa Takuboku and Russia). Tokyo: Kanrin shobō, 2006.

Yi Ho-ryong. *Han'guk ŭi anak'ijŭm* (Anarchism in Korea). Seoul: Chisik sanŏpsa, 2002.

Yi Hŭi-jŏng. "1910-nyŏndae *Maeil sinbo* sojae sosŏl yŏn'gu" (A study of the novels published in *Maeil sinbo* in the 1910s). PhD diss., Kyŏngbuk University, 2006.

Yi Hyŏn-hŭi, Sŏng-su Pak, and Nae-hyŏn Yun. *Kundae han'gugŏ sigi ŭi ŏnŏgwan, munchagwan yŏn'gu* (A study of the view of language and letters after the invention of Korean script). Seoul: Somyŏng, 2014.

Yi Hyo-sŏk. *Yi Hyo-sŏk chŏnjip* (Yi Hyo-sŏk: complete works). 8 vols. Seoul: Ch'angmisa, 1990.

Yi Ik-sang. "Yesulchŏk yangsim i kyŏryŏhan uri mundan" (Our literary world that lacks artistic conscience). *Kyebyŏk*, no. 11 (May 1921): 100–112.

Yi Ki-baek. *Han'guksa sillon* (A new history of Korea). Seoul: Ilchogak, 1999.

Yi Kwang-rin. *Han'guk kaehwasa yŏn'gu* (A study of the Korean Enlightenment period). Seoul: Ilchogak, 1999.

Yi Kwang-su. "Munhak e ttŭt ŭl tunŭn i ege" (To people who aspire to do literature). *Kyaebyŏk*, no. 21 (March 1922): 1–15.

———. *Yi Kwang-su chŏnjip* (Yi Kwang-su: complete works). 11 vols. Seoul: Samjungdang, 1977.

Yi Kyŏng-yŏng. "1920-nyŏndae ch'oban nodong undong ŭi punhwa kwajŏng" (The differentiation process of labor movements in the 1920s). *Chung'ang saron*, no. 8 (December 1995): 103–40.

Yi Min-han. "Ae ŭi ryŏk" (The power of love). *Chosŏn ilbo*, October 2, 1924.

Yi Sang-hwa. "Tokhuingsang" (A thought after reading). *Sidae ilbo* (Sidae daily), November 9, 1925.

Yi Sŏn-ok. "Cho Myŏng-hŭi chakp'um yŏn'gu" (A study of Cho Myŏng-hŭi's literary works). Master's thesis, Sukmyŏng Women's University, 1989.

Yi T'ae-jun. "Kŭ chŏnnal pam" (On the eve). *Haksaeng* (Student) 1, no. 5 (August 1929): 78–85.

Yŏm Sang-sŏp. *Yŏm Sang-sŏp chŏnjip* (Complete works). Vol 2, *Sarang kwa choe* (Love and sin). Seoul: Minŭmsa, 1987.

Yoo, Theodore Jun. *The Politics of Gender in Colonial Korea: Education, Labor, and Health, 1910–1945*. Berkeley: University of California Press, 2008.

Yu Chin-hŭi. "Nodong undong ŭi sahoejuŭi-jok koch'al" (A socialist study of the labor movement). *Kongje*, no. 2 (October 1920): 11–20.

Yu Nam-ok. "1920-nyŏndae tanpyŏn sosŏl e nat'anan peminijŭm yŏn'gu" (A study of feminism represented in short stories of the 1920s). PhD diss., Sukmyŏng Women's University, 1993.

Yukihito Hijima. *Ishikawa Takuboku*. Boston: Twayne, 1979.

Yun Pyŏng-ro. "Pinghŏ Hyŏn Chin-gŏn ŭi saeng'ae wa pip'yŏng" (A biographical study of Hyŏn Chin-gŏn). *Taedong munhwa yŏn'gu* 20 (January 1986): 101–19.

Yun Tong-ju. *Yun Tong-ju chŏnjip* (Complete works). Edited by Hong Chang-hak. Seoul: Munhak kwa chisŏngsa, 2004.

Index

A Ying (Qian Xingcun), 9
adaptation: vs. appropriation, 188n77;
    of Chekhov, 44, 124–27; and copy-
    right, 124; film, 188n77; vs. literal
    translation, 20, 21–22; and novels,
    189n78; and politics, 188n77; in
    serialized translations, 164–65;
    studies of, 28; terms for, 21–22;
    theatrical, 142, 188n77; and transla-
    tion, 25, 26, 123, 182; of Turgenev,
    143, 206n31; and world literature,
    129–30
"Aibiki" (The tryst; Turgenev), 140, 142,
    205nn24–25
"Ai ka" (Is it love?; Yi Kwang-su), 24
"Aims of the Youth Association" (Ch'oe
    Nam-sǒn), 62
Akita Toshihiko, 200n7
Akutagawa Ryūnosuke, 103
Alexander II (tsar of Russia), 155
American literature, 15, 40, 175, 182,
    189n81, 210n2
An Ch'ang-ho, 53, 54, 193n36
An Hwak, 31, 83, 86
An Mak, 35
anarchism, 42, 182, 211n15; of Tolstoy, 50,
    51, 52, 56, 63, 65, 193n26
Anderson, Benedict, 2–3, 4, 53
Anna Karenina (Tolstoy), 56
anticommunism, 175, 203n1

appropriation, 8, 35; vs. adaptation,
    188n77; of Chekhov, 98, 103, 108,
    109, 114, 115; cultural, 9, 96, 135; and
    Korean proletarian literature, 132, 133;
    productive, 98, 99, 100, 103, 108, 123,
    180, 199n2; of Russian literature, 42,
    43, 45, 68, 132–33, 172, 182, 205n24;
    of Tolstoy, 47, 79, 95, 96, 136, 138;
    translation as, 15, 16, 19, 99, 100, 123,
    124; of Turgenev, 139, 141, 154, 156, 158,
    159, 165
Arac, Jonathan, 185n12
Arishima Takeo, 70
aristocrats, Korean (*yangban*), 48, 62–63,
    115, 135, 160
Asō Hisashi, 150
"Asya" (Unrequited love; Turgenev),
    177–78
Atsuko Ueda, 94
authorship, 9–12, 186n30. *See also* writers

Ba Jin, 30
Bakunin, Mikhail, 208n76
Barbusse, Henri, 148
Bassnett, Susan, 12–13
Bazarov (*Fathers and Sons*), 154
Belinsky, Vissarion, 154, 208n76
Benjamin, Walter, 8
Berman, Antoine, 18
Bersenev (*On the Eve*), 143, 144, 163, 169

Harvard East Asian Monographs
(most recent titles)